WHAT'S

LEFT

OF

THEORY?

ESSAYS FROM
THE ENGLISH INSTITUTE

Since 1944, the English Institute has presented work
by distinguished scholars in English and American literatures, foreign literatures and related fields. A volume of papers selected for the meeting is published
annually.

Also available in the series from Routledge:

Comparative American Identities:
Race, Sex, and Nationality in the Modern Text
Edited and with an introduction by Hortense J. Spillers

English Inside and Out:
The Places of Literary Criticism
Edited and with an introduction by
Susan Gubar and Jonathan Kamholtz

Borders, Boundaries and Frames:
Essays on Cultural Criticism and Cultural Theory
Edited and with an introduction by Mae Henderson

Performativity and Performance
Edited and with an introduction by
Andrew Parker and Eve Kosofsky Sedgwick

Human, All Too Human
Edited and with an introduction by Diana Fuss

Language Machines:
Technologies of Literary and Cultural Production
Edited and with an introduction by Jeffrey Masten,
Peter Stallybrass, and Nancy J. Vickers

ROUTLEDGE

NEW YORK

LONDON

WHAT'S

LEFT

OF

THEORY?

NEW WORK

ON THE POLITICS

OF LITERARY THEORY

Edited by

JUDITH BUTLER, JOHN GUILLORY,

AND KENDALL THOMAS

Published in 2000 by
Routledge
29 West 35th Street
New York, New York 10001

Published in Great Britain by
Routledge
11 New Fetter Lane
London EC4P 4EE

Copyright © 2000 by Routledge

Printed in the United States of America on acid-free paper.

Cataloging-In-Publication Data available upon request from the Library of Congress.

CONTENTS

CONTRIBUTORS

MICHAEL BÉRUBÉ is Professor of English and Director of the Illinois Program for Research in the Humanities at the University of Illinois at Urbana-Champaign.

JOHN BRENKMAN is Professor of English at Baruch College, the City University of New York.

JUDITH BUTLER is Maxine Elliot Professor of Rhetoric and Comparative Literature at the University of California at Berkeley.

WILLIAM E. CONNOLLY is Professor and Chair of Political Science at the Johns Hopkins University.

JONATHAN CULLER is Class of 1916 Professor of English and Comparative Literature at Cornell University.

JOHN GUILLORY is Professor of English at New York University.

JANET E. HALLEY is Professor of Law and Robert E. Paradise Faculty Scholar at Stanford University.

MARJORIE LEVINSON is F. L. Huetwell Professor of English at the University of Michigan.

JEFF NUNOKAWA is Associate Professor of English at Princeton University.

GAYATRI CHAKRAVORTY SPIVAK is Avalon Foundation Professor in the Humanities at Columbia University.

KENDALL THOMAS is Professor in the School of Law, Columbia University.

MICHAEL WARNER is Professor of English at Rutgers University.

ACKNOWLEDGMENTS

We thank Stuart Murray for his assistance in organizing the submission of this volume of English Institute papers, Marjorie Garber and Andrew Parker, for prodding us along with humor and persistence. And we thank the English Institute for the chance to come together, to write for one another, and for posing for us some of the more vexed questions in literary studies to think about. At Routledge, we thank Bill Germano for his patience and insistence, Krister Swartz for his work on production, and Julien Devereux for keeping us on track.

John Brenkman's essay appears as "Extreme Criticism," in *Critical Inquiry* 26.1 (Autumn 1999).

William E. Connolly's essay appeared in a slightly different form in *Why I Am Not a Secularist* (Minneapolis: University of Minnesota Press, 1999).

Janet Halley's essay appeared first as "Gay Rights and Identity Imitation: Issues in the Ethics of Representation," in *The Politics of Law: A Progressive Critique*, 3rd ed., David Kairys, ed. (New York: Basic Books, 1988), pp. 115–146.

Gayatri Chakravorty Spivak's essay will also appear as a chapter in a forthcoming book.

Michael Warner's essay appears in altered form in *The Trouble with Normal: Sex, Politics, and the Ethics of Queer Life* (New York: The Free Press, 1999).

JUDITH BUTLER, JOHN GUILLORY, AND KENDALL THOMAS

FOR SEVERAL YEARS a debate on the politics of theory has been conducted energetically within literary studies. The terms of the debate, however, are far from clear. What is meant by politics? What is meant by theory? "Theory" more often than not appears to mean "poststructuralism," but it is unclear why (a) the history of literary theory should be collapsed into the synecdoche of poststructuralism and (b) whether poststructuralism, in its varied forms, can be referred to meaningfully as a unitary phenomenon. "Theory" sometimes operates as shorthand for a certain operation of formalism, the uncovering of the structural conditions and features of a text, a way of reading that culminates in a self-referential move, e.g. the text allegorizes some feature about textuality itself. The reigning suspicion toward this kind of formalism is that it suspends questions of context; if a text cannot thematize the world from which it comes, how can it constitute the basis of a politically informed reading? If, the argument goes, the text is not "about" something other than itself, it is certainly not "about" its world. This loss of referentiality is tantamount to the loss of political relevance.

There are, at least, two rejoinders to make to this characterization of theory. The first is that even if by "theory" one refers to the work of Derrida, de Man, Foucault, it is unclear that any of them are unequivocally formalist. For Derrida, the "form" of a literary text is always contaminated by that which exceeds its bounds, and the criticism that deconstruction levelled against the New Criticism from which it emerged was that a text cannot achieve and sustain formal unity. There is always that which calls the form into question, and that is not simply another formal element, but a resistant remainder that sets limits to formalism itself. Moreover, the question of context is not dismissed within deconstruction: it is simply held to be illimitable. This does not mean that one ought never to try to delimit a context, but only that every such attempt will be open to necessary revision. The appropriation and redeployment of poststructuralism in legibly "political" contexts by writers such as Stuart Hall, Ernesto Laclau, Homi Bhabha, Gayatri Chakravorty Spivak, Drucilla Cornell, Teresa de Lauretis, do not "apply" the theories of French poststructuralism to political "contexts," but recontextualize or "iterate" the theory in ways that augment its contamination and enhance its political salience. These redeployments of theory in the context of politically invested arenas—race, colonialism, sexuality, gender—are generally situated within a left academic discourse. Of course, there are those who would call into question the legitimacy of calling such theories "left," fearing a corruption of politics by theory, but this is clearly a sign of how far the "left" has departed from the theoretical tradition of Marx himself.

But is theory too formal and non-referential to have a significant bearing on politics?

There are those who fear that theorists abandon thematics altogether, holding literary texts to have a specificity as literary, to have formal features which are not easily transposable onto other kinds of texts, to be specifically literary interrogations into the workings of language which are divorced from the workings of the world. Clearly, the crisis in realism documented by Lukács, Adorno, and Brecht saw the very self-referentiality of modernist literature as politically significant: the breakdown of mimetic forms of realism exposed a world in which the relations of representation were radically altered by conditions in the world. To insist on transparent reference under such conditions is precisely to misread the very way social conditions produce and structure literary form and literary reference. On the other side, however, there are clearly still formalist critics who universalize this condition of the text and the autonomous role of theoretical criticism. Some fear that theory has itself become too "thematic," lost its pre- or post-ideological status, especially as it engages modalities of power. Thus, it seems, theoretically informed literary analysis that suspends all political judgment fears contamination from another direction: the contamination of theory by politics. If some of those who turn against theory in the name of politics do so by laying claim to referentiality and thematic criticism, then some of those who turn against politics in the name of theory do so by sacralizing the suspension of all reference to context. Both are projects of purity which do not recognize their fundamental dependence on the other. Theory has become impure as it engages the social and political world through the reading of literature, and thematics have no doubt become more difficult once we avow the modes of representation that permit—or fail to permit—of certain kinds of politically significant insights into our world.

This volume does not seek to rehearse the arguments for and against the thesis that (poststructuralist) theory is political. Rather, we seek to understand the conditions under which this question is posed, and to chart some of the ways that literary studies continues to intersect, in all its volatility, with left political thinking. Are there ways of pursuing a politically reflective literary analysis that have definitively left theory behind, and must "theory" be left behind for left literary analysis to emerge? Has the study of literature passed beyond its encounter with theory? If so, in passing beyond theory, has it remained unchanged? Does the recent cry for a "return to literature" signal the surpassing of theory, the fact that literature remains after theory? Or would we find that, upon such a return, we would still have to ask: in what does the literary consist? What is our access to it? Upon what presuppositions about language does literature and its criticism draw? Does literature remain (the same) after theory?

This volume does not "settle" these questions, and within its pages the reader will no doubt recognize the contours of the following discordant perspectives: whereas some of the animus against theory comes from those who seek to safeguard the literary text and forms of close, literary readings, some comes from an explicitly political position. Worrying that "theory" is but another formalism that loses sight of the material conditions of textual production, this form of leftist skepticism toward theory has sought to historicize the reading of literature, reintroduce the importance of context and intention and, in some instances, interrogate the conditions of literary reception and influence.

The history of this encounter between theory and literature proves to be difficult to narrate in progressive terms. For in its disseminated state, theory now arrives as part of historicism, as part of new materialist approaches to literary texts, and it often arrives in tandem with close readings of literary texts. Theory is not over, but it is no longer, if it ever was, in one piece.

Thus, a number of questions remain: Is there a specter of "high theory" that continues to inform the left work in cultural studies and new historicism that cannot be eradicated from its operations, and on which it remains fundamentally dependent? Has "theory" post–de Man been repudiated only to emerge as the animating specter of contemporary literary analysis, whereby "theory" is both disavowed and preserved in the reaction formation that has followed? Is theory still "poststructuralism" or has that very term become meaningless precisely as its dissemination and contamination in cultural and political analysis establishes a set of unanticipated meanings for the term? In a sense, the value of poststructuralism no longer forms the pivot of contemporary debate, but, rather, its place in new forms of cultural and political analysis is both inchoate and central. Although there are leftist positions that seek a full purging of the poststructuralist trace, panicking at the slightest trace of "jargon," they still contend with its specter as one of the ghostly conditions of their own emergence.

The extraordinary interest in social theory and the law that has recently emerged in literary studies has seemed to many to constitute an important redirection of the field toward political themes and active political investments in justice, freedom, and equality. Whereas some argue that literature should remain cordoned off from social science and social theory, others are relieved that literary studies has moved toward a more active engagement with social issues, with race studies, practices of gender and sexuality, colonial space and its aftermath, the interstitial cultural spaces of globalization. It may be that literary scholars make poor social theorists, as Richard Rorty has argued, but it

seems more likely that literary scholars bring insightful forms of reading to bear upon social and political texts that have great relevance for
the course of our collective lives. Moreover, as literary scholars continue to probe the cultural and social context of cultural production,
they need to overcome their ignorance of the law, of political theory, of
the shape and structure of social movements. Similarly, the texts produced within social theory and social science rely on metaphor,
metonymy, ellipsis, and allegory, and these dimensions of meaning
production go unnoticed by those who do not engage a literary analysis. The task will be to consider what role literature and the literary still
play within the context of this increasingly complicated social context.

This volume does not seek to answer the question of whether theory is necessary for the left or for literature, but does seek to evidence
an array of essays that rearrange these terms—"theory," "the left," and
"literature" —in less than predictable ways. Is it possible to leave theory behind for the left, or is what is "left" precisely what remains to
worked through in the new social registers of theory? Will the left leave
literature behind, or will literature emerge as a site for the negotiation
of progressive political readings? Will we continue to find the literary
appearing in non-literary texts, as dimensions of legal and historical
texts generally not approached in this way? Are we, as a profession,
ghosted by a formalism that never was? And how might we continue
to generalize the conditions of our practice without receding from the
world that calls upon us to engage in politically responsible ways and
the literary texts whose specificity and challenge it remains the task of
literary scholars to read?

GAYATRI CHAKRAVORTY SPIVAK 1

MARX

I
T IS PERHAPS no surprise that, in the absence of a "practical" left in the United States, a dwindling enclave in the academic and journalistic world continues to debate the theory-practice binary opposition with a vigor matched only by its lack of consequence outside the academy. But the U.S. academy is our home, and in so far as the consequences of this debate affect our hiring and firing practices, it is worth commenting on it in a strictly academic way. I should add here that our handful of elite universities, with larger and more managerial global spheres of influence, protect their conservatism with a viciousness not necessarily imaginable outside that charmed circle, ideologically controlling the constitution of their student body when the formal law of the land will not allow more visible lines of separation. In this sorry field, then, I begin, as usual, in the classroom.

FROM HAVERSTOCK HILL FLAT TO U.S. CLASSROOM, WHAT'S LEFT OF THEORY?[1]

Every couple of years for the last two decades, I confront the task of explaining to a new group of graduate students that, although the *difference* between use and exchange seems immediately available to intuition, use-*value* and exchange-*value* are in the *same* form—the value form. To put something in the value form means to abstract it, so that it can be measured. This is as true of use-value as it is of exchange-value. When we use something up, we do not in fact measure it.

(Today an exception might be made of foods with their nutritional value tabulated on the label.) But that does not in fact mean that the thing cannot be put in the value form. It is only in this sense that use-value is a fiction.

Marx was trying to explain the value form as the possibility of abstraction across the board because it was going to come in handy to explain the special character of capital, but the insight was altogether counter-intuitive. By this insight, use-value, generally a fiction, is not a fiction for capital. Capital consumes by measure. This is labor-power, not labor. It is the use of the use-value of labor, not the use of labor. Counter-intuitive lesson 1.

And then comes the other lesson, better known but commonly left unconnected with the first one: That the capitalist pays back less value (in the money form) than s/he borrowed (in the labor-power form). This is because when labor-power is used, it produces more value than its concrete pre-measurable personal base requires to reproduce itself potentially as measurable into use-value for capital: labor-power. Socialism will voluntarily keep the use of labor-power undisturbed in form but equitable in fact; and save the difference for redistribution.

It is essential to understand the abstraction involved in the value form, *whether in use or exchange*, in order to understand this argument. Commodification of labor into labor-power is a potentially good thing in this argument, for it alone can provide the wherewithal for social-ism. Use (concrete) over exchange (abstract)—more goods for the working class to use, and fewer for the capitalist to exchange—is far too Luddite a binary opposition to account for the theoretico-practical breadth of Marx's work. Ownership of the means of production, dic-tatorship of the proletariat, critique of reification, when anchored in this binary, cannot confront the self-determination of capital (I use the nineteenth-century expression advisedly) as globalization—global finance capital necessarily interrupted by world trade. On the other hand, if the counter-intuitive Marxian lesson—in the value form both use and exchange are abstract, and the capital-labor (power) relation-ship is that capital uses the abstract(ed labor)—is learnt, the socialist grabbing and saving the difference (surplus and/or interest) for redis-tribution can mean the difference between crisis-driven and strategy-driven globalization.

It is difficult to grasp this because Marx was ahead of his time. It is also difficult because working-class culture clung to a robust empiricism which was the muscular side of the querulous academic empiricism that commanded the authoritative translations—in the narrow as well as the general sense—into English.

From all accounts, Frederick Engels was not a querulous man. But he can be counted as Marx's first English "translator"—a metonym for the empiricist havoc that constructed a "practical" Marx who repeated "good common sense"—namely, use/concrete, exchange/abstract, alienation of labor a crime against the working class. No. Marx's tone is different: Labor for him is use of labor-power by capital. And, "[i]t is an extraordinarily cheap kind of sentimentality which declares that this method of determining the value of labour-power, a method prescribed by the very nature of the case, is brutal. . . . When we speak of capacity for labour, we do not speak of labour, any more than we speak of digestion when we speak of capacity for digestion" (C1, 277).[2]

Let us read one critical page of *Capital* (see next page for reproduction) to see the process at work.

Marx is theorizing and Engels is running interference, with the intention of making things clearer for the implied working-class reader. In the two previous paragraphs, Marx has been telling us that we must leave behind the intuition that value first appears in the exchange-relation, in quantitative abstraction. Marx urges the reader to make the difficult counter-intuitive move, to grasp abstraction in use-value. Of course, when we exchange, "the common factor in the exchange relation . . . is its value. We must now consider value independently of this [the exchange] form of appearance. A use-value or good [*Gut*] therefore, has value only because *abstract* human labour is objectified in it" (C1, 128–129; emphasis mine).

In the use form of appearance, value does not become intuitively manifest to us because we do not engage in exchange. But, as I suggest above, Marx's clear implication is that, unless we are able to think it, we will not be able to understand the relationship between capital and worker and the commodity will remain a fetish. Thus it is the role of the abstract—the spectral, if you will—that we must grasp rather than reject. Here we can see that he is clearly undoing the use(-value)/exchange(-value) binary opposition or semantic nexus that still haunts our common sense. Yet, as he

✱ ENGELS

their value might fall below that of bricks. In general, the greater the productivity of labour, the less the labour-time required to produce an article, the less the mass of labour crystallized in that article, and the less its value. Inversely, the less the productivity of labour, the greater the labour-time necessary to produce an article, and the greater its value. The value of a commodity, therefore, varies directly as the quantity, and inversely as the productivity, of the labour which finds its realization within the commodity. (Now we know the *substance* of value. It is *labour*. We know the *measure* of its magnitude. It is *labour-time*. The *form*, which stamps *value* as *exchange-value*, remains to be analysed. But before this we need to develop the characteristics we have already found somewhat more fully.)*

A thing can be a use-value without being a value. This is the case whenever its utility to man is not mediated through labour. Air, virgin soil, natural meadows, unplanted forests, etc. fall into this category. A thing can be useful, and a product of human labour, without being a commodity. He who satisfies his own need with the product of his own labour admittedly creates use-values, but not commodities. In order to produce the latter, he must not only produce use-values, but use-values for others, social use-values. (And not merely for others. The medieval peasant produced a corn-rent for the feudal lord and a corn-tithe for the priest; but neither the corn-rent nor the corn-tithe became commodities simply by being produced for others. In order to become a commodity, the product must be transferred to the other person, for whom it serves as a use-value, through the medium of exchange.)† Finally, nothing can be a value without being an object of utility. If the thing is useless, so is the labour contained in it; the labour does not count as labour, and therefore creates no value.

2. THE DUAL CHARACTER OF THE LABOUR EMBODIED IN
   COMMODITIES

Initially the commodity appeared to us as an object with a dual character, possessing both use-value and exchange-value. Later

---

* The passage in parentheses occurs only in the first edition.

† [Note by Engels to the fourth German edition:] I have inserted the passage in parentheses because, through its omission, the misconception has very frequently arisen that Marx regarded every product consumed by someone other than the producer as a commodity.

approaches the end of the clinching paragraph, Engels undermines the theoretical effort, crucial to the establishment of the point around which the lever of social justice will turn (C1, 132).

In the value form, use as well as exchange suffers abstraction. When labor is abstracted into labor-power, it is "used" for capital accumulation by the capitalist; only if it is still abstracted into labor-power can it be thus "used" by associated workers, for socialism. (The "ownership" of the means of production must *not* be understood on the model of collective private property here.) Instead, we get a bit of formula-talk, that generations of leftists have learnt by rote, leaving out the crucial words use-value and labor-power: "Now we know the *substance* of value," Engels writes. "It is *labour*." Yet Marx was attempting to emphasize the value *form*: not labor, but labor as labor-power. "We know the *measure of its magnitude*," Engels continues. "It is *labour-time*." For the Marxian argument this is irrelevant without the transformation of labor into labor-power. And Engels's next sentence, "the *form*, which stamps *value* as *exchange-value*, remains to be analysed" reinforces the very use-exchange semantic nexus that Marx was attempting to dislodge in the value form.

Between 1867 and 1873, Marx re-read the *Capital*. From the second edition, to which he wrote a magisterial Postface, he removed the Engelsian passage. Engels preserved it in a note. English translations restore it to the text. Rather a lot of the received pieties of left conservatism in the metropolis is this sort of "failure of translation," an inability or refusal to surrender to the counter-intuitive "original."

By chance I was reading both Plotinus on Beauty and Marx on the Commodity, for my undergraduate and graduate classes last semester. I was struck by the tenacity of Marx's classical training. Marx unpeels value in a style of argumentation remarkably similar to the Plotinian unpeeling of beauty. Marx was keen on Aristotle. His theoretical object choice is in step with Aristotle. Theory takes as its object things that are birthless and cannot be verbally articulated.[3] Marx is looking at the circuits of capital, the birth of whose originary accumulation cannot be philosophically grasped, only narrativized.[4] By shifting gears from philosophy to history, so to speak, another favorite move of classical German philosophy.[5]

In keeping with this methodological proviso, and still undoing the use-value/exchange-value split, Marx offers a few counter-examples. Keeping just "value" for the découpage of his labor theory, he consigns value-at-the-origin to Nature, where the possibility of measure exists as the incommensurable. Thus the very first counter-example—earth and air—has incommensurable use-value because human labor has not gone into its making. This, one may say remembering the Aristotelian notion of theory, is the birthless, unphrasable end of the forms of appearance of value. The other three counter-examples are: 1. use-value produced with labor but producing no commodity (the thinking of abstraction must be possible here); 2. use-value for others—"social" (*gesellschaftlich*) use-values—where abstraction must surely be thought, although the value is not deployed within general commodity exchange; and, finally, 3. arguing from the other side, Marx indicates the need to assume *Nutz*—sheer usefulness—in use as well as exchange, so that it cannot be kept separate for use-value alone. This hint of the complicity (folded togetherness) of usefulness and the abstract mensurability of value is unfortunately not clear in English translations.

After Marx's death, Engels explains away the counter-intuitive politics of theory by predicating the commodity only in exchange.

It was "Engels" who provided the decisive cuts. The history of the left rose and fell in them.

In the classroom, we give accounts of the world beyond. Only in that spirit, one can connect our problem of reading with the predicament of what Perry Anderson magisterially called "western Marxism" more than twenty years ago.[6] We remember that our failure in reading, anchored in so frail a thing as the disappearance of real language requirements in this era of the triumph of English is part of the picture. We are implicated in what we study. What we are recounting is what we now call a "cultural difference." British (U.S.) empiricism (pragmatism) over against continental rationalism, leading to a failure of reading (translation). It is with this intimate connection, not-quite-not-a-consequence, in mind that we turn to one possible temporizing of the predicament of Western Marxism.

After 1919, Western Marxism moved through cultural critique, varieties of the New Left, structuralist Marxism, and now Marxism on the deconstructive model. After 1989, capitalism triumphant has led through to globalization—nearly complete abstraction, finance capital. Deleuze and Guattari's fantastic insight, that capital was—let us say "almost"—the abstract as such and capital*ism* codes it—is no longer sufficient.[7] Finance capital is let us say "almost" the abstract as such and world trade codes it.[8]

In "Can the Subaltern Speak?," my point was that the British and the caste-Hindu reformers only concentrated on the visible violence of Sati, passed a widow remarriage law without any infrastructural involvement, and left the miserable rule-governed life of the "ordinary" Hindu widow unchanged.[9]

A structural homology may be advanced here. As long as we remain only focused on the visible violence of world trade, endorse the credit-baiting of the poorest rural women of the Southern hemisphere in the name of micro-enterprise without any infrastructural involvement, the subaltern remains in subalternity.[10] And we legitimate the world trade coding of the finance capital market by reversal.

In this situation, the untrammeled power of the abstract—financialization of the globe—economically and ideologically managed from within capital—world trade—cannot be managed—supplemented—by opposing perspectives from within. Today Marx's ghost needs stronger offerings than Human Rights with economics worked in, or the open-ended messianicity of the future anterior, or even "responsibility" (choice or being-called) in the Western tradition. The need is to turn toward ethical practices—care of others as care of the self—that were "*defective* for capitalism."[11] Marx must be turned around to those who lost in the capitalist competition again and again; in order to turn this ferociously powerful form of capital around to the social.

Caught in our "cultural difference," English-dominance and pragmatism, we cannot think of abstraction as useful—for capital and therefore for socialism. Caught in his "cultural difference," Europe-dominance and rationalism, Marx could not think this need. First, as an organic intellectual of industrial capitalism—he could only advise a public use of reason (understanding and turning around the spectralization of labor-power) from below. It must, of course, be admitted that, in his unrelenting analysis of what it was that the workers must free themselves from—namely the workings of capitalism—he did not devote as much time to the "how," beyond this faith in Reason. If only the worker grasps "this twofold nature of the labour contained in commodities [as labor and its spectralization, labor-power]," s/he will grasp the "blasting point [*Springpunkt*, modern German *Sprengpunkt*] of political economy," and revolution "is almost inevitable . . . if one makes a public use of one's reason . . ."[12] This is clearest in *Capital* 2, where Marx recommends the commodity-circuit explanation of capitalism to workers because

> The commodity capital, as the direct product of the capitalist production process, recalls its origin and is therefore more rational in its form, less lacking in conceptual differentiation, than the money capital, in which every trace of this process has been effaced, just as all the particular useform [*Gebrauchsform*] of commodities are generally effaced in money.[13]

Here are the rational bones within the flesh of the marketplace that will guarantee freedom from capitalism. (The money-circuit, the favorite mode of explanation of vulgar economists, is constantly described as "irrational.")

It is still only the story of "freedom from." When it came to the presumably postrevolutionary moment of "freedom to" establish socialism, no provision for something like an epistemic guarantee could be or was thought. Toward the end of his life, Marx gave a picture of a socialist community:

> If however wages are reduced to their general basis, i.e. that portion of the product of his labour which goes into the worker's own individual consumption; if this share is freed from its capitalist limit and expanded to the scale of consumption that is both permitted by the existing social productivity . . . and required for the full development of individuality; if surplus labour and surplus product are also reduced, to the degree needed under the given conditions of production, on the one hand to form an insurance and reserve fund, on the other hand for the constant expansion of reproduction in the degree determined by social need; if, finally both (1) the necessary labour and (2) the surplus labour are taken to include the

amount of labour that those capable of work must always perform
for those members of society not yet capable, or no longer capable
of working ... then nothing of these forms remains, but simply those
bases [*Grundlagen*] of the forms that are communal [*gemeinschaftlich*] to all social modes of production.[14]

What is not given here is why people as a whole would want to exercise the freedom to arrange for the upkeep of other people. The establishment of governments that enforce this are, first, again that reliance
on abstract structures that we are questioning here. Secondly, the
machinations of electoral politics do not usually support a cause
because of a desire to help others. Although Marx left the question of
the will to socialism begged, we cannot afford to do so. The post-Soviet
rhetoric of the indispensability of the U.S. is often couched in the language of a moral mandate (although the politicians know that it is no
more than lip service). A thousand people are not much of a specimen,
of course. But if the behavior of managerial passengers on international
flights over the last ten years gives a clue, the guess can be ventured
that, in full-swing globalization, the supposed inheritors of the
Enlightenment legacy as the torch passed from Europe do not insist on
the freedom to arrange for the upkeep of the species-being of others.
They get better and better at making money (manipulating the now
electronic spectral, as Marx had hoped the workers would the rational
spectral), but, when left to their own devices, their talk—and, rather
infrequently, their reading—would lead to the following rational
expectations: that they understand "power" as it is inscribed in a simple semiotic.[15] They understand simple sentimentality about "family"
as well as gender-struggle as the latter relates to the semiotic of power.
This sentimentality can accommodate "charity," stretching sometimes
to structured "community work"; all accompanied by the miraculating
power of "American" superiority, as it makes them superior as individuals.[16] Is this what Marx was shooting for? I think not, since his
assumption was an implicit entailment of the ethical in the agential
grasping of the spectral.

   At the other end of the spectrum, thinkers who can think collectiv-
ity cannot think responsibility and vice versa. In his latest book, Mahmood Mamdani charts the extent to which British colonial policy

constituted a monolithic "tradition" or "custom" in equatorial Africa in order to assign power to chieftaincy.[17] For him, the antonym of "tradition" remains "rights." Commenting on "a departure from the accent on individual rights in received liberal notions. . . . [C]ircumstances of birth prevailed over choice of association in shaping one's life possibilities," Mamdani relates this to other historically specific details but his attempt at understanding its "particular significance" (p. 202) misfires. If "birth" is given its full philosophical expansion as "the unanticipatable fall into time," it can form the shifting bedrock—Foucault's *socle mouvant*—upon which to base one's quest for remnants of "responsibility" in what is precisely not "liberal."

One cannot for a moment deny that the problems here are great. At least three types can be tracked here, the first peculiar to equatorial Africa, the other two common to other oppressed systems containing a certain degree of internal coherence. First, the establishment by colonial authorities of group-specific traditions gave ethnic rights to group members belonging to a region but only race-rights (comparable but, of course, not equal to the whites) to the out-of-state Black traveler. Can lines of generality, outside of rights-talk, and involving responsibility-talk as birth right, be inscribed here? I ask in ignorance. It seems at least as massive and intractable a problem as Marx's idea of entailing the ethical in the spectral. Secondly, these systems, if and when institutionalized, give rise to relatively inflexible hierarchies. We must compare them—discontinuous as the terms of comparison must be—to the power semiotics mentioned above; avoiding cultural conservatism, on both sides. But how does one weigh cultural systems? Another massive and intractable task. But so was the promise of full socialism. Thirdly, these systems, reactive to colonial domination of the males, often turn increasingly gender-compromised. At least for Southern Africa (this indicates the limits of my knowledge, not of the field), there is activist feminist work engaged here, in the framing of gender-sensitive constitutional law.[18] Hence the lineaments of "responsibility" in African tradition are, in Mamdani's reading, particularly difficult to track. In his reading, there may be nothing (authentic) left with which to associate labor in the interest of the social.

Discussing "tradition" in a vaguer "non-European" form, Michel de

Certeau speaks with rare understanding of "*collective fragments of memory* [which] constitute, whether consciously or unconsciously, the roots or the 'fixed points' by which a collective irreducibility is engraved in individual members."[19] Yet he too cannot get beyond the language of "collective rights as "capable of balancing the economy that, in the name of individual rights, exposes the entire social reality to the great universal light of the market and of the administration" (p. 157). On the other side, Lévinas's *autrui* is a non-phenomenological abstraction. His *visage*—too quickly translated as visage or face—is mostly a nominal construction from *viser*, to be directed towards, the verb of intentionality. The singular/universal remains a perennial moral dilemma, an ethical conundrum. Granted that this may be the outline of an irreducible experience of the impossible. But how can we loosen the bracket, how contaminate this austere landscape with the unevenness of grouped persons without falling into the abstraction of collective *rights*?

As I have argued elsewhere, the place of the subject of rights is empty because, even in statutory law, it must be written in the normative and privative language of abstract equality. To fill it with an impossible ethical singularity without jettisoning the usefulness of the abstract calculus is what we are contemplating here. Systems where responsibility inheres as birth right—thus programming an indeterminacy that frees it from the deliberations of conscience—can support a sense of "rights" alone when we have moved from "freedom from" to "freedom to." (This is responsibility in an "extra-moral sense," if you like, counter-intuitive to Enlightenment moralisms). "Rights," being altogether self- and selves-directed, is too weak a concept to make the move.

To go any further here would be to anticipate the argument.

METROPOLIS

Let us acknowledge the protocol of Marx's initial movement, from speculations about the subject of labor in the Economic and Philosophical manuscripts to the definition of the agent of production in the *Capitals*. This agent, only a part-subject, since its labor is part of an abstract flow, will turn the lever, *as* commodified labor, *of* political economy, *to* veer capital into *pharmakon*, a medicine always ready to

turn poisonous if the socialist dose falls short. Detractors and sympa-
thizers of diverse persuasions will grant alike that the epistemes or
mind-sets foreclosed by the capitalist/socialist teleology, defective for
capitalism, survive in more or less habitable ruins in unEnlightened
sectors and enclaves of the planet, as more or less recognizable
remain(s). Perhaps these are not ruins. The question to ask may be of
the order of " '*what remain[s] of a Rembrandt torn into small, very regular squares and rammed down the shithole.*' . . . As the remain(s)."[20]
The memorable opening lines of the counter-hegemonic right-hand
column of Derrida's *Glas*.

One can make a tight analogy here. The structural outlines of
responsibility-based cultural practices begin to atrophy into residual
scaffolding as industrial capitalist imperialisms impose the dominant
structures, whose motor is rights-based. (It needs to be said that as
soon as a culture systematizes responsibility, the contingency of
"responsibility" begins to atrophy even without the intervention of an
"alien" dominant.) Working para-sitically upon and under the dominant, they may at worst be no more than meaning-less connective
behavior—bits and pieces of syncategorematic social idiom—"small,
very regular squares." Rammed down the shithole of an ethnic practice determined by colonial policy, "what remain[s] . . . as the
remain[s]"?

This question, if read as the question of cultural identity, for which
reading there is, of course, no guarantee, shows that we are looking at
an effortful project of developing something de-formed and de-consti-
tuted, fragmented into disjointed joinings, through a species of prayer
to be haunted, which will both support and critique the institutional
supports that guarantee agency. It must be remembered that the success of the prayer to be haunted is unanticipatable. And you cannot
just call any attempt at multiculturalism a successful ghost dance: "at
certain points the dominant culture cannot allow too much residual
experience and practice outside itself, at least without risk. It is in the
incorporation of the actively residual—by reinterpretation, dilution,
projection, discriminating inclusion and exclusion—that the work of
the selective tradition is especially evident."[21]

By this astute reckoning, most metropolitan or postcolonial elite
"cultural" intervention is frankly "archaic" or part of dominant reap-

propriation that produces "culture" even as it thwarts the emergence of the significant emergent.

At the end of that chapter, Williams counsels observing the "pre-emergent." It is a measure of his strength that he does not counsel its plotting in some calculus. And it is in the space of this "observation" that we install the prayer to be haunted.

No mystical exercise this, but an effortful suspension of/from the calculus. Since the English institute has its being in the literary, let us consider a literary example before proceeding further. I do not have the political taste to offer an example via cultural identities outside of Europe. All I need here is an instance of the prayer to be haunted. I choose a text that moves you and can move most in my classroom.

Virginia Woolf "offers you an opinion upon one minor point—a woman must have money and a room of her own if she is to write fiction"—in a fictive space that she introduces in the robust mode of paradox: "[l]ies will flow from my lips, but there may perhaps be some truth mixed up with them; it is for you to seek out this truth . . ."[22]

She closes this nested or framed space of paradox with a line not written: "The very first sentence that I *would write here*, I said, crossing over to the writing-table and taking up the page headed Women and Fiction, is that it is fatal for any one who writes to think of their sex" (p. 104; emphasis mine). The lovely "unwritten" passage is put to rest with the long mesmeric vowels of high modernism taking a page out of impressionist painting: "the taxi took the man and the woman, seeing them come together across the street, and the current swept them away, I thought, hearing far off the roar of London's traffic, into that tremendous stream" (pp. 104–105).

When Woolf starts to speak, "in my own person" (p. 105), she urges what I can describe as the prayer to be haunted by the spirit of Shakespeare's sister, "buried where the omnibuses now stop" (p. 113), the singular spirit of all women (each woman) of talent who could not enter writing because they were not written in the socius as such. She urges her reader not to be confined in the mere calculus of rational expectations: "A thousand pens are ready to suggest what you should do and what effect you will have. My own suggestion is a little fantastic, I admit; I prefer, therefore, to put it in the form of fiction" (p. 113). And, in another striking paradoxical move, she concludes by unspeaking "a room of one's own and £500 a year" in the very last words of her book: "the dead poet who was Shakespeare's sister will put on the body which she has so often laid down. . . . [S]he would come if we worked for her, and . . . so to work, *even in poverty and obscurity*, is worth while" (p. 114; emphasis mine).

There is something like a relationship between this chiastic structure of a double paradox as a figure of what and how to do and the hesitant suggestions recently advanced by me to *Stiftung-Dialogik*, a Swiss foundation.[23] I started out from a simple mind-change:

> in the gridwork of electronic capital, we achieve something
> that resembles that abstract ball covered in latitudes and lon-
> gitudes, cut by virtual lines—once the equator and the trop-
> ics, now drawn increasingly by other requirements—
> imperatives?—of Geographical Information Systems. The
> globe is on our computers. No one lives there; and we think
> that we can aim to control globality. The planet is in the
> species of alterity, belonging to another system; and yet we
> inhabit it, on loan. It is not really amenable to a neat contrast
> with the globe. I cannot say "on the other hand."[24] I am sim-
> ply suggesting that, without an education into a drastic epis-
> temic transformation, capital—industrial and finance—
> cannot be persistently checked and turned around to the
> interest of the social. I am further arguing that this social
> practice of responsibility based on an imperative imagined as
> intended from alterity (a planetary self-representation, as it
> were) cannot today be related to any named grounding. This
> is where educating into the planetary imperative—assuming
> and thus effacing an absolute and discontinuous alterity and
> thus comfortable with an inexhaustible diversity of epistemes,
> from animism to postmodern science—takes its place.
>
> I am further suggesting that, rather than honoring the his-
> torical happenstance, that the rational machine of capital
> logic required the destruction of this understanding of the
> individual, and thus dismiss it as "pre-capitalist," we might
> imagine it animating and inspiriting the abstract structures

of democratic guarantees, which are indeed a great good. Speaking in South Africa, I have argued that democratic freedoms—both freedom from and freedom to—can be free as guarantees but can be exercised only when bound. To you, the European nation-state with the longest history of liberalism—and conscientious about multicultural policy—I say: bind it to a re-constellated planetary imperative to responsibility, seen as a right precomprehending becoming-human, where the proper name of alterity is not God, in any language. In the United States, at least, children's multicultural education divides into two broad areas: education into tradition and education into modernity. The following random example will give a sense of the divide.

On August 23, 1997, New York 1 News reported approvingly on two children's programs. One, called "Passing On," trained them in Caribbean dance steps. The other, where they got t-shirts, took them to the floor of the New York Stock Exchange. This too is children's education: relegating "tradition" to "culture" and a past museumized into a dynamic present being played out on the subject's involvement with the Stock Exchange.

If in the area of cultural practice, multicultural demands circle around religious observance and (usually female) dress code, in the arena of education, multicultural demands, since they are usually emergent from economic migration (even when ostensibly seeking asylum), remain content to accept this divide.

I am asking you to imagine something different, much harder, not a quick fix. Something that you will never hear in discussions of multicultural policy. I am daring to suggest that we have something to learn from the underclass immigrants, in the interest of a more just modernity: the remnants of a responsible pragma. I am asking if together, we can reinvent this pragma to fit, however unevenly, the democratic structures of civil society. I am therefore suggesting that both the dominant and the subordinate must jointly rethink themselves as intended or interpellated by planetary alterity, albeit articulating the task of thinking and doing from different "cultural" angles. What is new here is that the dominant redefines himself in order to learn to learn from "below," learns to *mean* to say—not just deliberately non-hierarchically, as the U.S. formula goes—I need to learn from you what you practice, I need it even if you didn't want to share a bit of my pie; but there's something I want to give you, which will make our shared practice flourish. You don't know, and I didn't know, that civility requires your practice of responsibility as pre-originary right.

To teach this saying is the support that cultural workers and educators can provide for the entire planet. It requires earning a right to win responses from both sides—responsibility once more.

I think the real winners in this transaction will have been women, on both sides. Let this remain a conjecture for the future anterior, to be opened up, again and again.

How is this to be done? Civil policymakers will have to learn some languages, clearly. The structure of general education will have to change some as well. The real requirement is diversified social tact, persuasion rather than coercion. I am not speaking of an easy or cheap change. But if the exchange is a two-way road, as I have proposed above, there can be no question of interfering with the languages of national and international governance, for those control the abstract structures of civil society.

Under imperialism, the colonized often suggested that they had the better spiritual and the colonizer the better material culture. This view has always been dismissed as, at best, disingenuous, and at worst hypocritical. It has repeatedly been pointed out that this slogan was one way of keeping women backward, as holders of spiritual culture. If structurally planetarized and persistently freed from the accoutrements of the cultural markers of migrant national origin on the part of the subordinate, and equally persistently freed from the nationalist prejudices of the dominant, the truth of this perception can be tested.

Otherwise, as it stands today, demands for "cultural" autonomy within a multicultural state is no more than a reaction to xenophobia and the lack of access to untrammeled upward class-mobility, combined with reaction-formation to cover over the guilt at having left the very "culture" that one wishes to conserve.

I have spent a good long time speaking of re-constellating the responsibility-thinking of pre-capitalist societies into the abstractions of the democratic structures of civil society—to use planetarization to control globalization—to locate the imperative in the indefinite radical alterity of the other space of a planet to deflect the rational imperative of capitalist globalization. It cannot be denied that I have been speaking of what may result in persistently critical institutional practice: politico-economic and ideologico-pedagogic accountability. The kind of lesson that I have learned from a more European ethical philosophy would suggest that institutional practice forgets ethical cautions, as follows:

Our life is lived as the call of the wholly other, which must necessarily be answered (in its forgetting, of course, assuming there had been a gift in the first place in the subject's unanticipatable insertion into temporality), by a responsibility bound by accountable reason. Ethics as experience of the impossible—therefore incalculable—is lived as the possible calculus that covers the range between self-interest and responsibility that includes the politico-legal. Justice and law, ethics and politics, gift and responsibility are structureless structures because the first item of each pair is neither available nor unavailable. It is in view of justice and ethics as undeconstructible, as experiences of the impossible, that legal and political decisions must be made, empirically scrupulous but philosophically errant. (Even this opposition, of course, is not tenable to the last degree.) The calculus of the second item in each pair such as the ones named above is imperative for responsible action, always in view of this peculiarity. These pairs are not interchangeable, but move on an unconcatenated chain of displacements. In each case, the "and" in the pair opens up the task of acknowledging that the copula "and" is a "supplement" covering an indefinite variety of relationships, since the supplement both supplies a lack and adds an excess.

When the thinking of this structureless structure turns to multicultural imperatives within a new Europe, it seems not to be able to move outside of thinking Europe as the giver—of hospitality. It circles and recircles *cosmopolitheia*. This supremacism won't do any more. In this new guise, alterity becomes a mere supplement as the ethics of alterity changes to a politics of European identity. We must give to it a proper name within a planetary graphic, not within a continental metonymy. If religion is the mobilizable instrument of the subaltern, this will accommodate many subaltern pasts, release it from the dated burden of mere messianicity. We cannot simply feel accountability in terms of border crossings and free frontiers. We must think our individual home as written on the planet as planet, what we learn in school astronomy. In this defracted view of ethics, Space may be the name of alterity, not time, not nation, not mother, not *visage* as intending.

As I have suggested above, few people know better than Mahmood Mamdani how very nearly erased are the traces of organized epistemes that are defective to capitalism. He has meticulously documented the construction of "custom" by colonial govermentality, in order to constitute itself thereby. Yet, if we are not committed to recovering an authentic origin, the lineaments of this hybrid ethos can perhaps yield, in the chanciness of the future anterior, and by way of effortful prayer, some restraining dynamic upon the abstract structure of civility into which they must be grafted. Otherwise, the Enlightenment leads to exploitation, and stagnant "custom" leads to genocide; and the promises of cyberpolitics do not produce an epistemic or ethical alternative.[25] One resource here can be the new virtualized demographic frontiers—connecting migrant groups to "mother" country—that establish Internet and other electronic shadow lines within the boundaries of the modern state. Is it merely to be "communitarian" to insist that, if not dismissed as reactionary, these shifting frontiers can offer a foothold for what's left of theory? Put in utterly practical terms, it involves a certain kind of left-work that is to be distinguished from both union organizing (old style empiricization of "spectrality") and human rights-ism (new style bourgeois moralist political blackmail).

Respect for, and systemic (rather than merely museal) integration of the para-capitalist mind-set of the migrant underclass into the efficient abstractions of civil society as an indefinitely continuing effort: such is the last-ditch model offered here for a metropolitan practice to "supplement Marxism." Living in a society where the only ethical model is a triumphalist corporate philanthropy matched by a trade-related Human Rights paradigm and global military policing, such offers can reflect no more than Gramsci's famous pessimism of the intellect and optimism of the will, expressed in a classroom that is increasingly committed to vocational professionalism. The next section will take a step backward to move toward a history of the vanishing present outside the metropolis. The object is to reconsider the metropolis—indeed, the urban, everywhere—as telos.

RURAL/INDIGENOUS

At the very beginning of *The Economic and Philosophical Manuscripts*, Marx writes a couple of sentences where the story of land-related agency still waits to be told.

Briefly, "agency" here is the name of institutionally validated action. Writing at the beginning of the consolidation of industrial capitalism, Marx's entire energy is and must correctly be devoted to showing the worker that s/he is the "*agent* of production," and this agency is validated by the institution of capital accumulation. This essay attempts to demonstrate, above, how Marx argues the turning (troping?) of this agency into social-ism rather than capital-ism. Such an argument requires an urbanist teleology, for its workshop is the factory:

> Let us therefore, in company with the owner of money and the owner of labour-power, leave this noisy sphere [the marketplace], where everything takes place on the surface and full view of

> everyone, and follow them into the hidden abode of production, on whose threshold there hangs the notice "No admittance except on business." Here we shall see, not only how capital produces, but how capital is itself produced. . . . When we leave the sphere of simple circulation or the exchange of commodities, which provides the "free-trader *vulgaris*" [still offering the mythic "level playing field" of the global free market] with his views, his concepts and the standards by which he judges the society of capital and wage-labour, a certain change takes place, or so it appears, in the physiognomy of our *dramatis personae*. He who was previously the money-owner now strides out in front as a capitalist; the possessor of labour-power follows as his worker. (C1, 279–280)

In spite of tremendous changes in the factory mode of production, its stagnancy and near–disappearance in postfordism, and the slow increase in importance of commercial and now finance capital, metropolitan theorists (Southern and Northern) are still caught within the urbanist teleology that Marx required. Thus it is quite unrealistic to expect Marx himself to have been prescient to a miraculous degree. Therefore Marx—in spite of all his homeopathic pharmacology of capital and labor (that the poison of commodification, when applied to labor, may lead to the medicine of socialism) and his lifelong sensitivity to originary indeterminacy (an opening we saw shut by "Engels")— could only think land and labor teleologically.[26] Indeed, it is a tribute to Marx's philosophical intuition that a trace of the road not taken remains in those notes scribbled by the young man of twenty-six trying to think wage through.

Sentence one: "It is therefore only for the worker that the separation of capital, landed property and labour is a necessary, essential and pernicious separation." Sentence two is separated and italicized in the manuscript. Marx *must* derive the agent of production through factory work. He buries the trace of an aporia lurking in that "necessary, essential, *and* pernicious" with an invocation of the finality of a merely human death: "*So for the worker the separation of capital, ground rent and labour is fatal.*" "Aporia" here is the "nonpassage" that Derrida ruminates upon in *Aporias*.[27]

If agency is validated action, for Marx this validation will come only from industrial capitalism. The rest is history. As the automobile commercial says, "You trade a commodity, you don't drive it." Marx had tried to self-drive labor-power, *as commodity*, without considering the episteme. Only agency here, for the *subject's* history is European and can be taken as given: if not Hegel, then the *Communist Manifesto*.[28] If a history determines consciousness, the ideology is German. We are living in the aftermath.

We are faced here with a world ravaged by the sheer rationalist convictions of capitalo-socialism, a predicament no less daunting than the confrontation with "Western metaphysics." Seeking to encounter the other of those convictions where the Enlightenment has not reached, as I have done for over a decade, with respect, humility, and a desire to learn, I cite Derrida's words for my metropolitan readers, hoping, in the iteration, in the इन्रing, to displace those words from the metropolis: "I [gave] in to the word *aporias*, in the plural, without really knowing where I was going and if something would come to pass, allowing me to pass with it, except that I recalled that, for many years now, the old, worn-out Greek term *aporia*, this tired word of philosophy and of logic, has for many years [*depuis de longues années*] imposed itself upon me, and recently it has done so with greater insistence [*de façon plus insistante*]" (translation modified).

The cited thought of non-passage is a passage.

Let us step back into the manuscripts again.

It is not often noticed that Marx's premature dismissal of the nation form of appearance, a tendency shared by most Western Marxists today, is concatenated or linked with the teleologization of the separation of land and labor that we noticed a moment ago. As Marx starts reading Adam Smith's *The Wealth of Nations* and taking the notes that form the first part of these manuscripts, the object of his analysis is named *Nationalökonomie* or "national economy." The lineaments of political economy do emerge as Marx takes notes, but the antagonist is still the *Nationalökonom*, sometimes almost a de-propriated (generalized) pseudonym for Smith. In some famous pages of the "Notebook on Capital" as assembled in the Dietz edition of the *Grundrisse*, Marx considers the genealogy of the nation-form in a secondhand way, via contemporary anthropology, looking forward to the separation of the subject from land, to the development of appropriate agency and its institution—industrial *and* postindustrial capitalism, toward urbanization.[29] By 1867, as the much-revised text of *Capital* is published, the critique *is* of *political* economy, the nation has disappeared, and Adam Smith is altogether de-propriated and de-authorized. The very first words of Marx's book are "the wealth of *societies.*" The *Grundrisse* had established the "national" as an atavistic residual: blood-tie to land. The "social" is the rational emergent, the result of the strategy driven manipulation of the abstract average. The argument is that we must progress from *national* wealth to *social* wealth, treating the problem of nation-thinking as a mere inconvenience, rashly brushed aside.

Now the *Umdrehung* or turning around of political economy is the embattled (*zwieschlächtig*) commodity-character of socialized labor. Unlike the automobile commercial, in Marx's hands this commodity is driven, traded, spectralized as futures. Labor's agency *is* in its commodity-character as labor-power. Labor can blossom or dance where body *is* soul as Reason holding the dancer *in* the dance as *zwieschlächtig*. This thinking is not immediately practicable. But no thinking has such closure. I have tried to show here how, perhaps unavoidably, even its *thinking* was not permitted. Engels's benevolent interpolations are emblematic of the impatience that insists that theory leave no residue, no remains. As we used to hear from the knee-jerk Marxists: theory and practice are united in the concept. From Western liberals of the left, with nothing left to lose, periodically: what's left of theory? And from the lone self-appointed "heir" of Marx: messianicity and the ghost dance. I continue to tease out the possibilities of the Marxian text.

I have argued elsewhere that it was in the untheorized space of "the social" that Marxism foundered. Here I have tried to outline the precipitate and derivative covering over of land and nation that allowed the word "social" to emerge. Yet, in the paragraph, precisely near the end of the chapter entitled "The *Schein* of Competition"—"illusion," yes, but also glow, lure, and even, in the echo of *Erscheinung*, carrying the normativity of appearance, which is a necessary form, illusion only if mistaken for the contentless (Marx cannot quite say form, or idea)— one can "read," in the language of hope, the trace of an avowal that the social cannot be merely the spectral as rational. Here are the concluding words of that paragraph, quoted above: "then [after all the socializing moves have been made] nothing of these forms remains, but simply those bases [*Grundlagen*] of the forms that are communal [*gemeinschaftlich*] to all social [*gesellschaftlich*] modes of production (C3, 1015–1016; translation modified).

Here is the trace of the community in the rational spectral: the urban telos carrying the "previous" formation of the *Gemeinschaft* in its subjunctive future. The translation loses the tiny nuance, massive in its implications, by rendering *gemeinschaftlich* as "common."

A non-passage, then, a "residual" invoked in so progressivist a system as Marx's must be! And the thought of non-passage forces a passage. Let us approach Marx's Eurocentric internationalism.

The question, "Why did capitalism not develop equally everywhere?" (implicitly asked and answered today by the waves of economic migration) had to be answered by some logic of difference by Marx. One of the notions that developed in response to this question was species-being [*Gattungswesen*]. At age twenty-six, Marx turned his back both on academic radicalism and street activism and began to read again. Those notes, obligatory before the days of the xerox machine, are the explosive first part of the *Economic and Philosophical Manuscripts*. In the latter parts, the young Marx writes from what he already knows, loosely affected by the reading whose tracks constitute the earlier sections. It is in this later section that he writes of species-being, the assumption that every human being is capable of, and must, take himself or herself as an example of being-human in general. No doubt this is a classical German philosophical cliché. But nonetheless, his conviction at that early stage was that socialism would make it possible for this to be empirically true in the case of each human being. It was therefore, at least in those early days, his practical motive force.

He was to lose this idea soon. But the idea that there was a difference that one had to account for and obliterate accompanies him into the new project of agent-formation. He comes, of course, to the idea of *Mehrwert*, literally "more-value" rather than the grander "surplus-value." The commonly narrative account of this formulation has been given at the opening of this essay. The more philosophical account would be to say that Marx sees that one can define the human being as being *more* than himself or herself, because s/he is worth more than him/herself with the production of "*Mehr*wert." This would be a naming of the human on a self-difference. But Marx wants a narrative or chronological account as, once again, he moves from a version of autonomy to a version of heteronomy—conclusions determined by "facts" rather than reflexion. In this case, the facts are an imaginative making of the probable (*poiesis*), rather than an *istoria*.[30] Marx and Engels lead themselves into the *story* of the Asiatic mode of production.[31] It is not enough simply to give it a decent burial. That allows us to forget that, although its factual correctness—that there was a mode of production in "Asia" where state tax and ground rent were the same—has long been disproved, *poiesis* did prove *philosophoteron*—better equipped to feed the love of knowledge—than *istoria*. That the main reason for lack of historical movement in "the developing world" was that the latter never produced real cities but only military encampments still carries a certain weight (its only serious competitor being an equally "poetic" cultural conservatism). It became the thing with which to adjudicate as to whether a country could be the locus of Communism as well.[32] The old Russian topos of the flight from Asia—Peter the Great and the initiation of "the Great Game"—was displaced in the great Lenin-Plekhanov debates. The notion accounted for either being different or being the same. And it was clinched around the impossibility of producing cities. In the new postcoloniality of the post-Soviet epoch, we should be aware that capitalist colonialism also urbanized. (This writer's birthplace, Calcutta, is one such urban formation.) Indeed, the Bolshevik Revolution, *mutatis mutandis*, can be read as Marx understood 1848.[33] A tremendous opening that, step by sequential step, served to consolidate the executive power of finance capital over a seventy-year span, and then dissolved itself. And through it all, the ideologeme of the City remained thoroughly embedded in the self-representation of "Europe" as the custodian of the Polis or Civitas.

This exercise on the edge of *aporias* has been to pass through to the history of the present. Here is the storying needed to keep the argument moving. It is the story of a storying—of the rewriting of the logical model of social justice into a narrative of population movements. The big international so-called non-governmental organizations (NGOs) that are, in fact, working for the Bretton Woods organizations, call themselves an international *civil* society (briefly, everything that is not the state) today. This exacerbates the weakening of the nation-states, which are increasingly powerless in the developing world, as the barriers between their fragile economies and international capital are gradually removed. And even in the so-called developed world, the international circuits of electronic capitalism (finance and trade) increasingly bypass the redistributive demands of the state. The particular phenomenon of the *non*-governmental organizations (hardly a substantive description) is a reaction to this. In this predicament Western Marxism has not been able to give up the narrative of movement from the rural to the urban. The most unfortunate consequence of this has been to describe transnationality—the characteristic of a certain capital-formation—as the movement of people. This leads Etienne Balibar to write off class-consciousness or agency-consciousness (quite distinct from theories of fully self-present subject-consciousness) and suggest that the best way to understand mass movements would be in terms of population movements.[34] And Derrida, in effect, transforms Marx—although in theory protected by the alterity of the *absolute arrivant*—into an *arrivant*, a species of migrant. The exilic hybrid as "marrano" becomes the name of the human condition, where "the secret keeps the Marrano even before the Marrano keeps it" (A, 81). In his brilliant recent work on hospitality, the figure is the foreigner at the door.[35] Any supplementation of this thinking will see that, for the subaltern in the narrow sense, the foreigner at the door is the World Bank, the IMF, and the World Trade Organization, sustained by the United Nations, fine-tuned by "the international civil society," often empirically represented by the hapless local field representative, not physically recognizable as "foreign" at all. Such a realization is no discredit to Derrida, who has always acknowledged the consequences that the thought of a divided origin is the "nonethical opening of ethics."[36] And this reminder of the narrow senses of *arrivant*, hospitality, foreigner will also be acceptable to the philosopher who has been ever mindful of paleonymy. Indeed, the asymmetry of interest that tips the balance for the migrant and the messiah is linked to the double bind of deconstruction. But his followers are not always alive to these checks and balances.[37]

Bound, no doubt, by my own double bind, I turn now to the subaltern in the South, the rural landless, the Aboriginal. Here also, literary examples will guide me into my argument. Let us remind ourselves that, in the initial redefinition of the Gramscian word "subaltern," as recorded by Ranajit Guha, it is the name of the space of difference inhabited by those who have no access to the lines of mobility within a society.[38] Let us also remember that there are no test cases, that singularities overflow definitive determinations—a caution Marx was obliged to deny.

Mahasweta Devi's novella, "Pterodactyl, Puran Sahay, and Pirtha," takes place in the shadow of the so-called green revolution. Puran Sahay—the settler Indian journalist (albeit "the settlement" was three thousand years ago)—travels to report the famine in Pirtha, an aboriginal area:[39] "The survey map of Pirtha Block is like some extinct animal of Gondwanaland. The beast has fallen on its face. The new era in the history of the world began when, at the end of the Mesozoic era, India broke off from the main mass of Gondwanaland. It is as if some prehistoric creature had fallen on its face then. Such are the survey lines of Pirtha Block."[40]

The figuring of geological time puts the (post)colonial-figuring instrument of the survey under erasure. The lineaments of the other of the human covers the self-and-other established by this old settler colony in antiquity. Since the remotely pre-capitalist colonizers (today's "Hindu" Indians) have inscribed themselves as postcolonials in the wake of the most recent Independence, this is an untold story.

The Mesozoic is invoked again in a passage where the pterodactyl has taken up the peculiar corporeality of a specter. This time, the ghost's otherness to the humans—however they themselves may be separated by ancient colonial history—is clear. The pterodactyl refuses the food laid out by the Aboriginal. And, as for the ancient settler, today's "real" Indian? "Who can place his hand on the axial moment of the end of the third phase of the Mesozoic and the beginnings of the

Cenozoic geological ages? . . . The dusky lidless eyes remain unresponsive" (PT, 155–156).

I can read this text as an unwitting reinscription of the Freudian uncanny.[41] With this second instance we have entered a doubly inscribed cave, an inner shrine room inside Bikhia's cave-dwelling. "Pterodactyl'"s cave is the home of the wholly other.

After the representation of the ghost's death, Mahasweta moves us through to yet another cave with all the accoutrements of a womb-archetype; the way down lies through an underground passage with dripping walls. The last cave, the place where the pre-human past is buried, is once again a place of the obliteration of historiography, as in the first figuration of the "extinct animal of Gondwanaland," the geography of survey maps has been overwritten. For in the final cave, Puran cannot tell if the wall-paintings are archaic or contemporary.

I can read this erasure of colonial, and indeed human, timing in order to take a step backward to move toward what I will call the spectralization of the rural, calling into question the urbanist teleology of the European tradition. For Devi's novella is framed in the green revolution—the first inkling, in the rise of neo-colonialism, after the dismantling of territorial imperialism, that land would be a major player in the gradual transnationalization of the pharmaceutical industry, the source of chemical fertilizers as well as chemical instruments of coercive contraception. The efficient cause for Puran's trip to Pirtha is a "famine" that cannot be constituted as evidence according to the statistical manipulation of the postcolonial state. And the counter-intuitive absurdity of family planning in a place that cannot be acknowledged as starving provides the contempt that is the pervasive tone of the text toward national policy.

After the European recession of the 1870s, Lenin already knew that the major theater of spectralization had shifted to commercial capital.[42] Already spectralized labor-power, use-value in capital accumulation, had lost its unique power to socialize capital as agent of production. One of the longest chapters in Lenin's book *Imperialism* is entitled "Banks." He could not envisage a World Bank yet.

The development of the spectralized capital dependent upon commerce through the circulating mediation of the banking system, with industry (theorized by Marx as labor-power) apparently invisible in a supportive infrastructural role—surplus-value invisible as anything other than interest, allows the explanation of capital that Marx had laughed at in *Capital* 2, to establish itself as the dominant explanation:

> The production process appears simply as an unavoidable middle term, a necessary evil for the purpose of money-making. . . . [E]nrichment as such appears as the inherent purpose of money-making. . . . [Money capital] is expressed as money breeding money. The creation by value of surplus-value is not only expressed as the alpha and omega of the process, but explicitly presented as the glittering money form. (C2, 137–138)

The apparent disappearance of labor-power (industry), and its concomitant use-exchange binary opposition, and the critique of reification, also still attached to considerations of industry, made it possible for academic post-Marxism to emerge. The criticism from the left, in other words, seemed to have nothing to do with the conjuncture, to metropolitan cultural radicals of various convictions. Time and space will not allow a discussion here of the various ways in which these intellectuals resolved their problems. It goes without saying that world economic behavior was largely untroubled by these controversies. Yet we must speak of the world in the classroom. And the same forces that substituted information command for knowing or learning (whatever that may be) in the classroom wrought a change in the nature of commercial capital—electronification.

Commercial capital works *through* banks. For finance capital, the bank is a matheme on the screen. If this is the morphological change in the determination of capital, the narrative support came from the fall of the Soviet Union. Globalization can now be seen as the establishment of the same system of exchange globally—made possible by electronification. Since this is also the method by which information can be stored and disseminated, it also causes (and is caused by) infoglut. At certain levels, this detailed proliferation of information helps globalization as such. Hence, TRIPS (trade-related intellectual property) on such things as biodiversity, human genome patenting, etc. On the more strictly "educational" levels, it creates a seductive simulacrum of learning. Global telecommunication is the industry which is linked to, but not identical with, globalization—in form; given that it must, unlike the circuits of finance capital, which are abstract—have a narrative (or at least decipherable) "content," it can be used for political manipulation, crisis management, and damage control.

For those of us still mesmerized by the urbanist teleology of the right and the left, the changes seen upon urban-built space are the most visible. It is possible, however, that the real terrain of globalization is the spectralization of the so-called rural. Again, the evolutionist narrative explanation and argument is that the former colonies must be "modernized." The development of bank-based commercial capital in neo-colonialisms showed up a fault-line in Marx's teleology. The urban had been an alternative. In postcoloniality, the rural was engaged directly.

Today's global front is in what can be called "the country," not the city at all. To learn that is to move from postcoloniality to globalism, from below. The space that is not the "global"—"global" being roughly synonymous with the old "social" minus the centralized pivot of socialism—is now thought *from* the centrality of the global: as the rural, the local, the ecological, the Aboriginal. In the age of biopiracy, databasing both indigenous *knowledge* and *body*, the *Encyclopedia of Life Support Systems* projected by UNESCO, must "define" the Aboriginal period as "associated with *inactive* approaches in which there is no concern for environmental degradation and sustainability."[43] It was, of course, as impossible for the Aboriginal to think sustainability as it was for Aristotle to "decipher . . . the secret of the expression of value," because of "the historical limitation inherent in the society in which [they] lived" (C1, 152). Yet the practical philosophy of living in the rhythm of the ecobiome must now be dismissed as "no concern."

The task, it seems to me, is not to cultivate this supremacist benevolence, but to revise—*re-viser*, re-turn—to rethink the separation of land and subject, the project that Marx was unable or unwilling to entertain fully because of "the historical limitation inherent in the society in which [he] lived." The story of industrial capitalist imperialism may be a contained episode in an epic temporization that is not necessarily unilateral.

From commercial to finance capital, transnationalization to globalization, it is the spectralization of the "rural" that is now the dominant. The silicon chip puts the "rural" into a general equivalent form—not

money but finance. Capital uses the spectrality of the "rural." The Global
Environment Fund is controlled by the World Bank and the United
Nations Development Program. Finance capital, the abstract as such,
cannot operate without interruption by the empirical. The haphazard list
below, involving the spectralization of the rural, is coded by world trade:

Biodiversity (the enormous variety of plant species in "Nature"), elec-
tronified for biopiracy (patenting them "illegally" with Northern
patents—though "legally" by unilaterally established latter-day "laws" by
the North, as in the famous Neem case); monocultures (mutant hybrid
high-yield seeds suppressing variety, in the process depleting and literally
"killing" the soil) produced by way of chemical fertilizers, themselves
blips on the screen. As the commercial says: "You see coffee, Sprint sees
data." Indigenous knowledge transformed into database. *Trade Related*
Intellectual property Rights and *Trade Related* investment measures abre-
actively punish the collectivities millennially working at the pre-measurable "rural" for not establishing property rights over its value coding.[44]
Deforestation-reforestation and the management of waters (for example,
cutting down forests that are important to indigenous life- and knowl-
edge-systems, and replanting with eucalyptus, that can produce 75%
pulp-wood but depletes the moisture in the soil and disturbs the balance
of living organisms in regions drastically; destroying mangrove and sali-
nating arable land to establish foreign direct export shrimp culture and
devastating long established human and other life-systems, and the like)
belong to the earlier (more commercial) phase but augment the latter.
And, the credit-baiting of rural women for phantom micro-enterprise is
the latest twist: small-scale commercial-in-the-finance-capital market,
where the perennial need of the rural poor is exploited for the commercial sector with no locally operated infrastructural change. This is an
important and complex issue that may be beyond the scope of this essay.
Suffice it to say that this invariable power choice of monocultures has
something like a relationship with the dismissal of literary production in
languages without capitalist power as "parochial."[45] It is with this connection in mind that I ask you to read the following remarks.

No conurbation is structurally necessary for the spectralization of
the "rural." As we have been insisting, "pure" finance capital—the
abstract as such—is impossible. In its coding through world trade (dis-

course of "level playing field") and the commercial sector (discourse of "money begets money" or "better than the moneylender")—it invokes land and the embodied female subject. And it is here that the always partially spectralized "rural" confronts the forces of the global face-to-face. Resistance networks long in place run interference for the operation of the globalizing agencies, which shift, twist, turn, and manage these crises as interruptions of their spectralizing global sweep. As a literary critic "reading" the social text in the broadest and most active sense, this unending series of interruptions, which I have learned to recognize by hanging out in the text of this new activism, can be rhetorically named the "irony" of the main text of global regularization, if we understand "irony" as "the permanent parabasis of an allegory (of globalization) . . . the systematic undoing, in other words, of the abstract."[46]

"Parabasis"—a step beside yet upon a ground—is when the Chorus stepped out to tell the public how to respond to the main text of the Old Comedy, the "freer" form of Greek drama of which Aristotle postpones discussion. No Marxist can be unmindful of the grandeur of the spectral motor of globalization as such. "The Moor" (Marx's nickname), as the dark double of the Enlightenment, wanted the agent of production to drive that motor by understanding its own spectralization as use-value of the capital that could become useful for global socialism. For this too-philosophical "revolution" he needed the narrative of the urban. We who criticize both the "pure" spectrality of a revolutionary program without epistemic support, as well as the urban as telos advanced metaleptically (substituting effect for cause), find in the negotiating-interruptive model of the constant turning around of globalization against the vicious greed of the super-power, an interminable and therefore more practical figure: a permanent parabasis. The model is eating (again and again) rather than book writing (once and for all, repetition unavoidable but unwelcome).

In the theater of metropolitan immigration we have proposed a model of give and take between responsibility-based cultural systems and abstract civil society and the rule of law. There politics and civil society are sustained by the European story of urbanization. In this new "spectralization," the paradoxical new complicity (folded togetherness) of the global, we must supplement the classic socialist method, even when unmoored from a telos- or job-security orientation; even when mindful of the feminization of labor and the disappearance of the factory in electronic postfordism. For unlike labor-power, the earth and the bios are not renewable. The incommensurable counter-examples cited in *Capital* 1 are here in the value form and not use-values at all: "A thing can be a value without being a use-value"; "You see coffee, Sprint sees data." The alternative line of land-related agency left behind in the *Economic and Philosophical Manuscripts* snakes forward in bursts, in ways that Marx could not have foretold.

This spectral "rural" is not the empiricity of green fields and vials of blood; it has, in the manner of catachreses, no literal referent.[47] Unlike what Paul Virilio thinks, it is not the metropolitan or transnational traveler whose experience of "com[ing] back to Paris from Los Angeles or New York at certain times of the year [when] you can see, through the window, passing over the pole, the setting sun and the rising sun" that offers us the new global time; showing "the beyond of the geographical city and the advent of human concentration in travel time."[48] The contempt in the following sentence is no more than an expression of the sanctioned ignorance of the European:

> The global metropolitics of the future electronic information highways in itself implies the coming of a society no longer divided so much into North and South, but into two distinct temporalities, two speeds: one *absolute*, the other *relative*. The cut [*coupure*] between developed and underdeveloped countries being reinforced throughout the five continents and leading to an even more radical rupture [*rupture*] between those who will live under the empire of real time essential to their economic activities at the heart of the virtual community of the *world city*, and those, more destitute than ever, who will survive in the real space of *local towns* . . .[49]

The time of seed and DNA is not "real" or "local" time, it is irrelevant to subject-speak, open only to an open place of agency. The definition of the "subaltern" is now being rewritten. It is the group that, although or perhaps because, cut off from ordinary lines of mobility, is being touched directly by global telecommunication: the spectrality of indigenous knowledge, the databasing of DNA-patenting of the most remote groups, the credit-baiting of the poorest rural women.

Arrived here, the writer of this essay no doubt reveals her double bind. But it seems that the epistemic undertaking here is not only messianicity, not only the responsibility of being human, but the mind-set that names the bios with the name of an alterity that harbors good and bad—the "sacred," if there is any. The infinite patience of learning so "unproductive" a mindset, from compromised sources—rather than declaring a futurity of new solitude-loving philosopher companions (theoretical), or protecting the intellectual property rights of the indigenous (practical)—has no place in an essay prepared for the impatience of publishers' deadlines in the international book trade. Its place is outside my classroom here.

CODA

1. From his flat in Haverstock Hill, Marx the rationalist wanted to build socialism with the bones beneath the flesh. He required an urbanist telos.

2. Actually existing socialism managed to strengthen the bones of capitalism in the long run.

3. Triumphant global finance capital/world trade can only be resisted with irony.

4. The model is actually existing Southern hemisphere–based network movements.

5. To strengthen this, metropolitan multicultural policy might strengthen the scaffolding of civil rights abstractions with the cement of cultural systems defective for monstrous self-enrichment.

6. Otherwise strong economic systems in the Northern hemisphere can offer a society with low unemployment, few social services, and tremendous gaps between the rich and the rest as "the good society."

7. Globalization studies might reconsider their urbanist telos and take account of the new system's engagement with the bones of the rural/indigenous.

8. The impossible solution is the infinite unguaranteed patience to learn to learn from below.

9. Otherwise corporate philanthropy and/or international protectionism see millions as only bodies or human capital.

10. This coda cannot be acted on from a U.S. classroom.

NOTES

1. I thank Jean Franco for her encouragement, and an astute first reading. I thank Jessica Forbes and Blythe Frank for their support, and unfailing good humor.

2. Karl Marx, *Capital: A Critique of Political Economy*, trans. Ben Fowkes (New York: Vintage, 1977), vol. 1, p. 277. Henceforth C1 in text, followed by page reference.

3. Aristotle, *The Nicomachean Ethics*, trans. H. Rackham (Cambridge, Mass.: Harvard Univ. Press, 1994), pp. 332–333. Translation modified.

4. The attempt to philosophize it leads to theology. It is "nothing else than the historical process of divorcing the producer from the means of production" (C1, p. 875).

5. Is it too fanciful to say that Marx is a strange sort of Kantian here, turning from the reflexive to the determinant judgment, from autonomy to heteronomy, in order not to participate in the poverty of a philosophy that goes too fast to solve problems? At any rate, Marx downshifts.

6. Perry Anderson, *Considerations on Western Marxism* (London: New Left Books, 1976).

7. This insight undergirds a large part of the political argument of Gilles Deleuze and Félix Guattari, *Anti-Oedipus: Capitalism and Schizophrenia*, trans. Robert Hurley et al. (Minneapolis: Univ. of Minnesota Press, 1996). It would be hard to isolate a specific passage.

8. *Foreign Policy in Focus*, a joint project of the Institute for Policy Studies and the Interhemispheric Resource Center, produces briefs that give the non-specialist an idea of these dynamics.

9. Pankaj Butalia's *Moksha*, an excellent documentary on Hindu widows leading a peculiar communal life in the holy town of Vrindavana carries English subtitles (middle-class sentiment emoting on their victimage) that do not reveal the strong cynical critique of the institution of marriage and a woman's lot in much that these widows said. A failure of translation, a difference in class culture. An appropriate elaboration therefore, for "Once Widowed in India, Twice Scorned," by John Burns of the *New York Times* (March 29, 1998), commenting on the widows' lot, again quoting, again pitying, again deploring their victimage. The subaltern is made to unspeak herself.

10. Even Chandra Talpade Mohanty's excellent lead essay in M. Jacqui Alexander and Chandra Mohanty, eds., *Feminist Genealogies, Democratic Futures* (New York: Routledge, 1997) is somewhat marked by this.

11. I use the words of the final Foucault because he was trying to understand ethics in its cultural-institutional coding, rather than in the deconstructive unmooring of the thematics of conscience. (Michel Foucault, *The Care of the Self: The History of Sexuality*, vol. 3, trans. Robert Hurley [New York: Pantheon, 1986]).

12. C1, p. 132; the last quoted fragment is, of course, a modification of Kant's famous lines: "But that the public should enlighten itself is more possible; indeed if one grants it freedom, it is almost inevitable [*unausbleiblich*]. . . . What may be called freedom is: to make public use of one's Reason [*Vernunft*] at every point" (Immanuel Kant, "What Is Enlightenment?," in Lewis White Beck, trans., *Kant on History* [New York: Macmillan, 1963]), pp. 4–5 .

13. Marx, *Capital: A Critique of Political Economy*, trans. David Fernbach (New York: Vintage, 1978), vol. 2, p. 131; hereafter in text as C2, followed by page reference.

14. Marx, *Capital: A Critique of Political Economy*, trans. David Fernbach (New York: Vintage, 1981), vol. 3, pp. 1015–1016.

15. Here is an example of a simple power semiotic, outside the context of my managerial specimens. At my university, one of the signs of "power," not necessarily connected with sheer intellectual or pedagogic excellence, is the square footage of your living quarters. The desire to give others space—as an ethical desire—gets quenched here, as of course, if you care more for your living than your being-othered, does any (irrational?) desire to live in a snug space.

16. As always, I use "miraculating" in the sense given to the word by Deleuze and Guattari, *Anti-Oedipus*, p. 10.

17. Mahmood Mamdani, *Citizen and Subject: Contemporary Africa and the Legacy of Late Colonialism* (Princeton: Princeton Univ. Press, 1996), pp. 203, 201.

18. See Susan Bazilli, ed., *Putting Women on the Agenda* (Cape Town: Ravan Press, 1991); and Neville Hoad, "Between White Man's Burden and the White Man's Disease: Tracking Lesbian and Gay Human Rights in Southern Africa," *GLQ: A Journal of Lesbian and Gay Studies* 5. iv (1999).

19. Michel De Certeau, *The Capture of Speech and Other Political Writings*, trans. Tom Conley (Minneapolis: Univ. of Minnesota Press, 1998), p. 161.

20. Jacques Derrida, *Glas*, trans. John P. Leavey, Jr., et al. (Lincoln: Univ. of Nebraska Press, 1986), p. 1b.

21. Raymond Williams, *Marxism and Literature* (New York: Oxford Univ. Press, 1977), p. 123.

22. Virginia Woolf, *A Room of One's Own* (New York: Harcourt, 1981), pp. 4–5. In this mode, Woolf cannily inscribes the connection between Western feminism and imperialism. Her fictive fiction-writing woman can do so because her "aunt, Mary Beton . . . died by a fall from her horse when she was riding out to take the air in Bombay" (p. 37).

23. Spivak, *Imperatives to Reimagine the Planet/Imperative zur Neuerfindung des Planeten*, ed. Willi Goetschel (Vienna: Passagen, 1999).

24. It is not a matter of using the word "planet" rather than the word "globe." One can say x and y, if one pleases. It is a matter of moving from world-thought as of

something you can control through spectralization (you believe); and of a self-placing where your other is indefinite, perhaps galactic. Such a shift can take on board self-and-other thinking all the way from aboriginal animism to postmodern science.

25. Here is John Perry Barlow on the cybernetic instant Enlightenment of Hmmma, a 14-year-old African boy. "See? The kid gets it. He is introduced to the computers and the Net, and 30 seconds later he knows the thing to do in this new economy is gain some attention. Advertise!" (Barlow, "Africa Rising," *Wired* [January 1998], p. 148). We are, of course, not discussing a collective problem solving by faxes and such, although what long-term effect the short-run successes have is another story.

26. Marx, *Early Writings*, trans. Rodney Livingstone and Gregor Benton (New York: Vintage, 1976), p. 282.

27. Derrida, *Aporias*, trans. Thomas Dutoit (Stanford: Stanford Univ. Press, 1993), pp. 12–13. Hereafter cited in text as A, followed by page reference.

28. It cannot be repeated often enough that both the *Communist Manifesto* and *The German Ideology* were written before Marx saw the revolution of 1848. That for me is the epistemic cut, not some attitude to humanism or Hegel.

29. Marx, *Grundrisse: Foundations of the Critique of Political Economy*, trans. Martin Nicolaus (New York: Vintage, 1973), pp. 471–493. It is as if there is a seamless continuity between Marx's nineteenth-century remarks and the United Nations publication *An Urbanizing World: Global Report on Human Settlements* (Oxford: Oxford Univ. Press, 1996).

30. Aristotle, *Poetics*, trans. W. Hamilton Fyfe and W. Rhys Roberts (Cambridge, Mass.: Harvard Univ. Press, 1991), pp. 84–85.

31. Similar implications of the Asiatic mode of production have been discussed at greater length in Spivak, *A Critique of Postcolonial Reason: Toward a History of the Vanishing Present* (Cambridge, Mass.: Harvard Univ. Press, 1999).

32. James O'Connor, *Natural Causes: Essays in Ecological Marxism* (New York: Guilford Press, 1998) shares many of the presuppositions of this essay, explains them with much greater scholarship and authority, but finally creates an articulation of ecologism and Marxism. I see a productive rupture where he sees a potential continuity. But we are allies.

33. Marx, "The Eighteenth Brumaire of Louis Bonaparte," in *Surveys from Exile*, trans. David Fernbach (New York: Vintage, 1974), pp. 143–249. For an alternative viewpoint, see Jon Eslter, *Ulysses and the Sirens: Studies in Rationality and Irrationality* (Cambridge: Cambridge Univ. Press, 1979), p. 102.

34. Etienne Balibar, *Masses, Classes, Ideas: Studies on Politics and Philosophy Before and After Marx* (New York: Routledge, 1994), p. 146.

35. Derrida, *De l'hospitalité* (Paris: Calmann-Lévy, 1997). As in the case of Balibar, this is the one moment in an otherwise dazzlingly brilliant work that remains opaque and insistent.

36. The earliest example I know comes from Derrida, *Of Grammatology*, trans. Spi-

vak (Baltimore: Johns Hopkins Univ. Press, 1976), p. 140. This move in Derrida is related to the impulse that makes Nietzsche investigate truth and falsity in "an extra-moral sense." The banality, the complicity with its opposite, of the general sense of a concept-metaphor, often escapes Derrideans. This is why he keeps rejecting "good conscience deconstruction," I believe.

37. The infinite delicacy with which he "corrects" Nancy on comparable grounds in Derrida, *Politics of Friendship*, trans. George Collins (New York: Verso, 1997), p. 48, n. 16 is exemplary.

38. Ranajit Guha, "On Some Aspects of the Historiography of Colonial India," in *Subaltern Studies* (Delhi: Oxford Univ. Press, 1982), vol. 1, p. 8. Checking the passage for reference, I see that he says something slightly different, but the difference may prove interesting to the reader.

39. For a nuanced scholarly account of how this should be responsibly stated, see Colin Renfrew, *Archaeology and Language: The Puzzle of Indo-European Origins* (Cambridge: Cambridge Univ. Press, 1988).

40. Mahasweta Devi, "Pterodactyl, Puran Sahay, and Pirtha," in Spivak, trans., *Imaginary Maps* (New York: Routledge, 1995), p. 99; hereafter PT, with page references following.

41. Sigmund Freud, "The Uncanny," *Standard Edition of the Complete Psychological Works*, trans. James Strachey et al. (London: Hogarth Press, 1961–), vol. 17, p. 245. Luce Irigaray's "Plato's *hystera*," in *Speculum of the Other Woman*, trans. Gillian C. Gill (Ithaca: Cornell Univ. Press, 1985), pp. 243–365 is also a reinscription of this text of Freud. The irony that Irigaray, victim of masculism, writes from below; and Mahasweta, descendant of colonizers, writes from above would, of course, be missed by the sanctioned ignorance of liberal multiculturalism.

42. V. I. Lenin, *Imperialism: The Highest Stage of Capitalism* (New York: International Publishers, 1993), p. 22.

43. *Encyclopedia of Life Support Systems: Conceptual Framework* (Whitstable, 1997), p. 13.

44. Najma Sadèque, *How "They" Run the World* (Lahore: Shirkat Gah, 1996), pp. 28–30. My only objection to this brilliant pamphlet is that it does not emphasize the production of the colonial subject in imperialism and thus cannot emphasize our complicity, which we must acknowledge in order to act. I keep quoting this text rather than some more "scholarly" work because of its directness and its simplicity, more appropriate to the general state of ignorance of the basic principles of these issues for the left academic in the human sciences.

45. I am referring, of course, to Salman Rushdie's remarks in the *New Yorker* (June 23 and 30, 1997, pp. 51–60), and the recent publication of Salman Rushdie and Elizabeth West, eds. *The Vintage Book of Indian Writing 1947–1997* (London: Vintage, 1997), containing writing only in English.

46. Paul de Man, *Allegories of Reading: Figural Language in Rousseau, Nietzsche, Rilke, and Proust* (New Haven: Yale Univ. Press, 1979), p. 301. I have altered two words. I invite the reader to ponder the changes. There are, of course, plenty of references to these movements in mainstream journals such as *The Ecologist* and

in the New Social Movement support groups in the United States such as the International Rivers network. In academic left literature not specifically connected to the Third World, the best we can do is something like O'Connor's "[t]housands of groups (formal and informal) and dozens of political parties in Africa, Asia, and Latin America are evolving programs that include elements drawn from both the old political Left and ecology. Clearly, radical ecology is becoming a force to reckon with, and to work with, and to defend and advance" (*Natural Causes*, p. 15). Although this statement overlooks the crucial difference between party politics and these alliances, it acknowledges their longterm existence and makes no claim to leadership. His chapter on "International Red Green Movements" (pp. 299–305) is the shortest in the book, and has the obligatory references to Mexico and the Narmada. Rosalyn Deutsche's *Evictions: Art and Spatial Politics* (Cambridge: MIT Press, 1996), certainly a breakthrough for New York–based Cultural Studies, faults "new social movements" for generally "positivist" understanding of social practice, without ever defining them. I have no doubt she is thinking of Euro/U.S.-based identity politics of one sort or another, including environmentalism; but cannot be sure. That she is not aware of the powerful global parabasis to which I am referring seems certain. Yet she faults "traditional left intellectuals" (undoubtedly confined to the phantom U.S. left and her own take on the gender-debates forever commemorated by the sixties so-called New Left): "Masculinism as a position of social authority is also about the authority of traditional left intellectuals to account for the political condition of the entire world. What measures does it take to reestablish this authority in the name of the public?" (p. 312). Deutsche celebrates "an essential limitlessness" (p. 275)—a species of anti-essentialist essentialism—where "public space" is finally seen to be "structured like a language." This is the problem with Derrideans that I refer to above. The lesson about the problem with making language your explanatory model of last resort might have been learned even from "Structure, Sign and Play in the Discourse of the Human Sciences," in Derrida, *Writing and Difference*, trans. Alan Bass (Chicago: Univ. of Chicago Press, 1978), pp. 278–293. Deutsche's basic good sense in the New York context is fortunately at odds with these theoretical pronouncements. She clearly knows that limitlessness requires the drawing of limits that must remain open, and thus is bound; that the structure of language is forever compromised with reference. (One interesting conclusion to be drawn from her work is that, even as the subaltern in the Southern hemisphere is the focus of spectral networking, the category of the "homeless," everywhere, fills the place of the earlier definition of the subaltern: beings cut off from all lines of mobility. On the homeless as subject of freedom, see Jeremy Waldron, "Homelessness and the Issue of Freedom," *UCLA Law Review* 39.2, pp. 295–324.) On the other side of the spectrum, it is interesting that, as of March 21, 1998 (Conference on "Does America Have a Democratic Mission?," University of Virginia), Lawrence Eagleburger, George Bush's Secretary of State, had not heard the words "New Social Movement!"

47. A picture of vials of blood appeared on the cover of the *Sunday New York Times Magazine* (April 26, 1998), to illustrate Lisa Belkin, "The Clues Are in the Blood,"

an article about tapping the DNA of Cebu islanders. I have commented on such "naturalized" explanations in terms of socialization of reproductive labor and slogans of owning one's body by way of a comparison of the work of Bangladeshi and U.S. feminism in *A Critique of Postcolonial Reason.*

48. Paul Virilio/Sylvère Lotringer, *Pure War*, trans. Mark Polizzotti (New York: Semiotext(e), 1997), pp. 13–14.

49. Virilio, *Open Sky*, trans. Julie Rose (New York: Verso, 1997), p. 71; translation modified. Virilio's book *Popular Defense and Ecological Struggles*, trans. Mark Polizzotti (New York: Semiotext(e), 1990), is all about European theories of war.

2

"LIKE RACE"

ARGUMENTS

Gay and lesbian advocates often claim that gay rights are just like rights already established for racial minorities or women by the black civil rights movement and the women's movement. Particularly when they argue to judges, who are formally if not actually constrained by precedent, and even when they make more general political appeals, advocates are opportunists looking for a simile: "Your honor, this is just like a race discrimination case; this is just like a sex discrimination case."

And indeed, sexual orientation and sexuality identities have formed important social movements that look like other identity-based movements. Gay men and lesbians, transgendered people, and other sexual dissidents have been able to create legal change and legal controversy on issues falling under almost every traditional rubric of law. Contract, tort, procedure, constitutional law, civil rights, family law, trusts and estates, employment law, housing law, taxation, regulation—sexually identified progressives have legal reform aspirations and achievements affecting all of these areas and more.[1] They have grass-roots and national organizations, including NAACP-like national legal reform offices staffed with full-time lawyers. They also have ferocious opponents convinced that, if they realize any of their reform aspirations, the entire national character will collapse. Sexual orientation and sexuality movements have the look and feel of identity movements of the contemporary sort.

But in important ways, they lack the substance. "Identity politics" is usually waged on assumptions that identity inheres in group members, that group membership brings with it a uniformly shared range (or even a core) of authentic experience and attitude; that the political and legal interests of the group are similarly coherent; and that group members are thus able to draw on their own experiences to discern those interests and to establish the authority they need to speak for the group. I will call these the "coherentist" assumptions about identity politics. Sexual orientation and sexuality identities don't support those assumptions very well.

Take lesbian identity for an example. One is a lesbian not because of anything in oneself, but because of social interactions, or the desire for social interactions: it takes two women, or at least one woman and the imagination of another, to make a lesbian. Lesbians have a huge range of experience and attitude relating to their sexual orientation: on issues as basic as whether being women makes lesbians really different from gay men, we don't agree. We are famously unable to agree with one another about what our collective political and legal interests are— for example, we don't agree about whether access to marriage should be a movement priority—and we are notoriously ready to punish any woman who purports to speak for us.

Similar things can be said about gay men, homosexuals, bisexuals (generic or male and female), transvestite/(pre-op, post-op, and non-op) transsexual/transgendered people, people living with AIDS/HIV, and sexual and gender dissidents of various, always changing, descriptions. Even more complex challenges to the coherentist assumptions about identity politics emerge when attention focuses on the question of the merger, exile, coalition, and secession of these constituencies, one from the other. Are gay men and lesbians "homosexuals," or, more properly, gay men on one hand, and lesbians on the other? Are bisexuals "homosexuals" or traitors? Is there a single social movement that seeks to relieve the social suffering of women who regard femininity as an engine of repression and transsexuals who identify as "women born in men's bodies"? Of people with AIDS, notwithstanding differences in the ways they became infected and in their access to expensive new treatments?

Sexual orientation and sexuality movements are perhaps unique among contemporary identity movements in harboring an unforgivingly corrosive critique of identity itself, and they have launched significant activist and theoretical impulses in the direction of a "post–identity politics." The term "queer" was adopted by some movement participants in part to frustrate identity formation around dissident sexualities. And academic and street-level queer theory challenge the coherentist assumptions about identity politics. The keynote of this critique of identity is deep, strong constructivism. Starting with the finding that modern homosexual identities have emerged only in fairly recent historical times, queer theory suggests that they do not exist prior to, but are instead produced by, their politics. Noting that homosexual identity and heterosexual identity are diacritically related—that each negatively defines and makes possible the social urgency of the other—queer theory suggests that homosexual identities create a necessary condition for the oppression of homosexual people, that is, the existence of a class of heterosexuals anxious to confirm their immunity from the designation "homosexual." Queer theory argues that identity is not the core truth and safe zone of authenticity and authority posited by our most widely shared assumptions about identity politics; instead it suggests that identity may be part of the problem.[2]

This insight poses ethical questions that are particularly pressing for advocates of identity groups. K. Anthony Appiah states the issue:

> Demanding respect for people as blacks and as gays requires that there are some scripts that go with being an African-American or having same-sex desires. There will be proper ways of being black and gay, there will be expectations to be met, demands to be made. It is at this point that someone who takes autonomy seriously will ask whether we have not replaced one kind of tyranny with another. If I had to choose between the worlds of the closet and the world of gay liberation, or between the world of *Uncle Tom's Cabin* and Black Power, I would, of course, choose in each case the latter. But I would like not to have to choose. I would like other options. . . .

> It is a familiar thought that the bureaucratic categories of iden-
> tity must come up short before the vagaries of actual people's
> lives. But it is equally important to bear in mind that a politics of
> identity can be counted on to transform the identities on whose
> behalf it ostensibly labors. Between the politics of recognition and
> the politics of compulsion, there is no bright line.[3]

The coherentist assumptions about identity politics make Appiah's statement appear merely disloyal. Those assumptions posit that identity preexists its articulation in politics, and thus assume away the constructive power of identity advocacy. They also assume away any difference between what Appiah, "as a" black gay man, might opt to do or become and the script set out for him in the politics of identity. But *if* advocacy constructs identity, *if* it generates a script which identity bearers must heed, *if* that script restricts group members, then identity politics compels its beneficiaries. Identity politics suddenly is no longer mere or simple resistance: it begins to look like power.

Appiah's challenge rests on the critical insight that power can be exercised not only to make people *do* things they would not otherwise do, but also to make them *become* people they would not otherwise be. One important theory of this second function of power was offered by the Marxist political theorist Louis Althusser, who posited that ideology could "'recruit[ ]' subjects amongst the individuals . . . or 'transform[ ]' the individuals into subjects . . . by that very precise operation which I have called *interpellation* or hailing, and which can be imagined along the lines of the most commonplace everyday police (or other) hailing: 'Hey, you there!'" Althusser elaborated this notion of "interpellation" further:

> Assuming that the theoretical scene I have imagined takes place in
> the street, the hailed individual will turn around. By this mere one-
> hundred-and-eighty-degree physical conversation, he becomes a
> *subject*. Why? Because he has recognized that the hail was "really"
> addressed to him, and that "it was *really him* who was hailed" (and
> not someone else).[4]

Althusser's description of interpellation has often been criticized for its depiction of the "subject" as abject, as completely powerless to resist or reshape the "hail" issued by ideology. That is an important criticism, but here I want to emphasize that his description is incomplete because it assumes that the interpellative call will always come from above, from a high center of power. Dealing with the challenge of Appiah's observation, however, requires us to imagine that interpellation, with all its invisible subjections, can come from below, from within resistant social movements.

As long as law and legal institutions help to build and protect identity-generating social hierarchies, legal reformers must invoke identity. But whenever activists invoke identity in ways that "transform" it, they may approach and even cross the dangerous line that Appiah specifies between advocacy and coercion; they may "interpellate" subjects just as invidiously as Althusser's imagined cop-in-the-street. How should a critical politics of law think about the possible coercive effects of identity-based advocacy? The features of queer legal movements that make them particularly inapt examples of the coherentist assumptions about identity politics also make them correspondingly useful for probing this long-deferred question.

SOME PRELIMINARY QUESTIONS

Departing from the coherentist assumptions about identity politics opens up some new versions of familiar problems. First, the coherentist assumptions make it important to know whether a given identity claim carries an accurate description of the identity base. But the question of accuracy is much more complex if identity claims have the power to transform the very identities they describe. Then, an identity claim's accuracy may be the product not of truthtelling but of its own social constructive power. So the question of accuracy must be complemented by additional questions, such as: does a description of the movement have the effect of making people see group members to be "like that," or does it make people see themselves as "like that"? Does a description of the group have the effect of bringing it into existence or repositioning its boundaries? To borrow a telling phrase of Ian Hacking, does a description help to "make up people"?[5]

Second and third, identity politics is frequently waged as a debate over whether a particular representational act, seen as a strategic move, is either useful or dangerous; and whether the act, seen as a self-interested or self-confirming gesture on the part of the person or subgroup making it, is either ethically acceptable or unacceptable. The first question is the question of strategy; the second is the question of "speaking for others."[6] On the coherentist assumptions about identity politics, these questions are sometimes framed with great facility because everyone supposedly knows who is being benefited or harmed, and who is being spoken for by whom. But without those assumptions, the questions of strategy and of "speaking for others" bring with them prior questions: useful or dangerous *to whom?* ethically acceptable or unacceptable *according to what normative view of identification or representation?*

Fourth, the coherentist assumptions about identity politics make it possible to have an extremely rich discourse of loyalty among group members. This is a useful political tool, allowing collective action often at the expense of group-member liberty. The discourse of loyalty encourages group members to believe that they can identify each other readily, to measure the degree to which group members are behaving in a way that fosters the group's interests, and to punish dissidents for disloyalty. The coherentist assumptions also make it possible to tell when one is speaking to outsiders, and thus support strictures against "washing dirty linen in public." But without stable assumptions about who belongs to the group and what their interests are, and about who can speak for the group, disloyalty loses much of its sting as an accusation and a new normative project opens up, of intragroup and non-group-based justifications for political action.[7]

These reframed questions about identity politics are particularly pressing for advocates of identity groups. Movement advocates enact two different meanings of the term "representation." They represent subordinated groups both in that they function as agents sent by the group on some mission for material change, and in that they manage the discursive rendering of the group. Keeping the second function of advocates in mind puts critical pressure on an important new branch of writing about the ethical obligations of lawyers representing disempowered social groups.[8] It posits that lawyers acting for subordinated social groups have a duty to strive for transparency in representing them. Lawyers for social groups should take the client group as they find it in the social world, defer if at all possible to its selection of goals and strive to "speak for" it only by saying what it would say itself if it were embodied as a lawyer. They are bound not only by the duties of loyalty normally imposed on lawyers representing clients, but the thicker and more culturally nuanced duties of loyalty imposed by coherentist identity politics—up to and possibly including a duty to withdraw from representation if the lawyer is not a bona fide member of the identity group. But as William H. Simon argues, lawyers' decisions to represent one client and not another, and to resolve conflicts within and between client groups, will "affect the contours of organizational power" *among the disempowered.*[9] Lawyers not only have special power to affect the goals and strategies of social groups[10]—they can do things that alter the social definition of the group itself. They can "make up people" in ways that weak constructivist views of group formation ignore.

To probe this form of power we need an ethics of representation that always keeps in focus the double meaning of "representation." This ethical inquiry has to be conducted, I think, on an assumption that asking the advocates of gay, women's, or disabled peoples' rights to give up "like race" similes would be like asking them to write their speeches and briefs without using the word "the." "Like race" arguments are so intrinsically woven into American discourses of equal justice that they can never be entirely forgone. Indeed, analogies are probably an inescapable mode of human inquiry and are certainly so deeply ingrained in the logics of American adjudication that any proposal to do without them altogether would be boldly utopian and is certainly beyond my aim here.[11] The following pages suggest that only *some* "like race" arguments are unjustifiably coercive; others, even though inescapable, join sexual constituencies to race constituencies in a shared exposure to danger that identity politics cannot even apprehend, that identity-based coalition politics can at least address, and that may cause us to seek identity-indifferent norms of distributive justice for adequate terms of analysis.

IDENTITY AS IMITATION

The imitative relationship between gay rights and sexuality movements and the women's rights movement has been vexed in the extreme, and warrants sustained ethical and strategic attention. In this essay, I defer that examination for a while, in order to focus on the problems raised by "like race" arguments.

The central legal achievement of litigation waged on behalf of the black civil rights movement was a historic succession of equal protection holdings: state-sponsored segregation was declared a violation of the Constitution, and the Court began to test its presumption (first announced in a case unsuccessfully challenging the Japanese-American internment) that other forms of race discrimination would also be found unconstitutional.[12] Seeking to find room under the aegis of these key equality precedents, gay and lesbian advocates often find themselves saying that sexual orientation is like race, or that gay men and lesbians are like a racial group, or that anti-gay policies are like racist policies, or that homophobia is like racism.

Thus early antidiscrimination briefs filed by the ACLU Lesbian and Gay Rights Project sought heightened scrutiny by arguing that homosexuals are like racial minorities: they derived from the race discrimination cases four or five "indicia of suspectness" and then argued that homosexuals as a group shared them.[13] The analogies appear in lawyers' political rhetoric as well: during the 1993 debates over Clinton's backfire effort to reform military anti-gay policy, one prominent gay legal advocate called the exclusion of homosexuals from the military "the apartheid of the closet"[14] and movement activists urged Clinton to imitate President Harry Truman's executive order banning racial discrimination in the military by abolishing anti-gay policy with a Trumanesque "stroke of the pen."[15]

To be sure, the "like race" analogy is not the handiwork of lawyers only. At about the same time that national gay rights litigators were presenting "indicia of suspectness" similes to courts, activist/theoretical work argued that homosexuals should understand themselves to constitute a community similar to those based on minority ethnicity.[16] And there are forms of imitation that seem almost unconscious, as if they were so deeply embedded in our culture of reform activism that they are repeated unthinkingly. For example, every time gay, lesbian, bisexual and transgendered communities stage a massive demonstration in Washington, D.C., they not only imitate the black civil rights movement's great 1963 March on Washington, but they do so in detail. When they selected the Lincoln Memorial as the event's grand proscenium and when they waged behind-the-scenes struggles over whether to frame the march as a bid for inclusion in America or as a more radical critique of it, they repeated key moments that, behind the scenes but crucially, structured the 1963 March.[17]

These imitations of identity present problems in three ranges of potential social obligation: within sexual orientation constituencies; between sexual orientation constituencies and the first constituencies of the civil rights model, African-Americans and other racial minorities; and at the "intersections" between race and sexual orientation constituencies, to borrow a term from critical race theory. I'll take all three up, in turn.

Within sexual orientation constituencies

To understand the internal dynamics, it is helpful to think about the position of identity-based thinking in modern pro-gay movements. Two useful distinctions are suggested by Eve Kosofsky Sedgwick and John Boswell. Eve Sedgwick distinguishes "minoritizing" understandings of sexual orientation difference, in which homosexual and heterosexual modes of life are understood to be taxonomically and socially distinct, from "universalizing" ones, which suppose homoerotic potential to be characteristically human. The former include not only "civil-rights models" of homosexual difference but "gay identity, 'essentialist,' [and] third-sex models"; the latter include "bisexual potential, 'social constructionist,' and 'sodomy' models" and Adrienne Rich's "'lesbian continuum.'"[18]

John Boswell offers a parallel distinction, between real and nominal understandings of sexual orientation identities. As Boswell notes, "Realists consider categories to be the footprints of reality. . . . They exist because humans perceive a real order in the universe and name it. . . . On the other hand, . . . [nominalists argue] that categories are only the names (Latin: *nomina*) of things agreed upon by humans, and that the 'order' people see is their creation rather than their perception."[19] Thus, on a nominalist view, "the category 'homosexuality' . . . does not so much describe a pattern or behavior inherent in human beings as it creates and establishes it," while realists insist that the "heterosexual/homosexual dichotomy exists in speech and thought because it exists in reality[.]"[20] Strikingly, minoritizing understandings of sexual orientation tend to be realist and universalizing ones tend to be nominalist.

These framings reflect not merely a range of descriptive options: people have *self-understandings* tied to minoritizing and universalizing, to realist and nominalist, models of sexual orientation. This is in part why these matters have such sharp ethical bite.

Ontologies of race are similarly understandable as either universalizing or minoritizing, as either realist or nominalist. When gay advocates turn to *legal* argumentation, and particularly to equal protection rights-claiming, their "like race" arguments tap into a deeply universalizing model of race, the integrationist ideal. Martin Luther King's famous invocation of race indifference in his "I Have a Dream" speech exemplifies the universalism of much civil-rights-era activism. His prayer-like invocation of a future in which "my four little children will one day live in a nation where they will not be judged by the color of their skin, but by the content of their character" is shocking to left sensibilities now only because the political meaning of race universalism has become so much more ambiguous since 1963.[21]

Arguments that anti-gay policies are like racist policies often maintain this universalizing representation of race. Thus Ninth Circuit Judge William A. Norris, in his brave 1997 speech attacking the military "Don't Ask, Don't Tell" policy, likened it to *de jure* racial segregation (it was "nothing more than another variation on the theme of invidious discrimination"), likened resistance to it to the black civil rights movement (crediting "all the countless gay men and lesbians . . . who have had the fortitude to expose themselves to the forces of bigotry, just as the Little Rock Nine did 40 years ago on the steps of Central High [in Little Rock, Arkansas]"), and predicted that society and even federal judges would soon say of it—as Arkansas governor Michael Huckabee had recently said of racial segregation at Central High— "Today, we come to say, once and for all, that what happened here 40 years ago was simply wrong. It was evil. And we renounce it."[22] This is very moving and very constructive, in part because it claimed only that the moral violation at Central High was like the moral violation of military anti-gay policy—not that blacks and gays are alike.

But often pro-gay advocates draw minoritizing models out of the legal representations of race *groups*, invoking a pictorial resemblance between racial minorities and gay men, lesbians, and bisexuals. I will consider below the ethical implications of the bid to shift our understanding of race implied in these "like race" similes. But first it seems necessary to observe the way in which these gestures operate within and among sexual orientation constituencies. The fact that minoritizing understandings of homo/heterosexual difference are so adaptable to the "like race" approach to advocacy means that pro-gay lawyers will be more likely to use them, and maybe also more likely to respond with indifference, obtuseness, and even hostility when universalizing models are proposed. At the same time, the utility to lawyers of minoritizing models makes those models more salient, more widely diffused, and more likely to take the shape of an identity "script" than they would otherwise be. The questions of accuracy, strategy, "speaking for others," and loyalty are all implicated in the resulting dynamics.

Consider two pictorialist "like race" arguments that have been particularly controversial: the arguments that gay men and lesbians are like racial minorities because they share an "immutable characteristic" or are a "discrete and insular minority." Immutability was one of the "indicia of suspectness" derived by gay rights litigators from judicial opinions treating legislation disadvantaging race groups and women as presumptively invalid—as "suspect." Some courts, in the course of justifying this aspect of equal protection doctrine, had observed that race and sex were "immutable characteristics," and pro-gay advocates argued that homosexual orientation was one too. In a related move, gay advocates looked to "the most famous footnote in constitutional law," Footnote Four of the Supreme Court's 1938 decision in *United States v. Carolene Products*. In this footnote Justice Stone laid out a new vision of the judicial role in enforcing the equal protection clause. The proposal was that courts were particularly obliged to protect minority groups that are chronically vulnerable in the political process, and that a good way of limiting the resulting judicial interference with political decisionmaking would be to accord special protection only to groups that were "discrete and insular"—paradigmatically race, national, and religious minorities.[23] Pro-gay advocates argued that homosexuals were similarly discrete and insular, and thus similarly vulnerable to exclusion and domination by legislative majorities.

Neither Footnote Four nor the many courts that observed that race and sex are immutable characteristics supplied their logic. The idea behind discreteness and insularity seems to have been that visually identifiable, socially and geographically isolated minorities were particularly susceptible to exclusion from or domination in the hurly-burly of pluralistic bargaining. The idea behind immutability must have been that race discrimination was particularly invidious because its victims could do nothing to sidestep it: blacks could not change the color of their skin, and thus come into compliance with the majority's preference for whiteness.

Major criticisms can be launched against these theories of subordination. For example, Bruce Ackerman very cogently used organization theory to argue that anonymous and diffuse groups (homosexuals were his prime example) can be just as subject to chronic exclusion from the political process as discrete and insular ones;[24] and an unexamined, and bizarre, premise of the "immutable characteristic" justification for heightened judicial protection seems to be that, if blacks *could* change the color of their skin, white majorities would be more justified in asking them to do so and punishing them with discrimination if they didn't. (To jump ahead a bit, query whether gay advocates should have done anything to weave this twisted concept of racism's wrongs deeper into the fabric of American law.) "Like race" pictorialism is, moreover, bad coalition politics because it concedes that groups that aren't "like race" have no claim to courts' equal protection solicitude;[25] and it is bad for the development of equal protection theory, among judges and elsewhere, because it promotes the idea that the traits of subordinated groups, rather than the dynamics of subordination, are the normatively important thing to notice. The coherentist assumptions about identity politics may make it hard to see that group traits—like discreteness, insularity, a perception of immutability, a focus on closetedness—are often the effect rather than the predicate of subordinating dynamics; they certainly have worked to obscure Footnote Four's primary focus on invidious majoritarian prejudice, and the immutability cases' persistent, primary concern with the irrelevance of the purportedly immutable trait to legitimate state concerns. The critique of coherentist identity politics, and simple good equal protection doctrine, merge here in a rejection of "like race" pictorialism.

The ethics of representation adds another layer to this critique. To be sure, it was a bold move for gay rights advocates to say that homosexuals were marked by an "immutable characteristic," inasmuch as a considerable proportion of anti-gay discrimination (unlike racial discrimination) is animated by a desire to convert lesbians and gay men to heterosexuality or to prevent gay people from coming into existence in the first place. And it was very much a part of the bold new outness of post-Stonewall gay communities in the Castro and Greenwich Village to claim that gay men and lesbians lived in discrete and insular enclaves (like racial and ethnic communities). But these representations could work oppression, like Appiah's "scripts." The "like race" similes very much took the minoritizing view of homo/heterosexual definition, and tended to suppress, hide, or outright deny universalizing ones. This tendency reached its apogee when gay-rights advocates claimed that some very preliminary and equivocal scientific studies suggesting that human sexual orientation might have some biological components proved decisively that homosexuality was a biological trait (supposedly like race).[26] The coherentist criticism of these arguments would be that they are *inaccurate*. But they may have been worse than that: they may have "made up people" in the sense that they persuaded gay men and lesbians that they were "like that." I think they did. In fact, I think they created a demand for gay gene experiments, which, in turn, did a great deal of interpellating of their own.

Second, how should we think about the problem of "speaking for others" involved in the selection of minoritizing representations for legal advocacy? The questions of strategy and "speaking for others" are linked here. Gay advocates who used these "like race" similes often did so because they believed they might *work*, might secure significant legal advances for gay men and lesbians across the board and relieve widespread suffering imposed on them by state-sponsored discrimination. "It doesn't matter that the simile is a little inaccurate," they would say; "judges fall for it, and once we secure some legal rights no one will remember the rhetoric we used to obtain them." This justification balances material benefits against "merely" symbolic harms. That framing of the "like race" debate carries with it coherentist assumptions about pro-gay identity politics, however, and sidelined the critical twist on the question: useful *for whom*? If the immutability argument had become the predicate for a legal victory, for instance, the resulting antidiscrimination case law could have left bisexuals out in the cold: after all, they can switch. And this was not merely a risk of future harm: the decision to run it displaced bisexuals as outsiders, nonmembers of the constituency on whose behalf gay and lesbian advocates spoke. This is a particularly striking case of interpellation from below, of representation working not only as service but also as power.

One way to avoid the ethical dilemmas posed here is to ask the question of loyalty. Here is a dangerous point in intra-group politics. When group members promote a duty of loyalty they implicitly ask internal dissenters to fall silent. But in this case, as in the case of double binds generally, the question of loyalty is a wash. Where pro-gay activists stake their arguments in universalizing forms, anti-gay activists can coopt them, saying homosexuality is a mere choice, or a mere set of acts from which one can abstain; anti-gay discrimination emerges in this formation as an effort to prevent the "spread" of homosexuality. But where pro-gay activists stake their arguments in minoritizing forms, anti-gay activists can coopt them too, representing homosexuals as pathological deviants who should be cured, killed, aborted, or at least hidden from view. Under these circumstances, it seems clear that the strategic move is not to ensure the ascendency of one model or the other, but to inhabit their cross-cutting vulnerabilities more consciously.

So the ethical weight of advocates' minoritizing representations must be gauged. The preferences of critical theory are pretty clear: lawyers should not impose minoritizing representations on the lively insubordination of queer politics. In stating that preference, critical theory has my deepest sympathies. But what about sincerely minoritized group members, and their desires for representation? What about the fact that sometimes minoritizing representations do work in the sense that they facilitate actual legal reform? (Imagine trying to argue a lesbian co-parent adoption case without making *any* reference to immutability.) And what about the note of communalism that sounds in so many critical appeals for universalizing, nominalizing representations? The current, wild race-to-the-courthouse individualism is disturbing precisely because it lacks any mechanism for intra-communal dialogue; but if such a dialogue were possible, who would be invited to join in it, and how could it be conducted without coercion? However hard those questions are, they can be stated more clearly, and understood more simply, if we bracket, or pretermit, "like race" similes when we deal with them.

Between sexual orientation and racially identified constituencies

To be blunt, "like race" similes have caused considerable friction between gay constituencies and race constituencies. "To equate homosexuality with race is to give a death sentence to civil rights," says Martin Luther King's niece Alveda Celeste King.[27] The African-American host of a call-in radio show objects to gay-rights ordinances, saying: "A lot of blacks are upset that the feminist movement pimped off the black movement. Now here comes the gay movement. Blacks resent it very much, because they do not see a parallel, nor do I."[28] Colin Powell, then Chairman of the Joint Chiefs of Staff and perhaps the most prominent African-American in mainstream politics, fought vigorously to maintain the military's anti-gay practices, and specifically objected to "like race" similes: "Homosexuality is not a benign . . . characteristic, such as skin color or whether you're Hispanic or Oriental. . . . It goes to one of the most fundamental aspects of human behavior."[29] These arguments go beyond criticizing particular "like race" analogies, like the immutability argument, to claim civil rights legalism as peculiarly dedicated to racial justice and to resist quite broadly the overall effort of gay constituencies to frame their justice claims in civil rights terms. What is at stake here? How should gay-friendly analysis understand these challenges and respond to them?

These questions suggest that the question of loyalty is a dangerous device for unpacking the ethics of representation. When the question is "loyal to whom?," the coherentist assumptions about identity politics make it easy to respond with glib composure: "To Us." But those assumptions were put into question by the very issue whether bisexuals belong to the group of homosexuals, and are quite demonstrably useless in the face of black resistance to gay "like race" arguments.

The controversy over "like race" arguments surely turns in part on obligations that pro-gay advocates owe to people who suffer not, or not only, sexual orientation discrimination, but race discrimination. I take it as axiomatic that pro-gay advocates should do everything they can to pursue racial justice. And so a key question emerges: how is identity imitation a way of becoming involved, indirectly but materially, in racial struggles, and how should we understand the resulting representational opportunities and normative tensions? And attached to that question is a deeper one, which I believe is an unacknowledged threat to identity politics generally: does identity imitation provide or block access to deep, identity-indifferent questions of distributive justice?

The intermovement ethics of representation posed by "like race" claims has been articulated in several ways, and I will try to tackle each approach in turn: first, the assumption that African-American criticism of these arguments can only be homophobic, on the one hand, or that it is authoritative because of the social epistemology of its speakers on the other; second, the argument that civil rights for gay men and lesbians are a natural right which can't be trammeled by an ethics of representation; third, the argument that gay civil rights claims should be muted because the stigma attached to same-sex sexuality, indeed to sexuality, might contaminate civil rights law for other constituencies; and fourth, the argument that gay "like race" articulations threaten either to transfer civil rights *resources* from racial minorities to gay constituencies or to transfer civil rights *meanings* between the groups in ways that will put racial justice claims in jeopardy.

1. To the challenge that gay "like race" arguments "pimp[] off the black movement," coherentist identity politics has two immediate answers, one amenable to gay coherentists, the other amenable to black coherentists. The former decry black criticism of gay "like race" arguments as manifestations of unregenerate anti-gay sentiment, while the latter call for deference to it as an authoritative expression by those in a position to know what is and is not "like race." Neither response is any more adequate than the coherentist assumptions upon which it is founded.

2. Believers in natural or formal rights have another answer: if gay rights are required by abstract justice, there can be no intelligible ethical

constraint on their assertion. That is, if rights are natural, primordial entitlements, they cannot justifiably be encumbered *at all, ever*. We have heard this argument in the marriage debates, when proponents of the gay marriage campaign assert that individual gay men and lesbians have a justice-based right to marry that supersedes any obligations arising from less primordial normativities (like the feminist critique of marriage, for instance). I take some satisfaction in the fact that, having let fly this boomerang, gay marriage campaigners encounter it again when individual gay men and lesbians defend their decisions to sue to obtain marriage licenses even though their cases would likely produce bad law because of bad timing or bad venue. As this dismal series of exchanges indicates, the natural rights argument is deeply tautological: in the absence of any agreed-upon metaphysics of formal rights, it merely posits that rights are definitionally entitlements that trump all other claims. It is a deeply individualist, deeply foundationalist argument, just as hostile to collective approaches to law reform as it is to any political, historical, or institutional analysis of rights discourse. Finally, no one on the left believes the natural rights argument except when he or she seeks immunity from strategic or communal criticism: those who assert it in support of gay marriage would probably be unwilling to say that Thurgood Marshall was wrong to craft a strategic run-up to *Brown v. Board of Education* and to suppress inopportune litigation when he could; and critical race theorists who defended rights discourse against the attack mounted by critical legal studies did so not in terms of formal rights but in terms of a rhetorically alert pragmatism.

3. An argument against "like race" assertions that may carry more water worries about contagion that homosexual stigma could bring to other areas of the law. It is, after all, entirely plausible that the stigma attached to homosexuals would facilitate legal retrogression harming racial minorities. Full-time gay rights litigators often comment that, when they say "Your Honor," they are often giving the judge his or her first opportunity to meet an openly gay person. Judicial homophobia is out there, and seriously affects the outcome of cases.[30] What if the resulting bad law is worse than anything that would have emerged in a race discrimination case, but is cited and followed in later race discrimination cases?

Case law, because of its analogical developmental style, is apt for mediating such movement-to-movement harms. Indeed, the danger seems to have materialized in *Bowers v. Hardwick* (1986),[31] aside from *Romer v. Evans* (1996)[32] the most important Supreme Court decision on a gay-rights issue to date. Michael Hardwick was engaged in fellatio with another man in the bedroom of his own home when a police officer came into the room to serve an arrest warrant on him. (There are good reasons to think that this intrusion was part of a campaign of anti-gay harassment that the Atlanta police were conducting against gay men generally and against Hardwick in particular.)[33] Prosecutors obtained a second indictment, this time on a charge of consensual sodomy. With the help of the ACLU of Georgia, Hardwick challenged the sodomy charge, claiming that Georgia's statute violated his rights to privacy under the U.S. Constitution. The privacy theory he invoked depended on cases that women's rights lawyers had won in their decades-long effort to establish rights to reproductive autonomy, particularly contraception and abortion. When the Supreme Court rejected Michael Hardwick's claim that constitutional privacy rights protected him from arrest for a private, consensual act of same-sex sodomy, they did so in shockingly harsh and dismissive terms that involved the Court in an ugly display of homophobia. The majority opinion derided arguments upon which Hardwick had prevailed in the Court of Appeals as "facetious," and the concurring opinion of Chief Justice Burger gratuitously cited Blackstone to describe same-sex sodomy as "'the infamous *crime against nature*,'" "an offense of 'deeper malignity' than rape, a heinous act 'the very mention of which is a disgrace to human nature[.]'"[34]

As disastrous as this defeat was for pro-gay legalism, it was at least as ominous for women's rights to reproductive freedom: *Hardwick* so deeply undermined the foundation of *Roe v. Wade* (1973)[35] that abortion rights advocates seriously faced the possibility that the Supreme Court could overturn it. In hindsight, it seems at least possible that some justices welcomed *Hardwick* onto their docket because its association with a stigmatized group gave them a chance to slam the door hard on privacy doctrine, and to put *Roe* in jeopardy.

If this is what happened—of course no one can say for sure whether it did or not—the gay rights litigation campaign set the stage for a crisis in the women's reproductive freedom campaign. But if women's rights advocates had approached Michael Hardwick and his lawyers when they were considering whether to "make a federal case of it," and had argued that the stigma associated with male-male fellatio was dangerous for the continued stability of reproductive rights that were crucial to women, they would have implicitly asked him to accept that stigma as a premise for his action. It was entirely appropriate to argue that his case should not be framed as a privacy claim because that misrepresented the public nature of the harm inflicted on him, or to argue that he should not file a lawsuit because the law in his district was not ripe to support his claim, or even to argue that fitting his claim to the existing structure of reproductive rights distorted them, but to ask him to forgo a claim because its overlay of stigma might injure others is to ask him to cooperate with—indeed, by his silence to reaffirm—a profound insult to his dignity. Asking homosexuals to modify their justice claims *precisely because they are exposed to acute and almost autonomic vilification* is to ask them to accommodate, even accept—indeed, through the "speech act of a silence,"[36] to endorse—that condition. That's asking too much.

4. The gravest argument against "like race" claims, and civil rights imitation generally, is that they may exhaust or divert civil rights resources—hard resources like jobs or funds for police retraining, or soft ones like a social/cultural appetite for antidiscrimination—away from the traditional constituencies of civil rights law to new constituencies that need it less. This is, I think, what some African-American critics apprehend when they object to gay rights legislation because it would "steal away the civil rights from under our very noses,"[37] when they worry that "the civil rights bandwagon is getting so full that it's not moving anywhere."[38] It seems extremely plausible to me that gay men and lesbians—who, relative to African-Americans, are whiter and far more likely to be economically just fine, thank you—don't need antidiscrimination protection as acutely as racial minorities but are more likely to get it. If antidiscrimination protection is a zero sum, moreover, we will not only get it, but take it away from people of color.

Particularly where hard resources are involved, it is alarmingly easy to see that winner-take-all civil rights contests can take shape. Affirmative action programs are rife with such contests, which pit one recognized civil rights constituency against another. For instance, in minority business enterprise programs, blacks and latinos have had ample opportunity to observe white women speed ahead of them in contests for finite resources.[39] Increasingly, we must tackle the problem as a question about whether a particular racial group with a unique history of racial disadvantage should take resources earmarked for affirmative action away from another racial group with a quite different history of racial disadvantage: for instance, magnet schools can become so attractive that their admissions policies are fraught with multiracial conflicts in which the position of Asian-Americans is deeply anomalous.[40]

If we maintain coherentist assumptions about identity groups, the problems are hard enough. We have about three choices, then: we could engage in a crude exercise in ranking oppressions, or undertake a distributive justice analysis borrowed from liberal theory, imagining the contesting groups as big, homogeneous individuals, or (the perennial cop-out of left multiculturalism) object to the size of the pie and go home. But two kinds of problems can make it hard to keep neat fences around resource disputes. First, a group seeking to engage in a zero-sum contest might not already have a civil rights identity, so the question whether it should be construed in identity terms needs to be answered first. Should learning disabilities be understood to be "like race" such that allocating educational resources to LD children is done through an antidiscrimination paradigm?[41] Here distributive justice meets identity politics, and the hardest problem is dealing with their analytic incommensurability. And second, the resource at stake might not be hard, like a finite public school budget, but might involve malleable cultural tolerances. Was the "ebonics" controversy about budget allocations dedicated to bilingual education or about respect and recognition? Here distributive justice meets critical theory, and the encounter throws up another range of problems sounding in analytic incommensurability. African-American objections to gay "like race" claims, understood sympathetically, involve both challenges.

To be sure, black critics of gay "like race" claims often challenge the amenability of sexuality to *any* antidiscrimination identity. But the argument that homosexuality is not a "status" "like race" but a classification based on conduct is deeply mistaken. This is not because the converse is true. Homosexuals *do* engage in homosexual acts (praise be). Rather, the distinctive danger attached to people currently designated homosexual arises because the relationships between sexual orientation identity and homosexual conduct are so slippery that they are always capable of becoming the vehicle for homosexual panic.[42] This doesn't make sexual orientation "like race," but it is (I think) a fully sufficient reason to invoke antidiscrimination norms to protect those harmed when vilified conduct and identity pinch.

A deeper challenge arises in the second problem, the claim that gay rights claims reallocate resources away from racial minorities that desperately need them. While it is quite possible that they may do so, in two important settings where this criticism was raised—the gays in the military fracas, and the conflict over gay rights ordinances—the impact of gay rights claims on black civil rights is better understood not as a struggle over a concrete zero-sum resource, but as a linguistic process in which black and gay civil rights constituencies, having become signs of one another, interact to shape soft limits affecting both constituencies.

Gay advocates sought a repeal of military anti-gay regulations in expressly "like race" terms. It would be possible to see this effort as a bid for hard resources. The analysis would posit repeal as a way to increase the number of white people eligible for a limited supply of government subsidized jobs. It would anticipate that white decision-makers in the military would feel more social solidarity with white gay troops than with black ones of any sexuality, and would promote the former more readily than the latter. Seen in this way, "lifting the ban" would have transferred a public resource from racial minorities to a new group of eligible whites.

This is an easy argument to make, so it is particularly striking that virtually no one made it.[43] A different justification for military anti-gay policy—unit cohesion—won the day, and it carries a subtler racial meaning. Apparently, the integration of women into the military, combined with the energetic sexual controversy provoked by the 1993 debates over military anti-gay policy, contributed to an upsurge in the number of sex harassment complaints. In those complaints black men have been disproportionately accused.[44] It seems at least likely that this disproportion emerges because black men are perceived by white women as sexually threatening in a way that white men are not. That is to say that disruptions in the male homosocial environment of the military has increased the level of sexual hostility there; and that sexual hostility in the U.S. defaults so readily to racialized tropes that (especially) black men in uniform face heightened danger.

I can't prove it, but I think that Colin Powell put in his ferocious defense of military anti-gay policy—a defense in which "unit cohesion" was the centerpiece—on something like this reasoning. But note that this is not a resource allocation problem. To make it look like one, you would have to say that the "good" of safety in the sexual culture is a finite resource that gay advocates implicitly propose to appropriate from black men in particular. But sexual tranquillity is not a finite resource: everyone could have it just as easily as no one. Under these circumstances it seems more direct to say that the ethics of "like race" arguments need to be worked out on a hypothesis that racial and sexual *meanings* are interconnected in complex discursive webs. Perhaps the best heuristic for understanding ethical challenges to "like race" arguments, then, is not the zero-sum competition between divergent coherentist identity groups, but the dynamics of language.

How those dynamics might work is suggested by a second controversy in which African-American critiques of gay "like race" claims were even more salient: the furor over gay rights ordinances and their attempted repeal through state-constitutional amendments. The centerpiece of anti-gay resistance here was a claim that "gay rights are special rights." It is conventional to read this claim to say "not like race." As Jane Schacter and Margaret M. Russell have amply documented,[45] conservative activists running Special Rights campaigns amplified the voices of African-American critics who said, "Gays were never declared three-fifths of human by the constitution," "I can't go into a closet and hang up my race when it's convenient," and "We say, 'No.' We will not agree to them saying they're just like us."[46] But more covertly the Special Rights campaign deployed a "*like* race" claim which mediated race and sexual orientation as indicators of each other, and which created rather than allocated a zero sum of antidiscrimination commitment.

The key is the rich range of signification packed into the term "special rights." The pro-gay ordinances that gave rise to the struggle I am describing added "sexual orientation" to a list of grounds already declared out of bounds for employers and public accommodations to consider. These grounds included race, ethnicity, and national origin—the classic civil rights grounds—and a hodgepodge of additional grounds that many civil rights laws now specify, from disability to marital status to veteran status and so on. The idea was to add "sexual orientation" to this list.

"Special rights" fundamentally misdescribed these reforms. Civil rights legislation bans especially bad treatment based on race, sex, and other specified grounds, and provides remedies and thus deterrence designed to put victims of discrimination on a level playing field with everyone else. It is formally neutral—men can sue for sex discrimination, whites can sue for race discrimination. Traditional civil rights legislation is "special" only in the sense—held by almost nobody[47]—that it invidiously removes a few arbitrarily distrusted grounds of decision from the free market. But there are three versions of antidiscrimination enforcement, all of them associated historically with very specified attention to racial minorities, women, and disabled people, that are more or less accurately described as *special treatment.*"

First, the entire "suspect classification" and "tiers of scrutiny" edifice built in Supreme Court doctrine under the equal protection clause recognizes that *blacks* are more likely to be hurt by race discrimination than whites, that *women* are more likely to be hurt by sex discrimination than men. This approach moves beyond formal equality to antisubordination and is, in one sense, "special": when considering any given axis of discrimination, it gives the chronically subordinated group particularized attention.

A second deviation from formal equality appears in arguments that equality requires accommodations to the particular needs of a protected group. These arguments are historically associated with efforts to integrate women and disabled people. And they involve "special treatment": when we say that women's equality rights include the right to pregnancy leave or that a wheelchair user's equality rights include the right to a ramp, we are saying that there is something particular, something distinctive, something special about their situation that requires attention. (The sophisticated justification for special rights of this kind is to point out that they are necessitated by norms that are special in themselves: workplaces that appear neutral but really assume male workers, public spaces that appear universally accessible but actually assume ambulatory users. But that justification only intensifies the specialness of this form of special rights.)

At the time of the ordinance struggles, both of these takes on antidiscrimination were controversial, but a third take—affirmative action—was the subject of a racial-justice firestorm. Like antisubordination models of antidiscrimination, affirmative action notices that blacks not whites need special assistance in a racially stratified society, that women not men are likely to be bypassed when higher-paying jobs are being distributed. And like "special accommodation" models of antidiscrimination, affirmative action goes beyond prohibiting discrimination to require affirmative steps to alleviate its effects. Affirmative action is "special treatment," then, in the sense that it undertakes positive steps for particular groups. Of course, by no stretch of historical accuracy is it a "special *right*": mainstream and constitutional law debates over affirmative action have stalled on the question whether it is *permissible*, never having gotten to the question whether it is legally *mandatory*. But it is a special remedy in several senses of the term.

The "special rights" campaign against gay rights ordinances was designed to free-ride on a strong anti–affirmative action backlash, and on milder backlashes against antisubordination and special accommodation models of antidiscrimination, that were primarily about white resentment of race-based redistribution, less acutely about male resentment of sex-based redistribution, and probably only marginally about accommodations for physical and other disabilities. In that sense, "special rights" subliminal "like race" analogy harmed gay men and lesbians, rather than helping them. At the same time, four elements of the "special rights" campaign hurt racial minorities and women. First, the association of homosexuals with various special-treatment backlashes united social conservatives with libertarian conservatives, facilitating a formidable coalition. Second, to the extent that the three forms of "special treatment" antidiscrimination focus primarily on racial and gender justice, the latter were under an unacknowledged subtextual attack. Third, the stigma attached to homosexuality made for an easy identification of the "queer"—"differing in some odd way from what is usual or normal: strange, . . . peculiar"[48]—with the "special," and muffled pro-gay activists when they tried to defend the ordinances as "normal" civil rights law. And fourth, possibly most damaging, the "special rights" accusation generated popular confusion about the relationship between formally neutral civil rights laws and affirmative action: if people could be convinced to vote against the former thinking they were the same as the latter, the very idea of civil rights legislation was undermined.[49]

This episode amply justifies African-American alarm about gay civil rights "like race" claims. But note that the question is not "will gay men and lesbians steal the civil rights from under African-Americans' very noses?" but "will an unholy alliance of social and libertarian *conservatives* do so?" The danger arises not because blacks and gays are alike or different, but because they can be flashed as signs of each other in a discourse that operates so smoothly it can remain virtually silent. And antidiscrimination fatigue is not the exogenous starting point of this operation, but its product. This pattern doesn't support ethical constraints on gay men and lesbians *deciding whether to make* civil rights claims, though it does suggest that imagining a rights-claiming project without anticipating or resisting the racial resignifications it may produce is to fail to imagine it well at all.

At the "intersections"

We have become accustomed to thinking of the intersections between sexual orientation and race as instantiated in persons—the black gay man, the latina lesbian—who inhabit a subordinated position in two (or three) categorical systems and who are thus particularly affected by anything said about their interrelations. But if my reading of "like race" claims in the gays-in-the-military debate and the Special Rights campaign is right, the seams joining and dividing sexual orientation and race are everywhere.

In a contribution to the "intersectionality" literature that expressly addresses feminist "like race" arguments, Trina Grillo and Stephanie M. Wildman discourage white women from using "like race" analogies to illuminate sexism. They note that "Analogizing sex discrimination to race discrimination makes it seem that all the women are white and all the men African-American. The experiential reality of women of color disappears."[50] Two ontological claims about racial and gender categories underlie this critique, and I would suggest that the ethics of intersectional representation are better understood without them. First, Grillo and Wildman posit that "To analogize gender to race, one must assume that each is a distinct category, the impact of which can be neatly separated, one from the other."[51] But it seems to me that the chief dangers of intersectionality arise not because the categorical systems are supposed to be independent, but because they are understood to impinge quite immediately on one another. And second, Grillo and Wildman posit that it is the *reality* of women of color that is obscured; similarly, Jane Schacter warns that "[t]he categorical lines drawn in the discourse of equivalents around protected groups *erase or distort the identities* of people who are part of more than one group."[52] For all their critique of feminist essentialism, these and many other "intersectional" formulations retain a strong ontological commitment to real identities. But it seems to me that "like race" arguments pose hard ethical challenges at intersections because they place the ontology of identity itself at risk in ways that are differently controversial in racial and sexual orientation discourses. To see this we need to shift from persons to discourses, from coherentist identity politics to critical theory.

If intra-gay identity wars can be roughly described as a tension between universalizing and minoritizing and between realist and nominalist understandings, so can disagreements about the ontology of racial differences. Minoritizing understandings emerge in ethnic solidarity, politics-of-recognition multiculturalist, and nationalist discourses of race; and universalizing understandings emerge in integrationist, hybridizing, mestiza, and strong-social-constructivist models. I will describe the related, less notorious tensions between realist and nominalist understandings in a moment; for now I'll simply note that they are implicated here just as they are in the framing of sexual orientation. My proposal is that gay "like race" arguments can tighten or loosen these tensions within racial discourse, and that this meta-intersectionality, if you will, is possibly more *political* than the face-to-face, largely phenomenological intersectionalities emphasized by Grillo and Wildman and others. Moreover, the interpellative difficulties that vex intra-gay ethics of representation are recapitulated here across a broader range of differences.

To put it simply, a "like race" argument that A is like B also implicitly claims that B is like A. Operating meta-intersectionally, "like race" claims can create interpellative links between gay minoritizing representations and racial universalizing ones; or, almost but not quite conversely, between gay nominal representations and racial realist ones.

Consider an example of the former case. When gay rights advocates began to invoke the "immutable characteristic" simile, they were working from a set of scattered, sketchy rationales occurring at happenstance in the race and sex discrimination cases. By translating these "immutable characteristic" references into an "indicia of suspectness" checklist, and implying that its items were not merely sufficient but necessary conditions for heightened judicial protection, they invited judges to "harden up" the law in this area. Which is just what judges did: federal district courts increasingly stipulated for immutability not as a mere factor but as a prerequisite for heightened scrutiny, even as they persistently concluded that sexual orientation was not an immutable characteristic. This development has made it harder for groups distinguished by theoretically mutable characteristics—fat people, for instance—to make antidiscrimination claims (why don't they just lose weight?).[53] Moreover, the "immutable characteristic" rationale is springloaded to harm racial minorities: its hidden assumption that racial discrimination would be morally acceptable if blacks could change the color of their skin leaps into prominence when employers tell black women on their payrolls that they can't wear braids, or latino employees that they can't speak Spanish (why can't they just conform to white cultural norms?).[54] Gay advocates making the immutability argument, then, bear some responsibility for a legitimation of universalizing understandings of race and a delegitimation of—indeed, a constriction of the social space for—minoritizing ones.

Almost but not quite conversely, there is a subtle tension between queer nominalism and a certain tendency of critical race representational choices to hew to realism. It seems to me that racial realism is not the sole property of nationalist and other minoritizing racial understandings; it appears also in hybridizing/mestiza/strong-social-constructivist versions of race-universalism. To look at just one example, in a coda "On Categories" to her book *The Alchemy of Race and Rights*, Patricia J. Williams makes a series of nominalizing gestures: "while being black has been the most powerful *social attribution* in my life, it is only one of a number of *governing narratives* or *presiding fictions* by which I am constantly reconfiguring myself in the world." "*[T]erms* like 'black' and 'white' do not begin to capture the rich ethnic and political diversity of *my subject.*" So far so nominalist. But Williams concludes: "I prefer 'African-American' in my own conversational usage because it effectively evokes *the specific cultural dimensions of my identity,* but in this book I use most frequently the term black in order to accentuate *the unshaded monolithism of color itself* as *a social force.*"[55] Those are the last words in this important strong-constructivist, racial nominalist book. I suppose that we could all agree that they bring in a certain realism.

Queer theory, on the other hand, is notoriously ready to abandon realism in its enraptured embrace with nominalism. The result in legal argumentation is a shift away from "like race" pictorialism and toward remedial theories that focus on the distinctive social and discursive dynamics of gay injury. My own argument that equal protection arguments should forefront not "who we are but how we are thought;"[56] Kendall Thomas's argument that sodomy laws should be understood to violate not a right to privacy but a right to be free from cruel and unusual punishment;[57] Lisa Duggan's recommendation that "like race" arguments be replaced with like-the-*relationship*-between-the-state-and-*religion*;[58] Toni Massaro's argument that equal protection claims should forgo "thick" social description and go "thin"[59]—all of these are crafted to make room for universalizing, particularly queer, understandings of sexual orientation in civil rights discourse.

For reasons known only to themselves, a majority of the Supreme Court in 1996 issued a favorable gay rights decision, *Romer v. Evans.* This important decision adopts an extreme form of nominalism. Holding Colorado's Amendment 2—which had barred the state in *any* of its subdivisions and agencies from entertaining *any* "claim of discrimination" based on "homosexual status"—unconstitutionally irrational, the Court persistently refused to base its decision on any social description of the group harmed by the challenged law. It describes and populates the class under consideration in a self-consciously nominal gesture: "the *named* class, a class *we shall refer to as* homosexual persons or gay men and lesbians[.]"[60] This is "a single *named* group"[61] defined by "a single *trait*."[62] "Homosexuals, by state decree, *are put* in a solitary class":[63] the Amendment "*classifies* homosexuals . . . to *make them* unequal to everyone else"; "It is a *classification of persons undertaken for its own sake*" and *in that sense* it is a "status-based enactment":[64] "[C]lass legislation . . . [is] obnoxious. . . ."[65]

It remains uncertain whether *Romer's* nominalism will appear in other equal protection decisions. But it is clear that, if it appears in the context of *race* discrimination, it will be inflected by an important racial trope that has no counterpart in the constitutional discourse of sexual orientation: the maxim, drawn from Justice Harlan's dissent in *Plessy v. Ferguson*, that "our Constitution is colorblind."[66] If understanding the distinctive dangers of race requires attention to "the unshaded monolithism of color itself as a social force," a queer shift toward nominalism could contribute, perhaps dangerously, to its doctrinal erasure. It seems to me that this is an ethical problem for gay advocates to consider, and that to do so we will have to make simultaneous use of distributive and critical tools that are not now designed to work well together.

CONCLUSION

When we say that something is "like race," we imply that we know what race is like. But do we? Ever since the Supreme Court's decision in *Adarand Constructors v. Pena*, which held that race-based affirmative action could be subjected to the same degree of judicial scrutiny that courts must apply to acts of overt anti-black racism,[67] there has been a strong strategic reason for equal protection rights-claims to take a new form, "*not* like race." As Stuart Minor Benjamin indicates in a fascinating article on Native Hawai'ian rights claims, the considerable edifice of special programs now dedicated under federal law to federally recognized mainland Indian tribes and under Hawai'ian state law to Native Hawai'ian cultural preservation could be erased from the landscape if native groups were understood to be "like race."[68] This reversal in the normative content of intra-group comparisons could hardly have been anticipated twenty years ago, but it is now part of the context of any "like race" claim.

In a situation this volatile, in which so many different kinds of social harms are so finely connected, it seems important to exercise considerable caution. Working within coherentist identity constituencies is not enough; forming coalitions across them, though crucial, is also not enough. When identity can be deployed to harm its own subjects, the search for equal justice also requires that we move beyond identity politics altogether.

NOTES

1. The best survey of this broad effort for legal change is the excellent monthly newsletter *Lesbian/Gay Law Notes*, ed. Arthur S. Leonard, New York Law School, 57 Worth St., NY, NY 10013.

2. Though disparate and internally disputatious, queer theory is probably all alike in being unimaginable without Michel Foucault's *The History of Sexuality, Volume I*, trans. Robert Hurley (New York: Vintage Books, 1980; rpt. 1978). Some key moments in the development of queer theory are: Eve Kosofsky Sedgwick, *Epistemology of the Closet* (Berkeley: Univ. of California Press, 1990); David M. Halperin, *One Hundred Years of Homosexuality* (New York: Routledge, 1990); Henry Abelove, Michèle Aina Barale, and David M. Halperin, eds., *The Lesbian and Gay Studies Reader* (New York: Routledge, 1993); and Michael Warner, ed., *Fear of a Queer Planet: Queer Politics and Social Theory* (Minneapolis: Univ. of Minnesota Press, 1993).

3. K. Anthony Appiah, "Identity, Authenticity, Survival: Multicultural Societies and Social Reproduction," in Amy Gutmann, ed., *Multiculturalism* (Princeton: Princeton University Press, 1994), pp. 162–63.

4. Louis Althusser, "Ideology and Ideological State Apparatuses (Notes Towards an Investigation," in *Lenin and Philosophy and Other Essays* 127, 174, Ben Brewster, trans. (New York: Monthly Review Press, 1971) (footnote omitted).

5. Ian Hacking, "Making Up People," in Thomas C. Heller, Morton Sosna, and David E. Wellbery, eds., *Reconstructing Individualism: Autonomy, Individuality, and the Self in Western Thought* (Stanford: Stanford Univ. Press, 1986), pp. 222–36.

6. See Gayatri Chakravorty Spivak, "Can the Subaltern Speak?," in Cary Nelson and Lawrence Grossberg, eds., *Marxism and the Interpretation of Culture* 271 (Chicago: Univ. of Chicago Press, 1988); Linda Alcoff, "The Problem of Speaking For Others," 20 *Cultural Critique* 5 (1991–92).

7. For a fascinating examination of loyalty to an identity group, see Ronald Garet, "Self-Transformability," 655 *S. Cal. L. Rev.* 121 (1991). David B. Wilkins provides a rigorous examination of how a group member who affirms loyalty to the

group should respond when group-based demands come into conflict with his individual ethical commitments; see "Should a Black Lawyer Represent the Ku Klux Klan?," 63 *Geo. Wash. L. Rev.* 1030 (1995).

8. See particularly Gerald P. López, *Rebellious Lawyering: One Chicano's Vision of Progressive Law Practice* (Boulder: Westview Press, 1992); Lucie White, "Subordination, Rhetorical Survival Skills, and Sunday Shoes: Notes on the Hearing of Mrs. G.," 38 *Buffalo L. Rev.* 1 (1990); and Anthony V. Alfieri, "Reconstructive Poverty Law Practice: Learning Lessons of Client Narratives," 100 *Yale L. J.* 2107 (1991).

9. William H. Simon, "The Dark Secret of Progressive Lawyering: A Comment on Poverty Law Scholarship in the Post-Modern, Post-Reagan Era," 48 *U. Miami L. Rev.* 1099, 1102–03 (1994).

10. William B. Rubenstein, "Divided We Litigate: Addressing Disputes Among Group Members and Lawyers in Civil Rights Campaigns," 106 *Yale L. J.* 1623 (1997).

11. Sharon Rush, "Equal Protection Analogies—Identity and 'Passing': Race and Sexual Orientation," 13 *Harv. Black Letter L. J.* 65 (1997). See also Cass R. Sunstein, "On Analogical Reasoning," 106 *Harv. L. Rev.* 741 (1993).

12. *Brown v. Board of Ed.*, 347 U.S. 483, 74 S. Ct. 686 (1954); *Korematsu v. United States*, 323 U.S. 214, 65 S. Ct. 193 (1944).

13. Under the Equal Protection Clause, courts recognize some classifications as "suspect" because their use in legislation or regulation always raises a judicial suspicion that invidious discrimination is at work. State action disadvantaging members of a "suspect classification" is subject to heightened judicial scrutiny. The "indicia of suspectness" were group traits that courts had often noted when holding that race groups and women were differentiated by "suspect classifications." For a gay rights brief hypostatizing these traits, see Brief of Amici Curiae Lambda Legal Defense and Education Fund, Inc., et al., in *Watkins v. United States Army*, No. 85–4006 (9th Cir.) (Aug. 30, 1988).

14. William N. Eskridge, Jr., "Race and Sexual Orientation in the Military: Ending the Apartheid of the Closet," 2 *Reconstruction* 52 (1993).

15. Clinton Collins, Jr., "Officer's Insubordination A Greater Threat Than Gays in Uniform," *Star Tribune*, Feb. 5, 1993, at 19A; Melissa Healy, "Clinton Aides Urge Quick End to Military Ban on Gays," *Los Angeles Times*, Jan. 8 1993, at A1.

16. Steven Epstein, "Gay Politics, Ethnic Identity: The Limits of Social Constructionism," 93/94 *Socialist Review* 9–54 (1987), rpt. in *Forms of Desire: Sexual Orientation and the Social Constructionist Controversy*, ed. Edward Stein (NY: Routledge, 1992), 239–93.

17. Scott A. Sandage, "A Marble House Divided: The Lincoln Memorial, the Civil Rights Movement, and the Politics of Memory, 1939–1963," 80:1 *J. of American History* 135 (June 1993).

18. Sedgwick, *Epistemology of the Closet*, 89.

19. John Boswell, "Revolutions, Universals, and Sexual Categories," in *Hidden from History: Reclaiming the Gay and Lesbian Past*, Martin Duberman, Martha Bauml Vicinus, and George Chauncey, Jr., eds., 17, 18–19 (New York: Meridian, 1989).

20. *Ibid.* at 19.

21. Martin Luther King, Jr., "I Have a Dream," in *A Testament of Hope: The Essential Writings and Speeches of Martin Luther King, Jr.*, 217, 220, James M. Washington, ed. (San Francisco: Harper & Row, 1986). On the gradual and partial displacement of universalizing by minoritizing models of race in the black civil rights movement, and the attendant increase in the importance of identity politics, see Harvard Sitkoff, *The Struggle for Black Equality* (New York: Hill & Wang, 1981).

22. William A. Norris, "Acceptance Speech," delivered at the Lambda Liberty Awards Ceremony, Los Angeles, CA, October 16, 1997 (available at Stanford Law School's Robert Crown Law Library website collecting primary documents about military anti-gay policy, http://dont.stanford.edu).

23. *United States v. Carolene Products*, 304 U.S. 144, 153 n.4, 58 S.Ct. 778, 784 n.4 (1938).

24. Bruce Ackerman, "Beyond *Carolene Products*," 98 *Harv. L. Rev.* 713 (1985).

25. Jane S. Schacter, "The Gay Civil Rights Debate in the States: Decoding the Discourse of Equivalents," 29 *Harv. C.R.-C.L. L. Rev.* 283 (1994).

26. For a discussion of these arguments, see Halley, "Sexual Orientation and the Politics of Biology: A Critique of the Argument from Immutability," 46 *Stan. L. Rev.* 503 (1994).

27. Teresa Moore, "King's Niece Slams Gay Rights: Oakland NAACP Chief Deplores Her Statement," *S.F. Chronicle*, August 20, 1997, at A17.

28. Lena Williams, "Blacks Rejecting Gay Rights as a Battle Equal to Theirs," *N.Y. Times*, June 28, 1993, at A1.

29. John Lancaster, "Why the Military Supports the Ban on Gays; Arguments Ranging from Privacy to AIDS Offered Against Clinton's Rights Pledge," *Wash. Post*, Jan. 28, 1993, at A8.

30. For discussion of a case in which a judge dismissed a domestic violence complaint involving a lesbian couple with disparaging remarks about "your funny relationships," another in which, in ruling against a gay plaintiff challenging the military's anti-gay policy, the judge referred to him as a "homo," and another in which the judge sentenced the murderers of a gay man to a less-than-life sentence saying he didn't "care much for 'queers,'" see David S. Buckel, "Unequal Justice for Gays in Hostile Courtrooms," *National L.J.*, August 18, 1997, at A20.

31. 478 U.S. 186, 106 S.Ct. 2841 (1986).

32. 517 U.S. 620, 116 S.Ct. 1620 (1996).

33. Kendall Thomas, "Beyond the Privacy Principle," 92 *Colum. L. Rev.* 1431 (1992).

34. *Hardwick*, 478 U.S. at 194, 197, 106 S.Ct. at 2847 (quoting 4 W. Blackstone, *Commentaries* *215).

35. 410 U.S. 113, 93 S.Ct. 705 (1973).

36. Sedgwick, *Epistemology of the Closet*, 3.

37. Moore, "King's Niece" (quoting Alveda Celeste King).

38. Jim Simon, "Battle Lines Blur over Gay-Rights Bill," *Seattle Times*, Feb. 27, 1994, at A1.

39. See, e.g., Steven A. Holmes, "U.S. Acts to Open Minority Program to White Bidders," *N.Y. Times*, Aug. 15, 1997, at A1.

40. Selena Dong, "'Too Many Asians': The Challenge of Fighting Discrimination against Asian Americans and Preserving Affirmative Action," 47 *Stan. L. Rev.* 1027 (1995); Paul Brest and Miranda Oshige, "Affirmative Action for Whom?," 47 *Stan. L. Rev.* 855 (1995).

41. Like gay men and lesbians, people with disabilities have quite deliberately and self–consciously framed their justice claims in "like race" terms. On this "like race" analogy in the psychology of deaf identity formation, see Neil S. Glickman, "The Development of Culturally Deaf Identities," in *Culturally Affirmative Psychotherapy with Deaf Persons*, ed. Neil S. Glickman and Michael A. Harvey (Mahwah, N.J.: Lawrence Erlham Associates, 1996), 115, passim; in deaf grass-roots activism, see Sharon N. Barnartt, "Action and Consensus Mobilization in the Deaf President Now Protest and Its Aftermath," 17 *Research in Social Movements, Conflicts and Change* 115 (1994); and in deaf antidiscrimination rights claiming, see Mary Ellen Maatman, "Listening to Deaf Culture: A Reconceptualization of Difference Analysis Under Title VII," 13 *Hofstra Labor L. J.* 269 (1996).

    On the way in which framing learning disabilities as an antidiscrimination identity occludes redistributive problems, see Mark Kelman and Gillian Lester, *Jumping the Queue: An Inquiry into the Legal Treatment of Students with Learning Disabilities* (Cambridge, MA: Harvard Univ. Press, 1997).

42. For my own expositions of this argument, see "Reasoning about Sodomy: Act and Identity in and after *Bowers v. Hardwick*," 79 *Va. L. Rev.* 1721 (1993); *Don't: A Reader's Guide to the Military's Anti-Gay Policy* (Durham: Duke Univ. Press, 1999).

43. The closest thing I've found is the strangely fretful prediction that "lifting the ban" might increase the appeal of military service to black gay men and lesbians and to low-income white homosexuals and thus change the demographics of the armed services, of John Sibley Butler, "Homosexuals and the Military Establishment," 31:1 *Society* 13 (1993).

44. Steve Komarow, "Army Forced Rape Charges, Women Say," *USA Today*, Mar. 12, 1997, at 1A (reporting NAACP's charges that, in all thirteen criminal sex harassment investigations at the Navy's Aberdeen Proving Ground, defendants were black men and accusers were white women).

45. Schacter, "The Gay Civil Rights Debate"; Margaret M. Russell, "Lesbian, Gay and Bisexual Rights and the 'Civil Rights Agenda,'" 1 *Afr.-Am. L. & Policy Rep.* 33 (1994).

46. Williams, "Blacks Rejecting." Social conservatives have encouraged African-Americans to regard gay civil rights claims with alarm. In his notorious "What Homosexuals Do" speech to Congress, then-Representative William Dannemeyer warned that "The road to Selma did not lead to the right to sodomy. . . . The freedom train has been highjacked." 135 Cong. Rec. H. 3511, 3512 (June 29, 1989). In the gays-in-the-military debate of 1993, the Reverend Lou Sheldon, head of the evangelical Christian Traditional Values Coalition, repeated the simile: "The freedom train to Selma never stopped at Sodom." Cindy Loose, "Gay Activists Summon Their Hopes, Resolve," *Washington Post*, April 18, 1993, at A1. The degree to which African-American alarm was indigenous, and the degree to which it was fomented by white conservatives, is unclear: I'll suppose it was some of both.

47. For a discussion of the attenuation of this strand of libertarianism in the U.S., see Kelman and Lester, 200–201, 298–99 nn.32–35.

48. "Queer," *Webster's Third New International Dictionary of the English Language, Unabridged* (Springfield, MA: Merriam-Webster, 1981).

49. For an examination of the extent to which this was an explicit goal of the conservative attack on "special rights," see Karen Engle, "What's So Special about Special Rights?," 75 *Denver U. L. Rev.* 1265–1303 (1999).

50. Trina Grillo and Stephanie M. Wildman, "Obscuring the Importance of Race: The Implication of Making Comparisons between Racism and Sexism (or Other -isms)," in *Critical Race Theory: The Cutting Edge*, ed. Richard Delgado (Philadelphia: Temple Univ. Press, 1995), 564–72, 568.

51. *Ibid.* For related arguments that are less directly focused on "like race" arguments, see Kimberle Crenshaw, "Demarginalizing the Intersection of Race and Sex: A Black Feminist Critique of Andiscrimination Doctrine, Feminist Theory and Antiracist Politics," 1989 *U. Chi. Legal F.* 139; Angela P. Harris, "Race and Essentialism in Feminist Legal Theory," 42 *Stan. L. Rev.* 581 (1990).

52. Jane S. Schacter, "The Gay Civil Rights Debate in the States: Decoding the Discourse of Equivalents," 29 *Harv. Civ. R.-Civ. L. L. Rev.* 283, 285 n.13 (1994).

53. *Cassista v. Community Foods, Inc.*, 5 Cal. 4th 1050, 1065, 856 P.2d 1143, 1153, 22 Cal. Rptr. 2d 287, 297 (1993).

54. On the relationship of cultural traits and racial group membership in antidiscrimination law, see Paulette M. Caldwell, "A Hair Piece: Perspectives on the Intersection of Race and Gender," 1991 *Duke L.J.* 365; Karl E. Klare, "Power/Dressing: Regulation of Employee Appearance," 26 *New Eng. L. Rev.* 1395 (1992).

55. Patricia J. Williams, *The Alchemy of Race and Rights* (Cambridge, MA: Harvard Univ. Press, 1991), pp. 256–57 (emphases added).

56. Halley, "Politics of Biology," p. 568.

57. Thomas, "Beyond the Privacy Principle."

58. Lisa Duggan, "Queering the State," 39 *Social Text* 1 (1994).

59. Toni Massaro, "Gay Rights, Thick and Thin," 49 *Stan. L. Rev.* 45 (1996).

60. *Romer* at 1623. Much of this paragraph appeared in my article "*Romer* v. *Hardwick*," 68 *Univ. of Colorado L. Rev.* 429, 439–40 (1997).

61. *Romer* at 1628.

62. *Romer* at 1628.

63. *Romer* at 1625.

64. *Romer* at 1629. See also *id.* at 1625 ("change in legal status"; "The change that Amendment 2 works in the legal status of gays and lesbians in the private sphere").

65. Romer at 1629, quoting *The Civil Rights Cases*, 109 U.S. 3, 24 3 S.Ct. 18, 30 (1883) (brackets and first ellipses in *Romer).

66. *Plessy v. Ferguson*, 163 U.S. 537 16 S.Ct. 1138 (1896) (Harlan, J., dissenting).

67. *Adarand Constructors v. Pena*, 515 U. S. 200, 115 S.Ct. 2097 (1995); see also *City of Richmond v. J.A. Croson Co.*, 488 U.S. 469, 109 S.Ct. 706 (1989).

68. Stuart Minor Benjamin, "Equal Protection and the Special Relationship: The Case of Native Hawaiians," 106 *Yale L.J.* 537 (1996). See also *Morton v. Mancari*, 417 U.S. 535, 553–55, 94 S.Ct. 2474, 2484–85 (1974) (distinguishing race from tribe in order to hold that affirmative action predecedents do not apply to the "special relationship" between federally recognized tribes and the U.S.).

MICHAEL WARNER   3

When you have police everything looks
queer.

ALONG CHRISTOPHER STREET, you   ZONES
can tell immediately that something is
wrong. In Harmony Video, for years   OF
one of the principal porn stores on New
York's most legendary gay strip, they   PRIVACY
now display $3.95 videos of football
teams, John Wayne movies, and music
videos by the fundamentalist pop singer
Amy Grant. Just up the block stands
Christopher Street Books, the store that
proudly bills itself as "New York's oldest
gay establishment." In the front room
it, too, sells bargain videos that seem to
have been unloaded by a desperate
wholesaler in Kansas: Bob Uecker's
"Wacky World of Sports," Spanish-lan-
guage children's cartoons. Whose idea of
gay merchandise is this? In the back
room where the peep show booths are,
they are showing films of wrestling matches. A few customers still come
in, mostly gay men over 40. They leave quickly.[1]

These surreal scenes are among the effects of Mayor Rudy Giuliani's
new zoning law limiting "adult establishments," which the city began
to enforce in the summer of 1998 after a series of court stays and challenges. As this book goes to press the court challenges are not over, and
won't be for a long time. The law has already allowed the city to pad-
lock dozens of stores and clubs, including a gay bookstore. But its
details contain many gray areas, and the resulting uncertainty and fear

have a much wider chilling effect than the raids. "We're just showing wrestling videos until some more rulings come down," says John Murphy, assistant manager of Christopher Street Books. So far, building inspectors have not threatened action against the store. But the new law forbids adult business within 500 feet of churches, schools, or other adult businesses, and the store is within a block of all three. "We've been here since before Stonewall," Murphy told me, "and there have never been complaints. The school and the church have no problem with us. Only the mayor." Murphy's anger is unmistakable, but it comes out in the flat intonations of despair. "The gay community used to fight this sort of thing. But no one seems to care anymore. And our clients aren't going to stand up and fight the law. Giuliani knew that before he started all this. But I thought some of the gay groups would fight harder."

Meanwhile, the street seems unnaturally quiet for a summer weekend. Ordinarily, in decent weather, the sidewalks overflow on Christopher, from Sheridan Square (site of Stonewall) down to the Hudson River. People come from all over the city to walk up and down, or to hang out at the piers by the riverfront. It's a queer scene: many of those who come are young black gays and trannies, mixed in with some tourists and the aging residents of the neighborhood. "This whole strip is going to die," says Murphy. "What do people come here for? Cruising. They cruise, then they get something to eat, then they go in for a drink, and the whole strip makes money." But the queer life of the street here had already been eroded, before the zoning law went into effect, by real estate development, by a rise in tourism, and most of all, by new policing and development on the riverfront. "You can hardly go down to the piers at all anymore," Murphy says. "They have curfews, they have fences, they have cops, there are undercovers everywhere." A few blocks down by the river, between two auto repair garages, stands West World, one of the few adult businesses still allowed under the new law. But there, too, business depends on the vitality of the Christopher Street strip, and the assistant manager is unhappy with the rezoning. "If you start taking out places, less people are going to come," he told the *New York Blade*. "We'd rather that they didn't close those other places." And he, too, says he has been surprised by gay apathy: "I thought the gay community was more politically connected than to just let things go."

In the mainstream press, the crackdown has been applauded left and right. A victory for "all decent New Yorkers," the *Daily News* called it. The *Times* agreed, calling rezoning an effective way to serve the "worthy purpose of protecting communities from the adverse impact of sex-related businesses." (The *Times* had editorialized in favor of the Giuliani plan on no less than seven occasions.) Many gay people as well think there would be nothing wrong with the death of Christopher Street. Neighborhoods change, times change. There will be new places to go. The gay neighborhood, for example, has already moved to Chelsea. And why not? No need to romanticize the West Village, or be nostalgic about it.

One problem with this view is that Chelsea has no noncommercial public space to match the old piers at the end of Christopher. Its strip along Eighth Avenue is wealthier, whiter, less hospitable to nonresidents. The trannies are not going to hang out at Banana Republic. And the disparity is only going to get worse. Developing the Eighth Avenue corridor from Chelsea to Times Square was the principal goal of rezoning.

Of course, there are other neighborhoods. Across town, for example, the old Jewish and latino immigrant district on the lower east side is fast becoming home to a mixed and queer scene, less pricey than nearby Soho, but already touted as the emerging fashion zone. Along with several new bars and restaurants, a new sex-toy store for women has just opened, called Toys in Babeland. But there, too, the effects of the zoning law are felt. Toys in Babeland is the project of two lesbian entrepreneurs from Seattle, where the parent store has been thriving for years. Clare Cavanaugh, one of the owners, told me that they are watching court rulings with a wary eye. (Sex toys are among the gray areas of the law.) In Seattle, their store has a large glass display window, lending queer visibility to the street and the neighborhood. In New York, the display windows stay empty, with nothing but discreetly drawn curtains. From the street, it looks like a podiatrist's office.

In Seattle, the store features a large selection of lesbian porn. In New York, the owners feel too unsafe to stock any. "It makes me sad," says Cavanaugh. "Women come in and want it. It's part of our mission to allow women to explore different parts of their sexuality. And when a woman comes in and says, 'I'm having trouble getting turned on,' I want to offer her a video. But I can't. We're taking chances as it is."

Farther downtown, the strip club Angels used to have a lesbian night. It was the only lesbian strip club in New York, and a place where even the "straight" nights featured lesbian or bisexual dancers as well as trannies. But its owner had been one of the most vocal opponents of the new law. When the court stay on the zoning law expired, Angels became a primary target for enforcement, one of the first in Manhattan to be padlocked.

Uptown, Times Square increasingly looks like a theme park for tourists. The few remaining gay bars in the neighborhood are being closed by the city. Cats, for example, was a neighborhood gay bar, and one of the very few that welcomed trannies. The police raided it at midnight one night, found a few clients with joints in their pockets, and closed the place. Other gay bars in the area have been closed by similar tactics. Only two gay bars remain, and both are conservative enough that, as one patron told the *Village Voice*, "you feel like you're in a gay bar trying to act straight."

All over New York, in fact, a pall hangs over the public life of queers. Much more is at stake here than the replacement of one neighborhood by another, or the temporary crackdowns of a Republican mayor. As in other U.S. cities, sex publics in New York that have been built up over several decades—by the gay movement, by AIDS activism, and by countercultures of many different kinds—are now endangered by a new politics of privatization. This new political alignment has strong support among gays and lesbians, and the conflicts now flashing up illuminate the growing rift between identity-based lesbian and gay politics and its queerer counterparts.

The new politics is proving difficult to resist. For one thing, it happens on many levels, so that its coherence is not always apparent. Zoning, for example, is only the most visible local form of the conflict. Consider the following developments as they affect the public sexual culture in New York.

1) In 1995, the New York City Health Department began enforcing the State Health Code, which prohibits oral, anal, or vaginal sex,

with or without condoms, in any commercial space. In the name of the health code, the city began padlocking theaters, video stores, and sex clubs—many of which had promoted safer sex. Some were allowed to reopen under court orders that even further restricted safer, and not just unsafe sex—in some cases banning solo or joint masturbation in theaters and even "exposed genitals."[2] The manifest contradiction of banning masturbation in the name of AIDS prevention caused neither the city nor the courts nor the local press to have doubts about this policy. Other businesses central to New York's culture of safer sex were chilled out of business by the harassments and publicity of the enforcement campaign. New sex clubs have since opened up to take their place, a fact that Gabriel Rotello points to as evidence that there has been no "sex panic" in New York.[3] But these new sex clubs, though numerous, are private, unadvertised, and in almost every case disconnected from any safer sex outreach. Even in the more or less aboveground sex businesses, like the West Side Club—all of which remain under threat of enforcement or harassment, and are thus compelled to deny that oral or anal sex take place—safer-sex materials are nearly invisible. In the gay bars of New York, almost without exception, the free condoms that used to sit in bowls on the bar are no longer available. The posters and pamphlets that were ubiquitous in the 1980s are nowhere to be seen. Coming to New York from Amsterdam, or Paris, or Sydney, one could not fail to notice the difference. Sex has gone under cover. The consequence seems to have been the nearly perfect obliteration of a visible culture of safer sex.

2) Since 1994, the piers along the Hudson River waterfront—a legendary meeting place for queers for decades, and more recently for youth of color—have been closed down, fenced off, subjected to curfew, and heavily patrolled, often by private police forces under contract to the state. Large stretches of the waterfront have been developed for upper-middle-class residences and tourism. Below the gay piers especially, the area down to Battery Park City has been turned into a tidy model of respectability. The city contracts the management of much of this space to private agencies, and already residents have been vocal in their resentment of nonresidents who come to use the parks. The waterfront redevelopment plan, a joint agreement between city and

state, currently contains no commitment to gay space or even open-use space on the waterfront.[4]

3) In 1997, the Anti-Violence Project in New York reported a dramatic upturn in arrests of gay men for cruising, often on public lewdness charges. Over 60 men were entrapped and arrested in one bathroom in the World Trade Center alone. Other arrests were made on the streets of the West Village and Chelsea. Men cruising or just nude sunbathing in the Ramble (the traditionally gay area of Central Park) were led off in handcuffs. Men of color, in these cases as in so many others, reported rougher treatment by police and higher levels of prosecution in the courts. The arrests were made not just by the NYPD, but even more by the MTA, the Port Authority Police, and the Parks Police. Sex workers, including transvestite and transgendered sex workers on the West Side, have also been harassed.

When the group Sex Panic! sought to help the Anti-Violence Project publicize these problems, the response from the local gay paper was simple denial. The numbers, it was said, though higher than previous years, were still no cause for alarm. But it has since become clear that the numbers were no fluke. In 1997, forty gay-bashings were reported to the police in the first eight months of the year; as I write, the same period of 1998 has seen 72 gay-bashings. Even while violence rises, the police themselves have become more industrious in efforts to entrap and arrest gay men—and not just in New York. In Los Angeles, intensified campaigns against gay bars, sex clubs, and cruising grounds were waged by a special task force, and the city has gone to such absurd extremes as to ban pedestrians from walking certain blocks more than once in a half-hour period. Other examples around the country have been documented by the website cruisingforsex.com, which posts regular "Cops v. Cruisers" updates. In the last two weeks of April 1998 alone, the report included examples of entrapment and harassment from Miami; Gainesville; Las Vegas; Columbus; Oklahoma City; Charlotte; Los Angeles; Fort Lauderdale; Norfolk; Montreal; Spokane; McComb, Mississippi; Frederick, Maryland; Wilton Manors, Florida; Pompano Beach, Florida; Pomona, California; Anderson, South Carolina; Havre de Grace, Maryland; Hallendale, Florida; Long Beach, California; Tupelo, Mississippi; Savannah, Tennessee; and Bakersfield,

California. Full information on the extent of the sex panics of the late 1990s is not available, and for a simple reason: the gay organizations have not gathered it.

4) Public space in general has dwindled in the city. The Giuliani administration, like the Dinkins administration before it, has awarded large tax abatements and other development incentives for corporations, often on the condition that the companies build or maintain a "public" area. (The Giuliani administration has granted a record $666.7 million in tax abatements, many of them to moving non-sex business into Times Square.) The result in the vast majority of cases is a sterile or semi-commercial area, closed to loiterers or the homeless, heavily patrolled, and inaccessible at night.[5]

5) Bars, dance clubs, and other venues of night life have been closed and harassed, sometimes for drug violations or on technicalities of cabaret license violations. (Bars can and have been fined or closed in New York if people standing at the bar are dancing.) Many actions against these venues are taken in the name of "quality of life," usually on account of noise complaints. Even the legendary Stonewall Inn has been targeted, as the West Village becomes a more and more high-priced and heterosexual neighborhood. Some bars, such as Rounds, the principal gay hustler bar, have been closed on such grounds even though neighbors were not complaining. The chill on New York's night life and youth culture has been noticed by everyone.

6) Finally, there is Mayor Giuliani's zoning amendment, passed by City Council in October 1995 by a 41 to 9 vote. The Zoning Text Amendment (N 950384 ZRY) has the following key provisions:

   a) A new definition of adult businesses. The old definition is a business "customarily not open to the public because it excludes minors by reason of age." The new one is vaguer and broader. It specifies businesses in which a "substantial" portion of materials or performances have "an emphasis upon the depiction or description of 'specified sexual activities' or 'specified anatomical areas.'" These areas include nudity, but also such things as "erotic touching of the breast, genitals, or buttocks." Included in this definition of "adult" are book and video stores, eating and drinking establishments, theaters, and other businesses. A preamble defines "substantial" as forty percent; but because that number is not in the text of the law itself, enforcement agents can broaden it. The Giuliani administration has announced its intention to close stores it considers "adult," regardless of the percentages. In many (but not all) of the court cases to date, it has succeeded.

b) Adult businesses are allowed only in certain zoning areas. Most of these turn out to be on the waterfront. Almost all are poor neighborhoods, low in political clout. Many critics have pointed out that the city's maps showing the areas reserved for adult businesses are misleading, as the majority of land listed as available is in fact unusable. It includes, for example, Kennedy Airport. The mayor's office added some new areas to offset this complaint, claiming that the additions expanded the legal areas by 40 percent. But the new areas turn out to be subject to the same complaints: they include land occupied by large hotels, corporate headquarters, department stores such as Macy's, and even City Hall itself.

c) Even in these new reserved districts, adult businesses are not allowed within:
  500 feet of another adult establishment; and
  500 feet of a house of worship, school, or day care center.
  (These are called "sensitive receptors" in the jargon of zoning.)

d) Adult businesses are limited to one per lot and limited in size to 10,000 square feet.

e) Signs on adult businesses are limited in size, placement, and illumination.

Enforcement of the bill is entrusted to building inspectors. The provisions of the zoning bill can be boiled down to three forms of isolation:

• from concentration to dispersal (the 500-foot rule keeps adult businesses from being close to one another);
• from conspicuousness to discretion (the signage regulations of the new bill are stricter than existing regulations); and
• from residential sites to remote ones.

All three impulses share the desire to make sex less noticeable in the course of everyday urban life, and more difficult to find for those who want sexual materials. In April, 1998, the city revealed that it would extend the new regulations to newsstand vendors, regulating the amount of pornography sold at kiosks. (At the same time, new restrictions and higher licensing fees were imposed on the kiosks.)[6]

The bill has been facing a court challenge on First Amendment grounds, brought by the New York Civil Liberties Union and the Coalition for Free Expression, a group representing owners of some of the city's adult businesses. The court challenge was made on two grounds, both widely recognized in the context of First Amendment law: secondary effects and reasonable access. In brief, because government is prohibited by the Constitution from regulating speech for its content per se, the zoning of adult businesses is justified on the basis of its "secondary effects"—falling property values, rising crime, etc. Those opposed to the bill argued that the city failed to show that adult businesses have these secondary effects. The city's own published research in some cases shows the opposite. Where there does seem to be a correlation between sex businesses and crime rates or low property values, the city has failed to show that the correlation is causal. It may very well be, of course, that porn stores go to those areas because rent and interference are both low. It must certainly be the case, too, that the low property values and crime rates result from other factors, like the proximity to the Port Authority bus terminal at Eighth Avenue and 42d Street, which draws porn stores because of the travelers. Despite the high scrutiny that should have been devoted to these factors to make sure that the city was not singling out porn stores because of their content—which, of course, everyone knows was exactly the case—the courts allowed the "secondary effects" argument to stand.

The other ground of the challenge, reasonable access, means that the city can only restrict adult businesses by zoning if the zoning plan continues to allow access to constitutionally protected forms of speech. On this score the challenge would seem to be especially strong, as the percentage of New York City land available for adult businesses—especially when nonviable sites such as City Hall Park are subtracted—falls well below the percentage that has been recognized in court precedents as allowing "reasonable access." And since most of the available land is in industrial waterfront areas that are badly lit, unpopulated, and remote from public transportation, forcing consumers into such areas is a way of imposing hidden costs for access. But as of this writing, the courts have upheld the zoning law. Judges thus far have been unwilling to regard the legal issues as serious.

The examples I have given thus far come from New York City, mostly under the administration of Mayor Giuliani. The most common reaction among queer New Yorkers is simply to blame Giuliani and wait, passively, for a better regime. But I have also noted that similar developments are taking place in other cities. Even within New York, the politics emerging in the areas I've listed is not always coordinated policy, and Mayor Giuliani's "quality of life" campaign is only partly responsible. Several city and state agencies converge in response to different pressures.

Most are not, in my judgment, driven primarily by homophobia. The closing of the waterfront, to take one example, involves agencies of both the city and the state, as well as a private security force, all acting in the name of a common vision of real estate development. The zoning issue was clearly driven by real estate interests, even more than by the petit-bourgeois moralism to which it gave such venomous expression. That is why the *New York Times* editorialized seven times in favor of rezoning; the New York Times Corporation is a principal member of the Times Square Business Improvement District. It was the Times Square BID, even more than Mayor Giuliani's office, that spearheaded the rezoning effort. The Disney Corporation insisted on eliminating the porn stores as a condition of its role in changing Times Square.

We are therefore confronted with a problem of political analysis. What lies behind this erosion of queer publics, since it seems local and uncoordinated, and yet widespread and systematic?

One common thread is the increasingly aggressive demand of market capital, which in the United States and elsewhere has seriously eroded the ancient ideal of an active public, a commonwealth. That conflict, however, is longstanding and has only an ambiguous relation to sex publics.[7] It isn't just "the market" that is chilling New York's queer life. The destruction of sex publics results from the new ways of resolving the conflict that have dominated the Clintonian era. The state is seen as responsible less for fostering a democratic public sphere than for ensuring the expansion of market capital. It is thought to be a servant of the market, rather than a check to the market. As it relies more on the corporate populism of private consumers and less on public citizens, it elaborates its rhetoric and its institutions to a normalized population and its forms of privacy.[8] This understanding of the relations among state, market, and public has become, in the late 1990s at least, a new common sense, one that appears as common sense partly because it arises in so many contexts that it seems to transcend the particularities and interests of any single context. From one point of view these developments are examples of economic privatization, the social or cultural effects of which may be complex. But more importantly, they also illustrate the consolidation of an unmarked national sex public, universalizing the norms of married couples, reproduction, and shared property.

The lesbian and gay movement has itself embraced those norms of privatization. The current conditions in New York vividly illustrate what happens when national and international forces are pushing the expansion of a market at the expense of public space and public autonomy, while at the same time lesbian and gay organizations decide that privacy and normalization are their goals. The trend toward privatization intersects with the history of lesbian and gay politics in a critical and destructive way. Gay men and lesbians collectively are exceedingly ill equipped at the moment to recognize or resist the shifts in public culture. The media that organize the lesbian and gay public have changed, along with the rest of the culture; they are increasingly dominated by highly capitalized lifestyle magazines, which themselves have been drawn into close partnership with the mass entertainment industry through the increased visibility of some gay celebrities and the increased use of gay-themed plots in mass culture. At the same time, a shift in the nature and temporality of the AIDS crisis has dissolved the counterpublic activism and collective will of the AIDS movement, now in spectacular disarray. Gay journalists are repudiating the legacy of safer sex, depicting lesbians as sexless homebodies whom gay men should imitate and gay male sexual culture as a zone of irresponsibility, narcissism, and death. Gay marriage is understood by many to offer a postpolitical privacy now described as the only thing we ever wanted. In this context the lesbian and gay movement has done almost nothing to resist the trends I have described. The erosion of public sexual culture, including its nonnormative intimacies, is in fact cheered on by lesbian and gay advocates.[9]

The Health Department campaign against public sex venues was not just cheered by gay advocates, but initiated by them, in an intense publicity and lobbying campaign led by a small group of gay journalists. In the dispute over the waterfront piers, Sal Silitti, a gay member of the Christopher Street Block Association, called for closing them down entirely, telling the Village Voice that they were responsible for "an influx of polluting revelers."[10] Both *LGNY*, the local gay paper in New York, and the news editor of *The Advocate*, a national gay magazine, responded to reports of public lewdness arrests by saying that if men were caught with their pants down, it was their own problem. *LGNY* also wrote that bar and club closings were proper enforcement of the law, and not a gay issue. When the rezoning of sex businesses was most contested in 1995, the gay playwright Terence McNally could only comment, "I don't want to live next door to a porn shop." (Later, in 1998, he expressed shock and outrage when the Catholic League, denouncing his own new play as obscene, nearly managed to prevent it from being staged.) In each case, in short, large numbers of lesbians and gay men— just how large we can only guess—embrace a politics of privatization that offers them both property value and an affirmation of identity in a language of respectability and mainstream acceptance.

Much of this reaction is familiar from the era of the homophile movement and later gay organizing.[11] What's new about the current politics is that it is understood as post-liberationist, a mark of gains already won. The history of queer public activity is now repudiated on the theory that its purpose has been served, that the highest goals of gay men and lesbians are now marriage, military service, and the elaboration of a culture in which sex plays no more of a role than it is thought to play in "mainstream" culture.[12] Privatization can sometimes be embraced explicitly, as in the rhetoric of Larry Kramer and Michelangelo Signorile, but more often it is tacit, as in the unmistakable decline of street activism throughout the 1990s.[13]

The "post-gay" rhetoric, however, can also mislead us into thinking that times have changed more dramatically than they have. In many ways, the conflicts over public sexual culture have changed little since World War II. Consider the following radio commercial, aired in New York City on May 10, 1998:

> They're cruising for sex all over New York. Sexual deviants are roaming our local stores and malls [sound of children laughing comes in], places that you shop, with your children. Monday, Fox Five's undercover camera catches perverts in very lewd acts in very public places [sound of jail cell closing & police siren]. Could you or your child be an innocent victim of . . . CRUISING FOR SEX? On the Fox Five ten o'clock news, Monday.

The Fox story was one of many such attempts to capitalize on the publicity following the arrest of pop star George Michael in early April, 1998, on charges of public indecency in a bathroom. Punitive journalism and police actions of this kind can be documented in great detail for every part of the United States, apparently undiminished since the McCarthy era. At least twenty local news programs around the country used the same gimmick during "sweeps" week in 1998, taking undercover cameras into gay cruising areas to arouse normal America's punitive instincts.[14]

It would be a mistake to see this tactic as simple homophobia. It is not that different from a local New York news story run in 1995 on gay sex clubs, in which the camera was led on a lurid undercover tour by gay journalist Gabriel Rotello, allegedly to expose unsafe sex. (Neither Rotello nor the reporter, Mike Taiby, thought it relevant that they had witnessed no unsafe sex.) Although the target, in these accounts, is sex between men, what matters to these watchdogs is not homosexuality per se, but public sex. They aim to exterminate a practice and the culture surrounding it, rather than an identity.

That is one reason why the punitive campaigns meet so little resistance, even in the late 1990s, from the lesbian and gay organizations. As countless studies of the tearoom and bathhouse cultures of sex have shown, many men who participate in public sex do not see it as an expression of political identity.[15] Many—a majority, in some studies— think of themselves as heterosexual. Many are married. Even those who consider themselves gay may be seeking in such venues a world less defined by identity and community than by the negation of identity through anonymous contact; they may be seeking something very different from "community" in a venue where men from very different worlds meet, often silently, for sex. Because the politics of resistance was early defined in the United States along identitarian lines, while many of the most policed sites have been those where sex happens, and not those associated with a distinct identity, the organized lesbian and gay movement has traditionally been reluctant to engage in a principled defense of sexual culture outside the home. Gay organizations such as the Human Rights Campaign have not been committed to challenging the regulation of sexual practice by the state and by public media. On occasion they have been worse than indifferent. Torie Osborn, former head of the National Gay and Lesbian Task Force, publicly lamented the fact that sex "dominates gay male—and now young lesbian—culture," arguing that sex "holds no promise for real change; it is consumeristic and ultimately hollow."[16]

Even the National Lesbian and Gay Journalists Association, in one of the few protests by gay organizations against the Fox news story, felt it necessary to preface its news release with a disclaimer by Karen Boothe, NLGJA president: "NLGJA in no way condones illegal sexual activity in public places." Here is the argument against the Fox story as the NLGJA conceives it:

> "Public sex [Boothe continues] is as foreign to the lives of most gay people as it is to most straight people. Males who engage in this practice with other males are usually those whose fear of societal condemnation makes them afraid to frequent clubs and bars where they risk being identified." Boothe said such stereotypical stories rarely examine the societal pressures that push people to have anonymous sex. What's more, day-to-day coverage on these stations often fails to present an accurate portrait of gay people living healthy and productive lives.[17]

Public sex, according to the NLGJA, is a temporary evil that will wither and fade when gay identity is made more freely available to all. It does not occur to Karen Boothe that dominant criteria for "healthy and productive lives" might be precisely the issue. She does not imagine that the kind of privatization she urges might be regarded by some as a real loss. She also does not consider that her yardstick of value is that of normalization. "Public sex is as foreign to the lives of most gay people as it is to most straight people," she says; but one might as well respond: so much the worse for most gay people and most straight people. The fact that public sex is not the statistical norm ought to have nothing to do with its value or its morality. (Sainthood, when it comes to that, is "foreign to the lives of most gay people.") Boothe succumbs to the hidden lure of the normal, the confusion between what "most" people do and what one ought to do. Though she was one of the few people to speak out against the homophobic press frenzy after the Michael arrest, she utterly fails to challenge the stigma against men who find each other outside the home. In this respect, little seems to have changed since 1950.

I do not mean to be singling out the NLGJA, as there is nothing exceptional about Boothe's comment. The press release articulates both the new common sense and the premises of identitarian organization. If your only tool is a hammer, the saying goes, every problem looks like a nail. The institutional framework of the lesbian and gay movement, predicated on identitarian thought, sees all sexual politics as requiring a more consolidated gay identity and a form of life more fully conforming to the institutions of privacy. Now that the movement is in a further retreat from its history of radicalism into a new form of post-liberationist privatization, it is not surprising that gay men and lesbians are often willing to repudiate their own sexual culture and its world-making venues. The result is catastrophic weakness.

This willing cooperation of the lesbian and gay movement in its own enfeeblement can be read in Mayor Giuliani's 1997 campaign strategy. In a 1995 letter to the Planning Commission, his opponent Ruth Messinger, then Borough President of Manhattan, called attention to the unequal impact of the law on gays and lesbians. Citing this letter, Giuliani kicked off his official 1997 campaign by mocking her stand against the law. He then featured this attack in his television ads as the centerpiece of his campaign. It was a dare rooted in shame. His strategy was based on a cynical calculation that New Yorkers would not support the city's tradition of openness and diversity, but more particularly that gay New Yorkers would not rally to protect sex businesses, and that Messinger would be isolated by the resulting stigma. It worked. The Stonewall Democratic Club, a gay organization, held a press conference supporting Giuliani's rezoning, asserting that Messinger had been misled by the advice of Sex Panic! and other radical, fringe elements who do not represent the views of the lesbian and gay "mainstream."

Fortunately, activists at some of the lesbian and gay groups did see the danger in rezoning. But their constituency never roused itself. Along with many others, I took part in a coalition of groups that decided to fight rezoning in the political process, even though it was clear that its ultimate fate would rest with the courts. One of the most troubling aspects of the issue was the erosion of public support for a diverse, publicly accessible sexual culture; without this erosion the bill would never have gained support, and its passage shows a desperate need for new kinds of organizing and awareness. The coalition against it included anticensorship groups such as the ACLU, Feminists for Free Expression, People for the American Way, National Coalition Against Censorship. It also involved a number of gay and lesbian organizations, such as Lambda Legal Defense Fund, the Empire State Pride Agenda, and the AIDS Prevention Action League. These latter groups joined the anticensorship groups for a simple reason, and it was this argument that Messinger echoed in her 1995 letter: the impact of rezoning on businesses catering to gay men and lesbians, but especially to gay men and other men who have sex with men, will be devastating. All of the adult businesses on Christopher Street can be shut down (or converted to outlets for football videos) along with the principal venues where gay men meet for sex. None of these businesses have been targets of local complaints. Since the Stonewall Riots of 1969, queers have come to take for granted the availability of explicit sexual materials, theaters, and clubs. That is how we have learned to find each other, to construct a sense of a shared world, to carve out spaces of our own in a homophobic world, and, since 1983, to cultivate a collective ethos of safer sex. All of that is about to change. Now, those who want sexual materials, or men who want to meet other men for sex, will have to travel to small, inaccessible, little-trafficked, badly lit areas, mostly on the waterfront, where heterosexual porn users will also be relocated, where risk of violence will consequently be higher and the sense of a collective world more tenuous. The nascent lesbian sexual culture is threatened as well, including the only video rental club catering to lesbians. The impact of the sexual purification of New York will fall unequally on those who already have fewest publicly accessible resources.[18]

It's also ironic that those who invoke AIDS in order to prevent anyone from having sex in a commercial space should also be trying to eliminate a porn trade that enables home consumption. Peep shows, masturbation, and porn consumption are, above all, safe. Porn stores are among the leading vendors of condoms and lube. And anyone with experience in AIDS education will tell you that the most successful tool against AIDS is a public culture of safer sex. Where will anyone find such a culture after the porn theaters, the bathhouses, the sex clubs, and the book and video stores have been closed? Does anyone who works in AIDS prevention think that it's a good idea to zone all public sexual culture down to the waterfront?

The Giuliani administration has already done much to undermine that public world in which men find each other safely for sex and share a commitment to risk reduction. The health department wants to drive all sex into the home, a policy that is inconsistent with what we know about HIV transmission and with the tradition of safer-sex education. A campaign against public sex is an easy sell in the Gingrich era. A campaign against unsafe sex is harder. And for some reason it seems to be difficult for many people to remember the difference. At the very moment when we most need an inventive and publicly responsible activism, we see one privatizing initiative after another. In the second era of AIDS, now that information has gotten out and the short-term responses have to be replaced with lifelong solutions, and now that we are facing individual and collective despair about that prospect, our public sexual culture has to be a resource, not a scapegoat. If we turn the shaping of that culture over to city officials and tabloid dailies, we will have failed the challenge and left countless men with even fewer resources to face a future that few of us have the stomach to imagine.

It has been very hard to mobilize even gay resistance to any of these measures, and the rhetorical requirements of organizing in this context entail some very difficult and very theoretical questions. Maybe only a minority among us are regular customers of sex businesses. Why should the others care? Are my arguments against the bill only going to protect gay male culture? Am I also committed to defending what is sold on Times Square, including the worst of heterosexual culture? What about NAMBLA? Will our position be justified on First-Amendment, civil-liberties grounds or on more substantive arguments about the benefits of public sexual culture?

WHAT'S PUBLIC ABOUT SEX?

There is very little sense in this country that a public culture of sex might be something to value, something whose accessibility is to be protected. Even when people recognize the combined effect of privatization initiatives—and in New York this effect is widely acknowledged—they find it difficult to mount a principled defense of a public culture of sex. Instead, they fall back on free-speech arguments. Although valuable, those arguments do not explain why you would want an accessible sexual culture. It should be clear by now that I intend to argue that a public sexual culture is not just a civil liberty—like the right to deny the Holocaust and march in Skokie—but a good thing, and that queer politics should make it a priority. This does not mean that I am arguing against privacy. Quite the contrary: The politics of privatization, in my view, destroys real privacy even as it erodes public activity.

To see how this could be so, it will be necessary to get over the common misconception that public and private are always opposites. There are so many competing definitions of public and private involved that it may be worth listing the main ones:

Public	*Private*
1) open to everyone	restricted to some
2) accessible for money	closed even to those who could pay
3) state-related	nonstate, belonging to civil society

4) official	nonofficial
5) common	special or personal
6) national or popular	group, class, or locale
7) international or universal	particular or finite
8) in physical view of others	concealed
9) outside the home	domestic
10) circulated in print or electronic media	circulated orally or in manuscript
11) known widely	known to initiates
12) acknowledged and explicit	tacit and implicit

13) "the world itself, in so far as it is common to all of us and distinguished from our privately owned place in it" (as Arendt puts it in *The Human Condition*).[19]

Matters are further complicated by several senses of private that have no corresponding sense of public, including:

14) related to the individual, especially to inwardness, subjective experience, and the incommunicable;

15) discreetly comported, in the sense of the French *pudeur*—expressible in English only through its opposite, impudence; and

16) genital or sexual.

None of these definitions are simple oppositions, or "binaries." Because the contexts overlap, most things are private in one sense and public in another. Books can be published privately; a public theater can be a private enterprise; a private life can be discussed publicly, etc. So it requires no stretch of the imagination to see that pornography, "public sex," cruising, sex work, and other elements in a publicly accessible sexual culture are public in some ways, but still intensely private in others. "Public sex" is public in the sense that it takes place outside the home, but it usually takes place in areas that have been chosen for their seclusion, and like all sex involves extremely intimate and private associations. Sex work is public in being accessible for cash, but still private in many of the same ways, as well as being a private trade. When people speak of "public sex," the crudeness of the term misleads us about what is at stake.[20]

The very concept of public sexual culture looks anomalous because so many kinds of privacy are tied to sex. One learns in infancy where one's "privates" are. This elemental relation to one's own body becomes the basis for a whole series of orientations: impudence and shame, modesty and display, upper and nether, clean and unclean, modest and lewd, etc. These charged polarities, with their visceral and pretheoretical force, come into play so quickly that it is often difficult, even with quite educated people, to discuss "public sex" and mean simply sex in spaces other than the home, or sex in commercial venues. It sounds like matter out of place, and in a way that triggers disgust. (The ability of sex in public places to reach such a primordial threshold of disgust, at once arbitary and unshakable, may of course be for many people part of its psychic and social appeal.)

Americans are most familiar with arguments for sexual liberties on grounds such as rights to privacy. Until the Rehnquist era, the Supreme Court on such grounds steadily limited the powers of the state to regulate sexual practice. The high point in this trend was the 1965 Supreme Court decision in *Griswold v. Connecticut*, authored by Justice William O. Douglas. The decision, which struck down a state law preventing the purchase of birth control, recognized a "zone of privacy" within which the government could not interfere with matters such as birth control. Twenty years later, the Rehnquist court shifted the direction of the law. *Bowers v. Hardwick* attached a new premise to Douglas's "zone of privacy": it is the heterosexual bedroom that is protected, regardless of what practices are performed or how the law refers to them. That is, laws that appear to ban oral or anal sex anywhere, even between married partners at home, cannot be invalidated by appeal to *Griswold* if the appeal is made on behalf of anyone other than married couples. (The Georgia sodomy statute was just such a facially neutral law.) The "zone of privacy" was recognized not for intimate associations, or control over one's body, or for sexuality in general, but only for the domestic space of heterosexuals. The legal tradition, in other words, tends to protect sexual freedom by privatizing it, and now it also reserves privacy protections for those whose sexuality is already normative. The privilege of heterosexual matrimony does not even need to be named, since it is able to pass in law simply as "privacy."[21] But at this rate it is hardly privacy at all in the sense that most people understand. If your zone of privacy requires the support of an elaborate network of state regulations, judicial rulings, and police powers, and if it is based on the prejudicial exclusion of others from the rights of association or bodily autonomy you take for granted, then your privacy is another name for the armed national sex public to which you so luckily belong.[22]

Richard Mohr, in *Gays/Justice* (1988), challenges the reasoning in *Bowers* on the basis of a strong conception of privacy: he argues that sex is "inherently private," and should be protected as such no matter where it occurs. The cultural taboo against public sex, he argues, stems from the phenomenology of the sex act—its exclusion of the everyday world of social status and individual will through somatic states of arousal, erotic personhood, and intimate relations. The very strength of that taboo, moreover, contradicts the state's claim to regulate consensual sex: "Across the range of actions for which there is an *obligation* to privacy, that very obligation generates, in turn, a right to privacy."[23] With an admirable consistency, Mohr defends the kinds of public sex common to gay male culture precisely on the grounds of their privacy:

> Many may find orgy rooms at bathhouses and backrooms in bars not to be private. This view is wrong, for if the participants are all consenting to be there with each other for the possibility of sex polymorphic, then they fulfill the proper criterion of the private in the realm of the sexual. If, as is the case, gay cruising zones of parks at night have as their habitues only gay cruisers, police cruisers, and queerbashers, then they too are private in the requisite sense; and, in the absence of complaints against specific individuals, arrests should not occur there for public lewdness.[24]

Involvement in a consensual sex act, for Mohr, presupposes a commitment to privacy, excluding all parties that have not consented and have not been chosen for participation. Consent distinguishes sex in public spaces from exhibitionism. And in spaces such as bathhouses and cruising grounds in secluded park areas, the assumption of privacy is reasonably grounded and should be respected.

Thus in the local news ad quoted above, one of the most fundamental falsehoods lies in the implication that "sexual deviants" cruising in bathrooms are seeking to annihilate both consent and the privacy it creates: they "are roaming our local stores and malls, places that you shop, with your children." In reality, it is the journalist himself who must transgress both consent and privacy: "Monday, Fox Five's *undercover camera catches perverts* in very lewd acts in very public places." The need to resort to an undercover camera contradicts the claim that these places are already "very public." It also contradicts the claim that "you or your child" could be an "innocent victim" of cruising, since it implicates you in the aggressional and voyeuristic project of "catching" those who have no desire to be caught, and who share a reasonable presumption that they will not be spied on.

Mohr's argument illustrates the intermingling of different senses of public and private in sexual culture. I think he is right to point to a kind of privacy—even intimacy—in the gay male practice of public sex, one that is very different from the privatization I see as characteristic of the new public morality. But I also think that Mohr's liberal arguments are somewhat one-sided in choosing to defend sex only on the basis of its consensual privacy. The practices of public sexual culture, including both cruising and pornography, involve not only a world-excluding privacy, but also a world-making publicness. The Fox News report is designed to undermine both. It replaces one privacy with another, one public with another: it violates the privacy of cruising in order to privatize the sex taking place there; and it reduces a rich public culture to inarticulate "deviants," consolidating instead a normal public in which it can be taken for granted that "you" have children, are at home, and go to "public places" in order to shop. The bad faith of this mass public is evident in the fact that the "deviants" are not imagined to have a rival point of view. And if the NLGJA protest is any indication, it must be admitted that the rival point of view remains badly inarticulate within the official publics of journalism and politics.

Within the culture of public sex, of course, very different recognitions and a very different articulacy are possible. The sexual cultures of gay men and lesbians are, after all, cultures in ways that are often forgotten, especially when they are treated simply as a mass of deviants looking for hormonally driven release. They recognize themselves as cultures, with their own knowledges, places, practices, languages, and learned modes of feeling. The naive belief that sex is simply inborn instinct still exerts its power, but most gay men and lesbians know that the sex they have was not innate nor entirely of their own making, but *learned*—learned by participating, in scenes of talk as well as of fucking. One learns both the elaborated codes of a subculture, with its rituals and typologies (top/bottom, butch/femme, etc.), but also simply the improvisational nature of unpredicted situations. As queers we do not always share the same tastes or practices, though often enough we learn new pleasures from others. What we do share is an ability to swap stories and learn from them, to enter new scenes not entirely of our own making, to know that in these contexts it is taken for granted that people are different, that one can surprise oneself, that one's task in the face of unpredicted variations is to recognize the dignity in each person's way of surviving and playing and creating, to recognize that dignity in this context need not be purchased at the high cost of conformity or self-amputation. Within this queer world we recognize, usually tacitly, that the norms of the dominant culture would quash the scene we're participating in. It is therefore best understood as a counter-public. But its openness, accessibility, and unpredictability are all marks of its publicness.

A public sexual culture changes the nature of sex, much as a public intellectual culture changes the nature of thought. Sexual knowledges can be made cumulative. They circulate. The extreme instances of this are in the invention of new practices or pleasures, as Michel Foucault noticed when he remarked that, with fist-fucking, gay men had invented the first wholly new sexual act in thousands of years. Even apart from this example, lesbians and gay men with relatively modest tastes can still recognize that their own bodies have been remapped by participation in a queer sexual culture, that each touch, gesture, or sensation condenses lessons learned not only through one's own experience, but through the experience of others.

The dominant culture of privacy wants you to lie about this corporeal publicness. It wants you to pretend that your sexuality sprang from your nature alone and found expression solely with your mate, that sexual knowledges neither circulate among others nor accumulate over time in a way that is transmissable. The articulated sexuality of gay men and lesbians is a mode of existence that is simultaneously public—even in its bodily sensations—and extremely intimate. But it is now in jeopardy even within the gay movement, as gay men and lesbians are more and more drawn to a moralizing that chimes in with homophobic stereotype, with a wizened utopianism that confuses our maturity with marriage to the law, and perhaps most insidiously of all, with the privatization of sex in the fantasy that mass-mediated belonging could ever substitute for the public world of a sexual culture.

When gay men or lesbians cruise, when they develop a love of strangers, they directly eroticize participation in the public world of their privacy. Contrary to myth, what one relishes in loving strangers is not mere anonymity, nor meaningless release. It is the pleasure of belonging to a sexual world, in which one's sexuality finds an answering resonance not just in one other, but in a world of others. Strangers have an ability to represent a world of others in a way that one sustained intimacy cannot, although of course these are not exclusive options in gay and lesbian culture. This pleasure, a direct cathexis of the publicness of sexual culture, is by and large unavailable in dominant culture, simply because heterosexual belonging is already mediated by nearly every institution of culture. Publicness in such a context is riddled with the bad faith of privilege, with the asymmetries of male domination, and with the banality of a normalized world. The resentment that even heterosexuals feel toward these conditions can often enough find expression in the demonization of the very queers to whom publicness might still mean something different.

But these differences, the learned knowledges of queer culture, do not find expression in conflicts over public sexual culture because of the hierarchies of shame and memory in official speech. The conflict focalized in the Fox report—and equally in the Giuliani zoning plan—is more than a conflict between the privacy of cruisers and the public discipline of the state and the media. It is a conflict between a dominant public and a counter-public, hierarchized by shame and silence. It isn't just cruisers who lose. It's everyone who belongs to the queer worlds that get more and more opaque to the normalized public view.

Writing in the *Village Voice* in 1995, Mark Schoofs quotes Council member Walter McCaffrey saying that customers of sex shops won't mind going to the waterfront because they "will feel much more comfortable going to someplace where they won't be seen." Schoofs continues: "This kind of 'comfort' is exactly what the right wing seeks, because it is not comfort at all. It is shame, and that emotion renders a person cowed, docile, and easy to oppress." This is why we don't hear more opposition to the bill, even though the extraordinary economic success of the industry shows that the porn trade has a broad popular base. Queers will be especially apt to understand this phenomenon, since it is so closely related to the effect that is called the closet. Common mythology understands the closet as an individual's lie about him- or herself. Yet queers understand, at some level, that the closet was built around them, willy-nilly, by dominant assumptions about what goes without saying, what can be said without a breach of decorum, who shares the onus of disclosure, and who will bear the consequences of speech and silence—by all of what Erving Goffman, in *Stigma*, calls "the careful work of disattention."[25] Speech is everywhere regulated unequally. This is experienced by lesbians and gay men as a private, individual problem of shame and closeting. But it is produced by the assumptions of everyday talk.[26]

This effect in the rhetoric of shame is more than simply an individual affect. It isolates contexts and publics from each other, dividing them by amnesias. The rhetoric of antiporn activism is full of terms like "sleaze," "filth," and "smut." These words, conceptually vacuous, do nothing to say why porn is bad. It is impossible to argue with them; their purpose is not to provide reasoned argument. Their purpose is to throw shame, to make a rival point of view seem unimaginable. This effect takes place in interactions between persons, where it is familiar enough, but also in the interaction between different contexts for speech—in the circulation of discourse. People in everyday life often have fairly frank and open ways of talking about sex; in some contexts, such as talk shows, that frankness runs to the extreme. In the context of zoning, that frankness gives way to an implausibly general air of innocence. In one public opinion survey conducted in 1990 by Penn and Schoen Associates, 84 percent of those polled said Americans "should have the absolute right to buy all magazines and books judged to be legal."[27] Yet in the context of the zoning debate, we have learned that large numbers of people will forget that opinion, supporting instead even more restrictive and punitive measures than those proposed by Giuliani. The language of shame, the scenario of the pure and vulnerable child, the fantasy of an undifferentiated community standard—such devices serve to hierarchize the contexts of sexual knowledge. They ensure that an amnesia-riddled official speech always trumps the knowledges of sexual culture, helping to thwart their tendency to cumulative and transmissible knowledge.

People commonly think public sex is the special province of gay men, those oversexed monsters of the urban alleys and the highway restroom. The same people who think this may have happily watched the movie *Risky Business*, in which Tom Cruise and Rebecca de Mornay fuck on the subway. They may have laughed their fucking heads off in the episode of *The Simpsons* when Marge and Homer romp around nude in public looking to spice up their sex lives. They may have identified deeply with the title characters of the show *Dharma and Greg*, who spend an episode competing with a friend to see who can have the most flagrantly public sex. They may own all of Madonna's albums. Yet the same people may think that there could be no defense for gay men who find each other in out-of-the-way corners of parks.

One advantage to thinking about the closet-effect this way is to see how it can persist even after individual identities are declared through coming out. Even people who are out will often go along with the rules of decorum, forgetting in any official context whatever they might have learned of the queer world. These tacit rules about what can be acknowledged or said in public are as much a closet as any, and a politics of identity will be inefficient in fighting it.

Interestingly, the Giuliani administration and other advocates of rezoning higher up in the political system did not speak the language of smut, filth, and shame. Giuliani did not condemn porn per se—at least not until his zoning plan received court approval. His arguments were limited to secondary effects and a rather vague, but politically potent language about "quality of life." This discretion had a legal rationale: he did not want the law invalidated in courts as a restriction on the basis of content. After the First-Amendment challenge to the law had been rejected by two courts, Giuliani shed that tact as though it were a hair shirt, and bragged openly that his tactics had succeeded in defeating the free-speech liberals. He also began advocating a more open deployment of shame, as the *New York Times* reported on May 16, 1998:

> Mayor Rudolph Giuliani, who prides himself on having a solution for everything, did not hesitate Friday when a caller to his radio show complained about X-rated video stores and topless bars in the caller's Queens neighborhood.
>
> "You know, one of the things you might want to do, which is perfectly legal: you can take pictures of people going in there," Giuliani said. "It really does cut down on business."
>
> The mayor, a former U.S. attorney, used his weekly call-in show on WABC-AM to give the caller, Don, a little free legal advice, pointing out that it is legal to take pictures of people on the street.
>
> "You know who goes into those shops, right?" Giuliani asked. "You know the kind of people who'd go in there. They probably don't want other people to know that." [28]

This was going a little far, even for the *Times*.

At another level, of course, the assumption of unanimity behind the phrase "quality of life" produces its own kind of shame. There is a circularity in this rhetoric, since it serves to reinforce the disrepute of adult businesses, and therefore helps to bring about the depression of property value that it appears to lament. More importantly from my point of view, the rhetoric of "quality of life" tries to isolate porn from political culture by pretending that there are no differences of value or opinion in it, that it therefore does not belong in the public sphere of critical exchange and opinion-formation. When Giuliani speaks of quality of life, he never acknowledges that different people might want different qualities in their lives, let alone that access to porn might be one of them.

The zoning bill seeks to privatize sex in part through this segregation of sexual matters from the public culture in which differences between people can be recognized. Like the other rightist initiatives I've mentioned, it rests in a fantasy that persons in their public capacities as citizens and historical actors are nonsexual; they are, as Lauren

Berlant puts it, "dead citizens."[29] Persons in their sexual capacities remain in the zone of privacy whose heterosexuality is legally mandated and whose isolation from public culture the zoning bill tries to preserve. These twin fantasies, of dead citizens and sexual subjects, require massive and complementary amnesias. Citizens must routinely forget everything they know about sex. And sexual subjects must routinely forget everything they know about public culture.

I have argued in my book *Letters of the Republic* that when the modern public sphere developed out of eighteenth-century print culture, one of its main assumptions was that citizens were abstract. Print culture allowed people to abstract themselves from their lives and their bodies, engaging a public that was by definition indefinite, not localizable, unnamed. Private interests, especially those having to do with the expressive life of the body, were left aside or transcended. As a result, the life of embodiment has always been a source of anxiety and dissonance in the public sphere. As the public sphere becomes less oriented to print and more oriented to electronic media, the bodies and expressive lives of politicians and citizens come more routinely into view in more and more unpredicted and troubling ways.[30] (This observation, of course, has come to seem banal during the course of the Clinton presidency.) The contemporary fantasy of dead citizenship is a new and more intensified version of a long tradition that sees people's physical persons as at best irrelevant to their citizenship. Pornography was the scandalous exception beginning in the eighteenth century, when it became a distinct genre for the first time, carrying all the potent charge of anticlerical enlightenment.[31]

Pornography and adult businesses jeopardize the amnesias separating sex and public culture in large part because of their physical orientation toward an indefinite public; they are media of acknowledgment. Having been reared in the bosom of Jesus, it happened that I never saw gay porn until I began graduate school. I had had sex with men for years on the side, but I didn't think I was gay. I thought I was just wicked. The first porn images I saw, in a magazine belonging to a friend, set me suddenly to think, "I could be gay." Why did those pictures trigger my recognition when years of sleeping with men somehow didn't? It's because the men in the pictures were not only doing what I wanted to do, they were doing it with a witness: the camera. Or rather, a world of witnesses, including the infrastructure for producing, distributing, selling, and consuming these texts. This whole world could be concretized in places like Christopher Street or Times Square, but also in the formal language of pornography. In order for the porn to exist, not only did some of its producers have to have gay sex, they and many others had to acknowledge that they were having it. What is traded in pornographic commerce is not just speech, privately consumed. It is publicly certifiable recognition. This is part of the meaning of every piece of porn, and what is difficult to communicate in the dominant culture is that the publicity of porn has profoundly different meanings for nonnormative sex practices. When it comes to resources of recognition, queers do not begin on a level playing field.

This function of porn, its implicit publicity, is what feels so scandalous about it. It is lost from view in those versions of antiporn feminism that describe pornography merely as objectification or violence. One of the things porn objectifies is acknowledgment. And it provides this acknowledgment not just for identities that are already organized and recognized as legitimate. Let's remember that partly because of the environment of shame and phobia, many users of porn find queer pornography in predominantly "straight" businesses. Many are people who have not come to think of themselves as gay, who would have no access to the gay world at all if they were required already to be uncloseted enough to enter gay commercial spaces. Others pursue pleasures that don't fit the gay/straight map, and the extraordinary diversity of the porn industry can be essential for them. Porn enables unpredicted forms of experience. For this reason it can be especially important for young queers, or for those who do not live in a gay neighborhood. Right now there is someone on Christopher Street who was drawn there by a hunger for that kind of acknowledgment. Those of us who have already fought our way to an identity and a supportive environment may feel that we no longer need that material evidence. But we still depend on rising generations of queers having access to it.

Only by recognizing the solicitousness of the right in monopolizing the resources of acknowledgment and the scene of citizenship can we even begin to understand why conservatives see this as an important issue. After all, heterosexuals, queers, people in couples, orgiasts, priests—all kinds of persons use pornography. Adult businesses catering to gays are a tiny minority even in Manhattan; only one specializes in lesbian material. The vast majority of the adult commerce is for presumptively heterosexual consumers. And given the increasing dominance of this market by video intended for home consumption, much of it is consumed in the very heterosexual bedrooms to which conservatives would like to see sexual culture confined. Yet some kinds of users are more at risk from the higher economic costs, and even more so from the higher costs of shame, and the consequent burden of having to live without resources of acknowledgment, information, and culture-building.

By intervening to cut off discussion and elaboration of the qualities of life, the zoning bill actually contradicts one important theme in the conservative vision of the state: the zoning bill, ironically promoted by those who routinely denounce government intervention and celebrate the market economy known as the "private sector," authorizes not only a massive state restriction on commerce but also state support for a particular vision of the good life. The bill brings the resources of the state into play in order to cultivate one form of life—already normative—by making it easier of access and acknowledgment than rival forms of life, which are not less legal, only despised and made artificially difficult.

The assault on legitimate pornographic commerce is particularly ironic given the enormous changes in the porn trade since the last attempt at zoning it out of New York, in 1977. Since then, the VCR revolution has made videotapes the lion's share of the porn trade. Unlike peep shows and stripper clubs, of course, videotape rentals are commonly taken to another space: home. Much of the panic about porn is not about what happens on Times Square, but about what people are doing with their home entertainment centers, which are harder for conservatives to regulate. There is no political gain in attacking the home consumption of commercial video. But if the video can be identified with its urban circulation zone, then—with a large dose of hypocrisy and no small irony—regulating it can be presented as a way of protecting the home from urban squalor.

The intervention of the state to weaken public sexual culture prob-

ably would not be possible without this an other forms of hypocrisy—
an ideology of space that demonizes some of the essential functions of
a city in order to idealize an impossibly purified privacy. For example,
what the Giuliani people hate most is the secondary effects of porn
concentrated in a neighborhood. The first aim of the bill's 500-foot
rule is to disperse adult businesses. Few of the bill's opponents challenged this provision. Even Manhattan borough president Ruth
Messinger, in her very thoughtful and closely reasoned letter to the
City Planning Commission against the bill, continued to support the
principle of dispersion.

But for queers the concentration of adult businesses has been one of
the best things about them. The gay bars on Christopher Street draw
customers from people who come there because of its sex trade. The
street is cruisier because of the sex shops. The boutiques that sell freedom rings and Don't Panic t-shirts do more business for the same reasons. Not all of the thousands who migrate or make pilgrimages to
Christopher Street use the porn shops, but all benefit from the fact that
some do. After a certain point, a quantitative change is a qualitative
change. A critical mass develops. The street becomes queer. It develops
a dense, publicly accessible sexual culture. It therefore becomes a base
for nonporn businesses, like Oscar Wilde Bookshop. And it becomes a
political base from which to pressure politicians with a gay voting bloc.
Lesbians and gay men continue to depend on this pattern in urban
space, no matter how much the promise of private identity—secured
through property, rights, and legitimate couplehood—might invite
them to repudiate the world-making scene of sex.

Phone sex, the internet, and sitcoms cannot take the place of this
urban space and its often unrecognized practices of sexual citizenship.
But that is what has been urged by columnists in the gay lifestyle magazines, chiefly Michelangelo Signorile. In his *Life Outside*, a jeremiad
driven by resentment toward the social network he ambiguously refers
both as "the party circuit" and as "gay culture," Signorile fuses that
resentment with a common rhetoric of antiurbanism. Fortunately, he
claims, two millennial trends can be identified: the "deghettoization"
and "deurbanization" of gay life in America. These, of course, are
pseudo-trends. Signorile has no evidence to support his claim that

either one is happening. He does quote a sociologist named Jerry
Kramer to support his notion that gay life is moving to the suburbs;
but even Kramer adds: "at least that's my perception. I would say it's
hard to tell how much of it is actually a movement out, and how much
of it is gays and lesbians who were living in the suburbs before and are
just coming out now because they feel more protected."[32] For the reasons I've given, however, the growth of a suburban or rural gay culture
would not lessen the importance of an urban one. To make that argument plausible, Signorile must rely on the rhetorical force of the
notion of a "gay ghetto."

This hoary bugaboo is time-honored, but deeply confused. No matter what aesthetic objections one might have to the styles and sociabil-
ity of a particular gay enclave, there has never been a gay ghetto in the
U.S. A ghetto is an urban district in which a minority is confined,
either by law (as in the Italian Jewish quarter from which the word
derives its name) or by poverty and systemic market effects (as in the
case of black American neighborhoods, which gives the term its current moral force). A neighborhood voluntarily created, freely entered
and left, and constituted only by massive concentrations of capital and
middle-class commerce can only be called a ghetto by those deaf to the
echoes of history or blind to the rules of power. A district like Christopher Street, in fact, is neither a ghetto nor a neighborhood, in the usual
sense of the terms. The local character of the neighborhood depends
on the daily presence of thousands of nonresidents. Those who actually live in the West Village—at this point increasingly straight—
should not forget their debt to these mostly queer pilgrims. And we
should not make the mistake of confusing the class of citizens with the
class of property owners. Many of those who hang out on Christopher
Street couldn't possibly afford to live there. Many are African-American, gay, and young. Where are they being zoned off to?

One of the most disturbing fantasies in the zoning scheme is the
idea that an urban locale is a community of shared interest based on
residence and property. In *The Death and Life of Great American Cities*
(1961) Jane Jacobs long ago noted that, "As a sentimental concept,
'neighborhood' is harmful to city planning."[33] Yet the ideology of the
neighborhood is politically unchallengeable in the current debate,

which is dominated by a fantasy that people are sexual only at home, that the space relevant to sexual politics is the neighborhood. The zoning bill is an ideal instrument for protecting the heterosexual zone of privacy because its procedural politics (Uniform Land Use Review Procedure, or ULURP) are set up to guarantee the dominance of the rhetoric of neighborhood at every step. The first requirement after the submission of the proposal was the meeting of every community board in the city, followed by the borough boards. Only then did the City Planning Commission hold public hearings at which non-neighborhood organizations could testify. But they were given much less weight, and in the public media the assumption remained that people have a right to control their neighborhoods.

Terence McNally, for example, seems not to have noticed that whether he wants to live next door to a porn shop is irrelevant to the question whether porn shops should be allowed next door by law. The antiporn organization Not In My Back Yard (NIMBY) somewhat fantastically asks us to suppose that we are considering only the narrow issue of porn in what it calls our back yard. But how many people in Manhattan have back yards? And does anyone, anywhere, have a porn store in his back yard? How does it come to pass that the nature of commercial urban space can be so flagitiously misrecognized?

The sexual culture of New York City serves people around the world, even if only as the distant reference point of queer kids growing up in North Carolina or Idaho, who know that somewhere things are different. Residents should not dictate the uses of the urban space around them to the exclusion of other users of the city. To do so is to fail to recognize what a city is. Urban space is always a host space. The right to the city extends to those who use the city. It is not limited to property owners. With the zoning scheme New York, perhaps the world's greatest metropolis, is pretending to be a suburb—though indeed one might want to ask whether a suburb is or should be in fact what it is in the NIMBY ideology.

In the hearings before the City Planning Commission, the objection was frequently made that New York's unique culture would be jeopardized by the bill. The Commission's only response comes at the conclusion of its report: "Suggestions made during the public testimony that the uniqueness of New York City precludes providing New York City *residents and neighborhoods* with protection against the negative impacts of these establishments are a disservice *to the many neighborhoods and individuals* of New York City and ignore the very real harm tending to stem from adult establishments." Even in the act of rebutting the objection, the Commission deepens its assumption that the right to the city extends only to residents and property owners, that propinquity of domicile alone gives citizens the right to a political voice on the issue.

A better model of urban space might be elaborated from Henri Lefebvre's *Le Droit à la ville (The Right to the City)*, where we read:

> The human being has the need to accumulate energies and to spend them, even waste them in play. He has a need to see, to hear, to touch, to taste and the need to gather these perceptions in a 'world.' To these anthropological needs which are socially elaborated (that is, sometimes separated, sometimes joined together, here compressed and there hypertrophied), can be added specific needs which are not satisfied by those commercial and cultural infrastructures which are somewhat parsimoniously taken into account by planners. This refers to the need for creative activity, for the *oeuvre* (not only of products and consumable material goods), of the need for information, symbolism, the imaginary and play. Through these specified needs lives and survives a fundamental desire of which play, sexuality, physical activities such as sport, creative activity, art and knowledge are particular expressions and *moments*, which can more or less overcome the fragmentary division of tasks. Finally, the need of the city and urban life can only be freely expressed within a perspective which here attempts to become clearer and to open up the horizon. Would not specific urban needs be those of qualified places, places of simultaneity and encounters, places where exchange would not go through exchange value, commerce and profit? Would there not also be the need for a time for these encounters, these exchanges? [34]

Lefebvre rightly recognizes that the organization of urban space into lived worlds is undertaken by the city's users—not its planners, builders, owners, or rulers. He also recognizes that the worldliness of the city is inseparable from the possibilities of waste, play, and sex—in other words, from its more or less queer appropriations, which must be freed to find their own articulation as a public horizon. Recent developments suggest that the gay movement is no longer oriented to that goal.

In November of 1997, an open meeting on these topics was held at the Creating Change conference in San Diego, a conference sponsored by the National Gay and Lesbian Task Force. The group drafted the following resolution, tailored to the language of movement organizing, but in the view of many, unconscionably bold:

A Declaration of Sexual Rights

The LGBT movement, feminism, and AIDS activism all have long histories of advocating the principles of sexual self-determination. These principles are under attack. In the name of "mainstream" acceptance, many are increasingly willing to embrace regulation and stigma for more marginal groups. And in the name of fighting AIDS, many disregard the need for HIV prevention to respect pleasure and the complexity of sex. Increasingly forgotten are the diverse pleasures, intimacies, and relations that sex enables.

In this context we reaffirm the following principles implied in the right to be sexual:

    1) the right to sexual self-determination;
    2) the right to publically accessible sexual culture;
    3) the right to a sexual life free from shame and stigma; and
    4) freedom from government intervention.

In light of these principles, we demand:

1. Respect for sexual diversity.
2. Decriminalization of sex practices.
3. An end to censorship and to restrictions on sexual information and public discussion of sex.
4. Recognition for the right of youth to sexual freedoms and self-determination.
5. A renewed commitment to universal health care.
6. An end to the scapegoating of HIV-positive people and PWAs, including those who are sexually active.

7. HIV-prevention efforts that affirm the right to be sexual and the need to sustain shared sexual cultures.
8. An end to state preference for dominant styles of households and relationships.
9. An end to harassment and legal sanctions against sex workers and the regulation of sexual spaces.
10. Advocacy for the above principles and demands by all progressive organizations.

This document can justly be accused of its own utopianism. It silently assumes that the reader will recognize that such offenses as rape can be criminalized for their coercive character, as distinct from their sexual character. It assumes that "youth" will be understood in a way consistent with meaningful consent, even if that is not defined by the current age-of-consent laws. And it speaks with some calculation in the language of individual rights, leaving aside the issues of public space and acknowledgment that I have been addressing in this chapter. Yet despite its limitations, the document has the ability to show us what an essential range of queer politics has by and large disappeared from the lesbian and gay movement. Its closing call for these organizations to rechart their agendas is one that I support.

In the culture of privatization, however, organizing a city's users on any footing other than identitarianism can be extremely difficult. How else will it be possible to bring into awareness the stake that the city's users—regardless of their identity—have in its queer space? How, especially as public sexual culture is either repudiated as the relic of a bygone liberationism, or defended merely as the indifferent expression of a civil liberty? Against these trends, my aim has been to bring to articulacy the publicness of sex publics, in all their furtive ephemerality, as a substantive good; to inspire queers to be more articulate about the world they have already made, with all its variations from the norm, with its ethical understanding of the importance of those variations, with its ethical refusal of shame or implicitly shaming standards of dignity, with its refusal of the tactful silences that preserve hetero privilege, and with the full range of play and waste and public activity that goes into making a world.

NOTES

1. The background conditions of this problem are succinctly stated by Jürgen Habermas, "The New Obscurity: The Crisis of the Welfare State and the Exhaustion of Utopian Energies," in his *The New Conservatism: Cultural Criticism and the Historians' Debate*, trans. Shierry Weber Nicholsen (Cambridge: MIT Press, 1989), 48–70. See also Lauren Berlant and Michael Warner, "Introduction to 'Critical Multiculturalism,'" in David Theo Goldberg, ed., *Multiculturalism: A Critical Reader* (Oxford: Basil Blackwell, 1994), 107–113.

2. I have made this argument in "Media Gays: A New Stone Wall," *The Nation*, July 14, 1997, 15–19; and "We're Queer, Remember?" *The Advocate*, September 30, 1997. See also Michael Warner, Douglas Crimp, Ann Pellegrini, and Eva Pendleton, "Sex Panic! Highlights Threats Facing Queer New York," *LGNY*, August 4, 1997.

3. "As Piers Close, Gay Protesters See a Paradise Lost," *New York Times*, September 14, 1997.

4. Indeed, it is a history marked by a depressing repetitiveness. See Gayle Rubin, "Sexual Politics, the New Rights, and the Sexual Fringe," *The Leaping Lesbian*, January 15, 1978; John D'Emilio, "Dreams Deferred: The Birth and Betrayal of America's First Gay Liberation Movement," in his *Making Trouble: Essays on Gay History, Politics, and the University* (New York: Routledge, 1992), 17–56; John D'Emilio, *Sexual Politics, Sexual Communities: The Making of a Homosexual Minority in the United States, 1940–1970* (Chicago: Univ. of Chicago Press, 1983); Donn Teal, *The Gay Militants* (New York: Stein and Day, 1971); Martin Duberman, *Stonewall* (New York: Dutton, 1993); Dennis Altman, *The Homosexualization of America* (Boston: Beacon, 1982); Scott Tucker, "Too Queer to Be Gay? A New Populist Group Fails to Support Sexual Minorities," *New York Native*, June 7, 1981; Konstantin Berlandt, "NOLAG: A Final Plea for Unity?" *Alternate*, June 1981, pp. 14–15; Nan Hunter and Lisa Duggan, *Sex Wars* (New York: Routledge, 1995); Karla Jay and Allen Young, eds., *Out of the Closets: Voices of Gay Liberation* (1972; repr. New York: New York Univ. Press, 1992); and Mark Blasius and Shane Phelan, eds., *We Are Everywhere: A Historical Sourcebook of Gay and Lesbian Politics* (New York: Routledge, 1997).

5. Whether the "mainstream" conforms to its self-understanding is, of course, a different matter. See Berlant and Warner, "Sex in Public," and Joshua Gamson, *Freaks Talk Back: Tabloid Talk Shows and Sexual Nonconformity* (Chicago: Univ. of Chicago Press, 1998).

6. The manifesto for this philosophy was Andrew Sullivan's "The Politics of Homosexuality," which originally appeared in *The New Republic* on May 10, 1993—just in time for the 1993 March on Washington. It is reprinted in Bruce Bawer, ed., *Beyond Queer: Challenging Gay Left Orthodoxy* (New York: Free Press, 1996), 60–85; and elaborated in Sullivan's *Virtually Normal* (New York: Knopf, 1995). Michelangelo Signorile, originally critical of Sullivan and Bawer, has increasingly

adopted their assumptions, often without realizing it; see his *Life Outside* (New York: HarperCollins, 1997), and numerous columns for *Out* between 1995 and 1998.

7. The Fox news story, along several others like it in other cities, was astutely analyzed by Richard Goldstein in *The Village Voice*, May 12, 1998. For the long history of such rhetoric, see George Chauncey, *Gay New York* (New York: Basic Books, 1994).

8. See, for example, the classic (if controversial) study by Laud Humphreys, *Tearoom Trade: Impersonal Sex in Public Places* (1970; rev. ed., Hawthorne, NY: Aldine de Gruyter, 1975); or, more recently, Clive Moore, "Poofs in the Park: Documenting Gay 'Beats' in Queensland, Australia," *GLQ* 2.3 (1995): 319–39. There are also instructive essays in William Leap, ed., *Public Sex / Gay Space* (New York: Columbia Univ. Press, forthcoming). And see Lee Edelman's "Tearooms and Sympathy" in his *Homographesis* (New York: Routledge, 1994).

9. *The Advocate*, Sept. 6, 1994, 80.

10. National Lesbian and Gay Journalists Association, press release, May 11, 1998.

11. Opposition to the zoning bill came from several directions. The main legal challenge has been made on First-Amendment, civil liberties grounds, and a number of anticensorship groups have joined together to that end. But the more vocal opposition has been from the right, especially from those in the outer boroughs who see the bill as dumping Manhattan's trade in their neighborhoods. Community Board 10 in the Bronx, for example, voted unanimously to oppose the bill because the list of sensitive receptors is not comprehensive enough:

Community Board 10 opposes any and all adult establishments from being located within the Board 10 district because the Adult Establishment Zoning Text Amendment does not address the proximity of such businesses to ball fields; residential homes regardless of whether or not they are situated on residentially zoned property; parks; cemeteries (due to religious ceremonies which take place here); cemetery property; motels, hotels; homeless shelters which operate day care activities; senior centers; post offices; and the city's designated waterfront greenbelt areas used for recreation by adults and children.

Other boards voted to extend the 500-foot rule to 750 or 1000 feet. Opposition from the right nearly derailed the bill when it came before the City Planning Commission; many community boards in the outer boroughs opposed it. But the same opposition allowed the Giuliani administration to describe itself as the reasonable middle ground. The *New York Times* has editorialized in favor of the zoning bill as a reasonable compromise on at least three separate occasions. (The *Times* is also a member of the Times Square Business Improvement District, the major agitator behind the proposal.)

12. This paragraph amplifies remarks by Nancy Fraser, "Rethinking the Public Sphere: A Contribution to a Critique of Actually Existing Democracy," in Craig Calhoun, ed., *Habermas and the Public Sphere* (Cambridge: MIT Press, 1992), 109–142.

13. The preceding paragraph summarizes the much lengthier account in my "Public

and Private," in Catharine Stimpson and Gil Herdt, eds., *Critical Terms for the Study of Gender and Sexuality* (Chicago: Univ. of Chicago Press, forthcoming).

14. On the legal distinction the literature is, of course, copious; but see especially Kendall Thomas, "Beyond the Privacy Principle," *Columbia Law Review* 92 (1992): 1359–1516.

15. See Lauren Berlant and Michael Warner, "Sex in Public," *Critical Inquiry* 24.2 (Winter 1998): 547–66.

16. Richard Mohr, *Gays/Justice: A Study of Ethics, Society, and Law* (New York: Columbia Univ. Press, 1988), 96.

17. Mohr, *Gays/Justice*, 105. Mohr has updated this argument, with reference to the sex panics of the 1990s, in "Parks, Privacy, and the Police," *The Guide*, January 1996.

18. Erving Goffman, *Stigma: Notes on the Management of Spoiled Identity* (1963; repr. New York: Simon and Schuster, 1986), 41.

19. The definitive study, of course, is Eve Kosofsky Sedgwick, *The Epistemology of the Closet* (Berkeley: Univ. of California Press, 1990).

20. Quoted in Marcia Pally, *Sex and Sensibility: Reflections on Forbidden Mirrors and the Will to Censor* (Hopewell, N.J.: Ecco Press, 1994).

21. "Giuliani Urges Photos Be Taken of Patrons Entering Sex Shops," *New York Times*, May 16, 1998.

22. Lauren Berlant, *The Queen of America Goes to Washington City: Essays on Sex and Citizenship* (Durham: Duke University Press, 1997).

23. On this history, see Lynn Hunt, ed., *The Invention of Pornography: Obscenity and the Origins of Modernity*, 1500–1800 (Cambridge: Zone Books, 1993).

24. Michael Warner, *The Letters of the Republic: Publication and the Public Sphere in Eighteenth-Century America* (Cambridge: Harvard University Press, 1990); and "The Mass Public and the Mass Subject," in *Habermas and the Public Sphere*, ed. Craig Calhoun (Cambridge: MIT Press, 1991), 377–401; also in *The Phantom Public Sphere*, ed. Bruce Robbins (Minneapolis: Univ. of Minnesota Press, 1993), 234–56.

25. Michelangelo Signorile, *Life Outside* (New York: HarperCollins, 1997), 195.

26. Jane Jacobs, *The Death and Life of Great American Cities* (1961; repr. New York: Modern Library, 1993), 146.

27. Henri Lefebvre, *Writings on Cities*, trans. Eleonore Kofman and Elizabeth Lebas (Oxford: Blackwell, 1996), 147–48.

4

EXTREME

CRITICISM

Like many who came of age in the 1960s, I was led to literary studies because of a passion for poetry and politics. In turn, the emerging projects in theory, which in many respects were an attempt to consolidate intellectually what had been learned and hoped for in the political and social movements that had arisen in the sixties and were then declining, illuminated the possible relationships between literature and politics in startling ways. The turn to looking at the question of culture, as the determining setting of literary practices and forms, then contributed to the origins of cultural studies in the United States.

The passion of literary intellectuals for politics goes back to the eighteenth century and has manifested itself in everything from the literary-political reviews that have accompanied virtually every literary and political movement all the way to the temptations for writers and critics to become fellow-travelers, functionaries, or tourists of the revolution. Today the vitality of the interplay of literature and politics in intellectual life is in trouble.

Why?

Cultural studies, in this its moment of ascendancy, exhibits an exuberant ignorance of itself. It takes great pride in going beyond literature, high culture, and disciplinarity. It defines itself as just this threefold transcendence. But what exactly is the practice of cultural studies?

For starters, cultural studies *is* literature. It exists through its journals, essays, conference papers, and books. It occupies a significant slice of contemporary print culture—though a considerably smaller one than, say, the world novel.

Second, insofar as the dubious concept of high culture has a reliable meaning in our society, cultural studies—whatever aspects of culture it studies—itself belongs to high culture. To do cultural studies requires an extraordinary level of educational attainment, the mastery of rarefied styles of discourse and argument, and, most importantly, a methodically alienated attitude toward ordinary cultural objects, practices, and experiences. It bears all the marks of the elite and specialized training on which it depends.

Third, as regards disciplinarity, cultural studies' methods, topics, and discursive norms are, on inspection, narrower and more uniform than those of a traditional history department.

So, while cultural studies defines itself as going beyond literature, high culture, and disciplinarity, what defines cultural studies is that it *is* literature, high culture, and a discipline. In the swollen annals of intellectual mystification, that approaches perfection.

The confusions afforded by this self-misunderstanding are multiplying. *Social Text* discovered the dangers of hopscotching disciplines; it's hard to do critical science studies if you can't tell a quark from a lark. When it comes to the question of literature and politics, the obfuscations are dire. Take the recent *PMLA* forum on "cultural studies and the literary." For the official publication of the Modern Language Association to invite interventions on the role of cultural studies at once accurately confirms and rightly legitimizes the presence of cultural studies in literature departments; it also implicitly acknowledges the intellectual conflicts and academic tensions that this presence fosters. But the discussion is skewed right off by the term "the literary," a decoy concept if there ever was one. Nearly all of the thirty-two contributors to the forum took the bait. The only sensible manifestation of "the literary" as a concept establishing a field of research came from the Russian Formalists, but nobody is talking about them. Otherwise, it's little more than the buzzword of those English department sentimentalists who proudly, defiantly announce their love of literature as a first line of defense against ideas.

As soon as cultural studies is pitted against "the literary" literary studies is reduced to either its most formalistic or its most ineffable dimension. Worse yet, it is cast out of any meaningful relation to politics. Except negatively: the proponents of cultural studies castigate the elitism of literature, while the defenders of literature fend off the intrusion of politics and ideology. The hard question—*what might the active relation between cultural studies and literary studies be?*—and the vital question—*what is the relation of literature and politics today?*—immediately drop from sight.

Two of the contributors whose own work and institutional activism have helped define cultural studies, Cary Nelson and Patrick Brantlinger, latch onto "the literary" and fire away at a target anybody could hit. Nelson's broadside leads to the pronouncement that "every body of theory" in the past two decades "has found a way to install literary idealization at the heart of its enterprise."[1] It does not occur to him that there may be something beyond idealization at work in the fact that Derrida crystallized a theoretical project through a reading of Mallarmé, Kristeva through Lautréamont, Said through Conrad, Jameson through Balzac, Gilbert and Gubar through the Brontës, Baker through Ellison, Deleuze through Proust, Lacan through Sophocles, Barthes through Racine, and on and on. These crystallizations of theory did not idealize "the literary" but found their own indispensable resources and sources in literature. Without them, cultural studies itself would be devoid of interpretive procedures and any intellectual framework whatever.

When Brantlinger then declares that literature "fits into [the] agenda [of cultural studies] only tangentially—perhaps merely as one more ideological illusion to be critiqued, together with God, the nation-state, individualism, and 'free market' (multinational) capitalism,"[2] who's illusioning who? (Though I should admit, up front, that when I get done defending literature, I'm going on to a spirited defense of the nation-state and individualism and, more obliquely, of the free market and, only tangentially, of God. But I'm getting ahead of myself.)

Because cultural studies fails to recognize that cultural and social criticism, including its own variety, are thoroughly a part of literary culture, it is at the moment menacingly contradictory in its attitude toward literary studies. Nelson calls for "a serious dialogue between literary studies and cultural studies" and, in an apparent gesture of magnanimity, comically repeated by half a dozen contributors to the *PMLA* forum, reassures us that, well, yes, there will always be room for . . . Shakespeare! But when it comes right down to it he seems poised to shovel out the Aegean stables of literariness: "we can't yet know what it would mean," he muses, "for the discipline to make cultural studies central and serve it fully, though it might mean that literature would no longer be our main preoccupation."[3] Literary intellectuals unpreoccupied with literature.

To recover the question of literature and politics from this chorus of performative contradictions, it's necessary to foreground the social and the aesthetic dimensions of the concept of literature.

First, the social problematic: literature is the social practice of writing. Despite the cultural studies polemicists' frequent obligatory homages to Raymond Williams, they've lost track of his most fundamental insight: the history of literature is coextensive with the social history of literacy. Few societies have achieved universal general literacy, and fewer still have democratized education beyond a basic level. The social "unevenness of literacy and learning" in Williams's phrase implicates all social practices of writing in complex processes of social hierarchy and democratic leveling, of specialization and dissemination, of educational privilege and deprivation, of exclusiveness and reappropriation.[4] Recognizing that a particular body of writing is "elite" is merely the start of inquiry, not its conclusion; the term does not have an unambiguous value, positive or negative. The place of print culture within culture as a whole is a dynamic, politically polyvalent question, complicated since the first third of the nineteenth century by the fact that the public sphere has had to reach all segments of society. The advent of mass media, which cultural studies seems to think relegates literature to the shadowy past, has merely shifted once more the place and dynamics of print culture. The social practices of writing, including the artistic ones, remain as pertinent as ever to the effective forms of literacy and learning and to the public sphere of information, opinion, and criticism.

Second, the aesthetic problematic: taking literature in the narrower sense of those social practices of writing that are artworks, the study of literature requires the study of literary form. The polemical evocations of "the literary" obviously allude to this aspect of literary studies but misunderstand it. There are formalist and nonformalist approaches to form, and the fruitful antagonisms and interactions between the two have shaped modern criticism. Propp, Jakobson, and Genette are formalists, Lukács, Bakhtin, Adorno, and Jameson are not, but they are all preoccupied with problems of form. I side with the nonformalists. Modern aesthetic theory from Hegel to Adorno has shown that the formative or constructive power of an artwork lies in its capacity to draw contradictory contents, imperatives, and modes of expression into some new form. Adorno identifies the beautiful—in a way that has important corollaries in Nietzsche, Heidegger, and Macherey—not with the finished form of an artwork but with the discontinuous moments of illumination that happen as a result of—or in a counter-movement to—the striving for formal coherence. The work's inner form gives shape to a rift it cannot overcome in the heterogeneous, incommensurate materials it works on. "Glory be to God for dappled things—" writes Gerard Manley Hopkins in the poem "Pied Beauty":

> All things counter, original, spare, strange;
>   Whatever is fickle, freckled (who knows how?)
>   With swift, slow; sweet, sour; adazzle, dim;[5]

What an artwork works on—let's simplify a bit with secular reference to the novel—is the material of its own medium (language or discourse) and the content it represents (some historical lifeworld).

The social and the aesthetic problematic of literature thus meet in the problem of form itself. They also meet through the institutionalization of the public realm. The social practice of writing implicates literature in the polity's forms of publicness. The aesthetic experience of inner form, I want to argue, is also implicated in publicness. Among the most suggestive passages in Kant's *Critique of Judgment* is the section titled "Of Beauty as the Symbol of Morality." Its key assertion restates and extends his central tenet that the experience of the beautiful "gives pleasure with a claim for the agreement of everyone else," which has most often been construed by Kant's advocates and detractors alike as equating the universalism of aesthetic judgment with some uniform standard of taste. Kant writes:

> Now I say the beautiful is the symbol of the morally good, and that it is only in this respect ... that it gives pleasure with a claim to the agreement of everyone else. By this the mind is made conscious of a certain ennoblement and elevation above the mere sensibility to pleasure received through the sense, and the worth of others is estimated in accordance with a like maxim of their judgment.[6]

Kant's insight here can be restated, in pragmatic terms, against the grain of his own search for intrinsic mental structures. The experience of the beautiful happens as a claim for the assent of others: only insofar as I tacitly appeal to others that *this is beautiful* do I experience beauty; conversely, my experience of beauty tacitly carries within it this appeal to others. The artwork's appearance in a public realm and my own participation in that public realm with others are, in other words, *internal* to the experience of artistic form.

Aesthetic "judgment" is enabled by a material, institutionalized space of expression and criticism. The so-called universality of the judgment is thus conditioned by the education, cultivation, and discourse of the participants in the public sphere. In the guise of formulating a "*critique of judgment*," Kant evokes, to anticipate on Hannah Arendt's phrase, the "worldly space" of *criticism*, that is, the democratic underpinnings of publicness. The beautiful is a symbol of the morally good in the sense that I affirm "the worth of others" in my tacit appeal for their agreement. However, since my experience of the beautiful is enmeshed in the practices of criticism, and since the appeal to agreement takes place on the socially uneven terrain of educated sensibility, aesthetic judgment is in fact drawn into the fray of critical contention and dispute. Estimating the worth of others does not celebrate a communal standard but prompts a task of persuasion. Add to this the post-Kantian view that artistic beauty arises not from harmonious form but from the illuminating, dappled countermovements to formal coherence. Inner form is, therefore, the regulative ideal of aesthetic experience not in the sense of an established or anticipated standard of taste but, on the contrary, an open-ended, contentious *valuing* at stake in literary and political criticism.[7]

In sum, literary form is the crux of the question of literature and politics in two respects. On the one hand, without grappling with inner form, criticism can't really grasp the work's material or its content, that is, its artistically rendered language and lifeworld. And, on the other hand, the aesthetic experience of form is implicated, through its necessary tie to critical discourse, in the social and political conflicts inherent in the formations of the public sphere.

There is a loss of form in current criticism, especially the very criticism that purports to link literature and politics. The reasons are undoubtedly multiple, and beyond the scope of this discussion. I want simply to suggest how this loss of form manifests itself in one significant trend in contemporary criticism, namely, the gender/race/class paradigm that has helped orient so much important political criticism of culture and literature.

As typically deployed, gender/race/class has given rise to a new allegorical criticism that deflects the problem of inner form in favor of a hermeneutic that scans a text's network of signifiers in search of its purported representation or "construction" of gender, race, and class. But networks of signifiers are a dime a dozen in literary texts; without the constraining obligation to read those signifiers off the inner dynamic of form, a reading is free to attach the signifiers it gathers up to any framework of meaning (any constellation of signifieds) it chooses, and it is the gender/race/class grid that supplies that framework. The grid is flexible because its three categories can variously be construed as problems of identity, difference, hierarchy, or power. The problem is not that the interpretive procedures start on the side of social content. Nonformalist approaches to form have often done so. The problem is that they seldom get to the question of form, and a part of the reason for that failing is the way gender/race/class is used to identify the social contents and political context of the artwork in the first place.

There has been no lack of skepticism, even irritation, with the prevalence of gender, race, and class in cultural studies. Kwame

Anthony Appiah and Henry Louis Gates, Jr., opened their introduction to the special issue of *Critical Inquiry* titled "Identities" in 1992 by suggesting that these terms, the "holy trinity of literary criticism," were threatening "to become the regnant clichés of our critical discourse"; they called for more attention to the "multiple intersections" of gender, race, and class to overcome reductive conceptions of identity.[8] Gates would later voice a more general skepticism toward what he termed the gender-race-class *mantra*, and denouncing this mantra has since then itself become a kind of mantra.

I am not wanting to repeat either incantation. Much of the most original and penetrating literary and cultural criticism today turns on questions of gender, race, and class. The new social movements of the last several decades—civil rights and Black Power, feminism, the gay and lesbian movement—inspired these efforts in critical discourse to give consistency to politically charged interpretations of literature and culture. What is flawed is the assumption in this search for a method that the gender/race/class *paradigm* tacitly provides a coherent account of social relationships as a whole and thus can reliably undergird and justify particular interpretations.

There are actually two versions of gender/race/class. The one is a paradigm of identity constructs, the other a paradigm of social inequalities. While gender, race, and class are crucial components of social lifeworlds and of politics, and therefore essential to understanding the contents and the contexts of literature, both versions of the paradigm tend to eschew the complexities of analyzing lifeworlds—the recalcitrant, heterogeneous, experienced content the artwork works on. And they are confused about the relation of gender, race, and class to the prevailing values and institutions of Western democratic politics.

The identity paradigm is particularly inadequate in addressing crucial questions of class-formation and distributive justice. Consider the question of the formation of middle classes. Does the cause of social justice in developing societies, for example, require the growth or the elimination of the middle class? Marxism, Stalinism, and Maoism have all linked social progress to the elimination of the middle class; in the Soviet Union and China this was a deadly, nearly genocidal project. Is there a peaceful and judicious path to eliminating the middle class? Or, on the contrary, as Octavio Paz has eloquently argued, does the possibility of combining democracy with development depend on the expansion of middle classes?[9] These historic questions cannot possibly be addressed by construing the question of the middle classes as a problem of identity. Closer to home, take the question of the making of the black middle class, originally in the first decades of the twentieth century and then again, dramatically, in the last thirty years. Is it best understood as a bundle of identity markers ("classism") or as a major progressive achievement of twentieth-century black political movements and social reform? The question is seldom even raised, for the simple reason that the gender/race/class paradigm of identity has nothing to say about it.

The other way of construing gender/race/class has been to take it as a kind of map of the macro-inequalities of modern societies. As a rough sketch of the social relationships from which significant political movements and debates emerge, the gender/race/class paradigm of inequality is certainly valid. But its radical tenor and utopian underpinnings depend on a tacit appeal to macro-*equalities* of gender, race, and class. And there the paradigm becomes hollow. With respect to gender and race, it runs afoul of the fact that its own theoretical categories cannot reconcile equality and difference, for the simple reason that equality and difference cannot be reconciled *by theory*; that task can only be carried out in the unending, undecidable conflicts and initiatives within the polity and civil society, culture and law.

The appeal to macro-equalities is a *faux* totality. It derives from Marxism's appeal to the possibility of a classless society as the basis for analyzing the dynamics of class societies. The inequalities paradigm not only puts race and gender in a false parallelism to class, it also ignores that the theoretical benchmark of a classless society is in shambles. For there is today no viable vision of a radically egalitarian society, that is, of a radically egalitarian industrialized, urbanized, mass society. That is the squandered utopia of 1848–1989. Its shadowy persistence in the gender/race/class paradigm suggests how uncertain we radical intellectuals now are about how to refashion a vision of social justice that Marxism preserved for a century and a half by assuming that the synthesis of modernization and egalitarianism was a realizable goal. The gender/race/class paradigm is, in this sense, an intellectual bulwark against the extreme historical pessimism to which the egalitarian imagination has of necessity succumbed. In an intellectual culture—like ours—that craves optimism, gender/race/class resurrects the rhetoric of egalitarianism in the absence of its possibility.

Though "politics" and "the political" are omnipresent terms in current cultural criticism, the traditions of Western democratic thought and the institutions of Western democratic practice have an unsettled place in this discourse. These traditions and institutions are frequently cast as ideological illusions, a hegemonic structure of power, or the West's ethnocentric modernity. I agree with Michael Walzer's argument in *Spheres of Justice* that social justice is a question of the distribution of goods and therefore of the cultural and political conflicts over the interpretation of goods and the principles of their distribution; I also agree with his argument that the *setting* of such deliberations, debates, and distributions is the *political community*, that is, the polity. "The community," he writes, "is itself a good—conceivably the most important good—that gets distributed. But it is a good that can only be distributed" insofar as people are "physically admitted and politically received [into it]. Hence membership cannot be handed out by some external agency; its value depends upon an internal decision."[10] I further agree with Walzer that within the realities and horizon of contemporary history, the necessary form of political community is the modern nation-state, with all the limitations and dangers that go with it. Political membership and participation are a question of citizenship.

When it comes to questions of rights, freedoms, participation, self-rule, and citizenship, the liberal and republican traditions of Western democratic thought cannot be superseded. They are the living though damaged and burdened tradition of Western political life. The supposition of much current cultural theory is that these traditions are defunct or can be transcended or are merely complicit in the evils of capitalism, racism, or "the West." The temptation to invalidate these traditions, rather than affirming their vitality while assessing their historical burden and criticizing their damaged actuality, has given rise to a style of political and cultural criticism which variously announces itself as post-Enlightenment, postmodern, postpolitical, or post-nation-state.

The liberal framework of rights and freedoms and the republican framework of self-rule and political participation, though always in tension and frequently contradictory, both hinge on the individual. The negative liberty of right and the positive liberty of participation are individual liberties. By contrast, the social-democratic framework of distributive justice hinges on the state's role in channeling, blocking, and regulating the effects of a capitalist economy; the deliberative and decision-making procedures of the state—legislative, bureaucratic, and juridical—are the site of a kind of endless contestation over liberal and civic imperatives pursued by various social movements, interest groups, alliances, trade unions, and mass parties.

Modern democracy requires these three interlocking but conflicting frameworks: the liberal, the civic-humanist, and the social-democratic. As a shorthand reference to the sorts of issues in political thought generated by these interlocking, conflicting frameworks, we might think of the work of, respectively, Isaiah Berlin, Hannah Arendt, and Jürgen Habermas. I take their utterly marginal, occasionally vexed place in current cultural theory to be a kind of symptom of the latter's disregard for the actual setting of contemporary political life.

I want quickly to refer to two tenets of Arendt's political thought because they bear directly on the concept of publicness that underlies the problem of literature and politics. For Arendt, the democratic *polis* is the human creation which institutes the very possibility of freedom. It indissociably links freedom to publicness. She states this tenet as follows: "Without a politically guaranteed public realm, freedom lacks the *worldly space* to make its appearance."[11] Her second tenet follows from this, and derives from Aristotle, namely, that the highest form of human self-realization is political participation. Citizenship, we might say, is the highest form of subjectivity because within it and from it stem all forms of human freedom. These notions run significantly counter to the tendency in current theory to define political subjectivity in terms of the Althusserian interpellated subject or the Foucauldian subjection to power, both of which have then led to endless dithering over the definition of agency. From Arendt's civic-humanist perspective, political identity resides in political participation. The citizen has to be formed, educated, socialized to the practices of participation. The formation of the citizen is a socialization into agency within the rule-governed institutions of the democratic polity. The all important work of political criticism, in word and deed, by individuals and groups, of challenging exclusions from citizenship or historically burdened and damaged forms of participation or the very rules governing actual institutions requires a commitment to the norms and ideals of the worldly space of the citizen.

The announcements of post-Enlightenment, postmodern, postpolitical, post-nation-state mistakenly aspire to step outside these norms and ideals of the democratic tradition. Such announcements promise a radical break, foreshadow some fateful turning in the course of modernity, a separation from three or four centuries of modern culture and politics. As intellectuals of all self-descriptions—public, organic, and otherwise—get pumped up for the year 2000, these announcements are taking on a millenarian tone. For just as our intellectual culture craves optimism to hide its darker uncertainty about the future of freedom and justice, so too its mania for announcing post-modernities hides a profound confusion about the directions and possibilities of contemporary history. *Fin-de-siècle*! The end of modernity! Millennium!—these are pretty heady notions for thinkers and seers who just a decade ago, in the years and months leading up to 1989, had no inkling of the imminent collapse of Soviet communism, plausibly the punctuating event of the twentieth century, perhaps of the entire era that began with the revolution of 1789.

Contrary to the vistas of end and *post-*, our moment of intellectual life is, I suspect, a miniaturized Zeitgeist. It announces radical breaks without analyzing actual transformations. Unsettled about the meaning of the past and present, it makes futuristic noise about the traditions it is ever about to overcome. With respect to democratic traditions and institutions, the allure of post-Enlightenment, postmodern, postpolitical, post-nation-state visions is profoundly affecting the language and values of political criticism. To sharpen the sense of what's at stake, I'm going to comment on two examples.

Post-Enlightenment. In 1989, in the wake of the fatwa issued by the Ayatollah Khomeini against Salman Rushdie, the editors of *Public Culture*, Arjun Appadurai and Carol A. Breckenridge, wrote an editorial critical of the way many Western intellectuals and the Western media defended Rushdie and castigated the Islamic leaders and crowds who were denouncing The Satanic Verses and threatening its author. They questioned the excesses and ethnocentrism in the outcries, including Rushdie's, against Islamic politics and saw in Western liberals' attitudes an ethnocentric attachment to Enlightenment interpretations of free speech. Their editorial culminated with the following remark:

> In our view, the politics of *The Satanic Verses* is partly about the rights of people to resist reading, and especially to resist reading what they have been told by others whom they hold in respect they should not read.... Some groups in the Islamic world are saying that criticism—socially, politically, and collectively constructed—can precede the individual act of reading.[12]

"Performative contradiction" is rather too polite a term for Appadurai and Breckenridge's hypocrisy. Here are two scholar-editors whose own life practice has value and validity to the exact extent that their own writings and what they publish in their journal exercise critical reflection, free expression, and skepticism toward doctrinal authority. Without the so-called liberal public sphere neither that exercise nor its controlling values would have the worldly space in which to happen. When Appadurai and Breckenridge then defended their editorial by asserting that "we intended to ask whether the enlightenment values about freedom of expression were beyond debate and thus rather like the values of Khomeini's Islam,"[13] they absurdly equated commitment to freedom of thought and expression with commitment to theocratic rule and religious authority. One can always, of course, debate Enlightenment values, but Khomeini's *fatwa* was the moment to defend freedom of expression.

The fretting over ethnocentrism is a smoke screen. While it is always relevant to criticize the tendency of Western liberals to believe freedom is uniquely or intrinsically Western, the Rushdie controversy has been about the perilous struggles in the Islamic world to institutionalize spaces of free expression and critical thought.[14] Those freedoms are not the essence of the West. Nor are they, on the other hand, merely its ethnocentric prejudice or its own particularistic values. Such freedoms have their precedents in other cultures, and they have been and remain the product of continual struggles in the West.[15] For those of us whose lives as writers and teachers require those freedoms, the struggle for them is relevant across borders and cultures.

The battle has long centered on writing and reading. In Stendhal's *The Red and the Black*, Julien is examined in theology upon his arrival at the monastery by the Abbé Pirard, who is highly suspicious of the methods of Julien's former teacher Chélan; Julien knows the Bible but nothing of the Church Fathers. The Abbé reflects:

> "A thorough, but too thorough, knowledge of the Holy Scriptures."
>
> (Julien had just spoken to him, without being questioned on this score, about the real time in which Genesis, the Pentateuch, etc., had been written.)
>
> "To what does this endless reasoning about the Holy Scriptures lead," thought the Abbé Pirard, "if not to *free inquiry* [*l'examen personnel*]; that is to say, the most dreadful Protestantism?"[16]

When the editors of *Public Culture*—nice title—abandon the struggle to foster discomforting scenes like this one everywhere in the world, touting instead "the rights of people . . . to resist reading what they have been told by others whom they hold in respect they should not read," that is, their "rights" not to have rights, post-Enlightenment has distilled itself down to its baldest contradiction. As an antidote, it's worth reciting a bit of Enlightenment scripture that remains unsurpassed after more than two centuries of intellectual struggles, namely, the opening paragraph of Kant's "An Answer to the Question: 'What is Enlightenment?'":

> *Enlightenment is man's emergence from his self-incurred immaturity. Immaturity* is the inability to use one's own understanding without the guidance of another. This immaturity is *self-incurred* if its cause is not lack of understanding, but lack of resolution and courage to use it without the guidance of another. The motto of enlightenment is therefore: *Sapere aude!* Have courage to use your *own* understanding![17]

The maturing of contemporary thought does not lie in believing we can think *beyond* or *post-* that motto.

Postmodern. In 1995, the W. E. B. Du Bois Distinguished Lecturer at the City University of New York was Robert F. Reid-Pharr. His lecture was provocatively titled "Speaking through Anti-Semitism: The Nation of Islam and the Poetics of Black Counter-Modernity." Responding to the controversy set off in 1993 by Nation of Islam minister Khalid Mohammad's anti-Semitic speech at Kean College, Reid-Pharr sets out to examine a significant hypothesis, namely, that the anti-Semitism voiced within the Nation of Islam expresses a tradition of black anti-modernity or "counter-modernity," the "very real Black alienation and skepticism in relation to the entire project of modernity: rationalism, civility, universalism."[18]

Reid-Pharr's own intellectual framework is drawn from Zygmunt Bauman's postmodern critique of modernity, centering on the claim that "the substance of modern politics, of modern intellect, of modern life, is the effort to exterminate ambivalence."[19] Bauman argues that European anti-Semitism arose, in Reid-Pharr's words, because "Jews and gypsies represent a threat to the structures of modernity, particularly the nation-state, precisely because they somehow seem to escape the yoke of definition."[20] Reid-Pharr then argues that Africans and African-Americans, like Jews, have been alienated from the project of modernity because made to represent the ambivalence that Western rationalism and universality engender and then seek to destroy. Since racist ideology itself associated Jews and blacks, the Nation of Islam's project of anchoring black identity in opposition to whiteness reencounters the figure of the Jew as an identity-threatening ambivalence, white and not white; the Nation's anti-Semitism is "calculated to demolish the ambiguity that the Jew represents in relation to the Black community." "Caught up . . . in the same ideological structures of modernity against which it purports to struggle,"[21] the Nation of Islam adapts anti-Semitism as an expression of black alienation from modernity by transfiguring Jews into the quintessential figure of whiteness.

The dialectical elegance of this formulation obscures some problems. The premise drawn from Bauman that European anti-Semitism derives directly from the so-called project of modernity and the nation-state is deeply flawed. Nazism was, in fact, an anti-modern ideology and mythology in the service of militarizing, racializing, and de-democratizing the nation-state and characterized Jews as emblems of modernity, capitalists and workers, rationalists and communists. By embracing the postmodern critique of political modernity, Reid-Pharr validates the antimodern experience which he finds *expressed* in black anti-Semitism, even as he rejects the expression itself: "I believe that anti-Semitism from any quarter is morally reprehensible," and, further, "that it mitigates against the further advancement of African Americans."[22] He thus implies that what's required is some kind of postmodern expression of black alienation from modernity, freed at once from anti-Semitism and from modern rationalism, civility, universalism.

What gives this indistinct postmodern politics its aura of validity? So long as the politics of the Nation of Islam, from W. D. Fard through Malcolm X to Louis Farrakhan, is analyzed primarily as a trope (an "expression," a "poetics," a "speaking through anti-Semitism") played off a purely theoretical paradigm of Western modernity (modernity = extermination of ambivalence), the meaning of the movement and its ideologies looks central to the African-American experience of modernity. But if the movement and ideology are, instead, played off the other political and ideological movements that have shaped African-American participation in modern politics, everything looks very different. The three most influential black political thinkers and activists in American history—Frederick Douglass, W. E. B. Du Bois, and Martin Luther King, Jr.—were all political modernists. Each took up the leading *modern* trends in the political discourse of his time and *advanced* them by forcing that discourse to comprehend racism in the United States. And each of them pegged the cause of freedom and justice to the transformation of the polity through black political participation and citizenship. Black civitas was the guiding thread of their respective criticisms of American democracy. Only by bracketing this more central tradition of the African-American political response to modernity can Reid-Pharr make the Nation of Islam a key if distorted cipher of a vaguely defined postmodern politics.

The language and values of political criticism are ill-served by this bracketing. The most disturbing impasse in Reid-Pharr's essay is his failure to suggest any perspective on how to counteract the anti-Semitism fostered by the Nation of Islam. He says, "I have imagined my audience as primarily Black, progressive, and anti-anti-Semitic," but the urgency and difficulties of enacting that anti-anti-Semitism are set aside: "If we can disengage for a moment from the particular sting we feel when we hear that it is the Jew who keeps the Black oppressed, what we find is very real angst and melancholy, in a word, alienation, in relation to the Black experience of modernity."[23] The deciphering remains an empty exercise, for it cannot generate a moral-political criticism of anti-Semitism. I'm not suggesting Reid-Pharr should supply a programmatic plan for answering anti-Semitism in the black public sphere or at large. His work is in political theory and cultural interpretation. But the rhetoric of his essay is relevant. Even the most theoretically inflected, methodologically sophisticated reflection on politics and society traces, as it were, the contours of the public sphere at large through its terms of persuasion and its argumentation. My criticism of Reid-Pharr's rhetoric is that it traces a closed circle in which theory supposes it can *understand* anti-Semitism *without contesting* its manifestations in the polity. He treats anti-Semitism as the distorted symbol of a deeper truth rather than a set of beliefs and values held by fellow citizens and to be disputed. Further, I consider this kind of retreat from the uneven battle over values, beliefs, and persuasive symbols to be characteristic of postmodern conceptions of the political.

Appadurai and Breckenridge and Reid-Pharr exemplify how post-Enlightenment, postmodern themes in several currents of contemporary theory, in aspiring to step outside or invalidate the traditions of Western democratic thought, authorize a misguided political stand that in effect undermines or forestalls the possibilities of democracy itself. But, of course, a part of my thesis is that the link between theory and politics is never quite so organic or inevitable. I therefore want to take up a kind of converse example, Judith Butler's *Excitable Speech*, in which an altogether progressive political stand seeks its justification or rationale in many of these same currents of contemporary theory.

I agree with every political position Butler takes in *Excitable Speech*: she is against speech codes; she's against antipornography legislation; she's against restrictions on the speech and sexual conduct of gays and lesbians in the military; she's against the censoring assault on the National Endowment for the Arts; and she reviles the Supreme Court as wrongheaded, nearly delusional, in ruling that an act of burning a cross in front of a black family's house was protected by the First Amendment as an exercise in free speech and unravels the Court majority's willful opacity about the history and reality of race relations in the United States.

What I question is the status of the theoretical arguments used to support these views, the theory that claims to establish "a politics of the performative." Butler's opening chapter persuasively turns J. L. Austin's theory of speech acts against those who use it to justify restrictions on hate speech on the grounds that such speech *is* action.[24] But as a legal and political matter, her argumentation is quite misleading. What she's ultimately advocating is that speech is best answered by speech not the police, that it's better to sustain, even stimulate a contentious public sphere of free expression in which all manner of discourses and counterdiscourses contend. But you don't need Austin's logic of speech acts to arrive at or argue for this position. Moreover, contrary to Butler's procedure, you cannot derive the positions she advocates from Austin's theory as such. While her argumentation starts with Austin's pure, logicizing categories and meticulously builds up to the legal and political controversies, those controversies could not happen, could not make their appearance, except for the worldly space already created by an entire set of democratic institutions and practices, in particular the liberal public sphere and the right to free speech guaranteed by the Constitution and ultimately enforced by the nation-state's monopoly on legitimate violence. Like Habermas, Butler relies on the idea that there is something in the *logic* of language or communication that determines the horizon of democracy. Arendt shaded the question significantly differently, arguing that human beings attain their "highest possibility in the faculty of speech and the life in a polis" in Aristotle's sense "that Greeks, living together in a polis, conducted their affairs by means of speech, through persuasion, and not by means of violence, through mute coercion."[25] It's not the logic of speech but the practices of persuasion that anchor democratic life. Persuasion draws on beliefs and values, as does the underlying commitment to the polis and freedom in general.[26]

I have no quarrel with Butler's implicit beliefs and values. Like Foucault, she is a libertarian *manqué*: she exhibits a deep commitment to a radical conception of individual liberty, but does not affirm the principle of individual liberty. Instead, she seeks to justify her stand via an ostensibly anti-individualist theory of the subject, language, and power.

If made explicit, the libertarian commitment would raise some hard questions. As is more obvious in Foucault's work, libertarianism in European thought has a complex lineage: it is part aristocratic, anchored in eighteenth-century male libertinage; and part anarchistic, anchored in radical proletarian resistance to modernization. Walter Benjamin's remark that Europe had lacked a radical conception of freedom since Bakunin held true until the appearance of *Discipline and Punish* and *The History of Sexuality*. But to carry the aristocratic and anarchistic traditions into the lifeworld and politics of the relatively stable Western democracies of the late twentieth century encounters two sets of problems. On the one hand, the exercise of individual liberty requires the protection of the liberal rights and freedoms guaranteed by the modern democratic state. Neither the aristocrat's privileged standing apart from the polity nor the anarchist's refusal of its legitimacy has relevance today. Foucault did not solve this conundrum, though he was clearly aware of it in his last writings. On the other hand, a libertarianism that embraces, as Foucault and Butler do, and rightly so, I believe, radical freedom in sexuality, political and artistic expression, public assembly, and so on, has to come to terms with the other branch of modern libertarianism—that is, the neoliberal branch—which grounds radical freedom in the individual's right to the unfettered pursuit of material gain and generally rejects the role of the state in communal provision. All manner of thorny questions about the meaning of freedom and individuality and the role of the state are nested in these different strands of libertarianism. It, too, in short, is a living but damaged and burdened tradition.

Back to literature and politics once more. Through a kind of pragmatist restatement of Kant, I have argued that the aesthetic experience of the artwork's inner form arises from our participation in publicness. Modern aesthetic receptivity is our *individual* experience only by virtue of being enmeshed in the public realm or worldly space of artistic expression and criticism. At the same time, Kant's account of aesthetic experience shares with Arendt's account of the democratic polity a normative reference to personhood. Aesthetic experience tacitly makes symbolic reference to "the worth of others" in the claim and appeal that *this is beautiful*; political participation tacitly makes practical reference to the cultivated, self-realizing citizenship of others in the claim and appeal that *this is unjust*. The double norm of publicness and personhood is thus at the heart of modern aesthetic and political experience, of the artwork's inner form and the polity's practices of deliberation and persuasion.

The Greek polis gave Aristotle the figure of personhood in the form of the *zoon politikon*; the Enlightenment, the stirrings of modern democratic revolution, and the aesthetic claims of the beautiful gave Kant the figure of personhood in the form of "one's own understanding" and the "worth of others." I'm calling these concepts *figures* of personhood because they carry a strong normative, even symbolic charge in Aristotle and Kant. And they resonate with religious figurings of person. *Your body is a temple*: while this symbolization originates in Jesus's polemic with Jews regarding his divinity (John 2:21) and is then taken up by Paul, with characteristic severity, to denounce fornication (I Cor. 6:18–19), it has been continually reappropriated and rewoven in Western poetry and ethics to express the intimations of the sacred in eroticism and love, the integrity of the person in moral and sexual relations with others, and the rights of the individual in moral and political relations with institutions and governments. Like all symbolizations of moral experience, *your body is a temple* is polysemous and ambivalent; it is susceptible to politically regressive as well as progressive uses. But the Foucauldian body, the Lacanian mirror-stage, and the Althusserian interpellated subject are hardly less ambiguous, and most certainly are less resonant. It is indeed hard to imagine these theoretical constructs truly doing the work of articulating sexual freedom, individual inviolability, or essential human rights more effectively than the enlightened commitment to the integrity of the person tinged with the symbolism of the sacred.

NOTES

1. Cary Nelson, "Forum," *PMLA* 112:2 (March 1997), p. 276.

2. Patrick Brantlinger, *ibid.*, p. 266.

3. Nelson, *ibid.*, pp. 277, 276.

4. Raymond Williams, *Writing in Society* (London: Verso, 1984).

5. *The Poems of Gerard Manley Hopkins*, 4th Edition, ed. W. H. Gardner and N. H. MacKenzie (New York: Oxford University Press, 1970), pp. 69–70.

6. Immanuel Kant, *Critique of Judgment*, trans. J. H. Bernard (New York: Hafner, 1966), pp. 198–199.

7. Among Kant's commentators, Heidegger provides the strongest unconventional reading of the idea that the experience of the beautiful is, in Kant's phrase, "devoid of all interest." He assails the conventional reading, which he attributes to Schopenhauer: "If the relation to the beautiful, delight, is defined as 'disinterested,' then, according to Schopenhauer, the aesthetic state is one in which the will is put out of commission and all striving brought to a standstill; it is pure repose, simply wanting nothing more, sheer apathetic drift." Heidegger interprets Kant differently: "Whatever we take an interest in is always already taken, i.e., represented, with a view to something else. . . . Whatever exacts of us the judgment 'This is beautiful' can never be an interest. That is to say, in order to find something beautiful, we must let what encounters us, purely as it is in itself, come before us in its own stature and worth. We may not take it into account in advance with a view to something else, our goals and intentions, our possible enjoyment and advantage. Comportment toward the beautiful itself, says Kant, is *unconstrained favoring*. We must freely grant what encounters us as such its way to be; we must allow and bestow upon it what belongs to it and what it brings to us." Heidegger's purpose is to create a rapprochement between Kant's aesthetic and Nietzsche's, despite Nietzsche's own conventional, Schopenhauerian reading of Kant. He cites Nietzsche to the effect that what is beautiful is "an expression of what is *most worthy* of honor," and then claims this is the Kantian conception of beauty: "For just this—purely to honor what is of worth in its appearance—is for Kant the essence of the beautiful." Kant's *unconstrained favoring* and *disinterested delight* he then equates with Nietzschean *rapture*: "the beautiful is what determines us, our behavior and our capability, to the extent that we are claimed supremely in our essence, which is to say, to the extent that we ascend beyond ourselves. . . . Thus the beautiful is disclosed in rapture. . . . If the beautiful is what sets the standard for what we trust we are essentially capable of, then the feeling of rapture, as our relation to the beautiful, can be no mere turbulence and ebullition." Cf. Martin Heidegger, *Nietzsche, Volume I: The Will to Power as Art*, trans. David Farrell Krell (New York: Harper & Row, 1979), pp. 108, 109, 111, 113.

The *valuing* that occurs in the experience of the beautiful does not measure the artwork against an established standard; Heidegger gets at this through the idea that the beautiful "corresponds to what we demand of ourselves" (p. 112). There is something unprecedented about what is beautiful, something beyond the scope of our existing interests, representations, goals, intentions, and so on. Nietzsche and Heidegger encapsulate their sense of aesthetic rapture in their pseudo-aristocratic vocabulary of honor, nobility, and rank, and they seek in aesthetic experience intimations of what the age may hold of greatness and supremacy. Their idiom is antimodern. In Heidegger's own essays on art and poetry, his aesthetic valuings clearly bear the mark of his reactionary and authoritarian beliefs. My argument is twofold. On the one hand, aesthetic experience *is* a valuing that reaches beyond established taste and standards; on the other hand, that valuing is embroiled in the contentious, democratic or proto-democratic public realm of contending political convictions and historical visions. The conservative convictions and visions of a Heidegger are there to be contested; actively contesting them requires aesthetic valuings as forceful as his own.

8. Kwame Anthony Appiah and Henry Louis Gates, Jr., "Editors' Introduction: Multiplying Identities," *Critical Inquiry* 18 (Summer 1992), p. 625.

9. See, for example, Octavio Paz, "Revolt and Resurrection," *One Earth, Four or Five Worlds: Reflections on Contemporary History*, trans. Helen R. Lane (New York: Harcourt Brace Jovanovich, 1985), p. 81.

10. Michael Walzer, *Spheres of Justice: A Defense of Pluralism and Equality* (New York: Basic Books, 1983), p. 29.

11. Hannah Arendt, "What Is Freedom?" *Between Past and Present: Eight Exercises in Political Thought* (New York: Penguin, 1977), p. 149.

12. *Public Culture* 1:2 (Spring 1989).

13. *Public Culture* 2:1 (Fall 1989), p. 123.

14. For a pointed reply to Appadurai and Breckenridge's editorial, see Michael M.J. Fischer and Mehdi Abedi, "Letters to the Editor," *Public Culture* 2:1 (Fall 1989), pp. 123–126.

15. In an extremely important essay, Amartya Sen has cut through the ethnocentric and anti-ethnocentric obfuscations that surround so many discussions of "Western" democracy and "Asian values." Against the ethnocentrism of Western liberal ideologues, he points out that there is no continuous unfolding in the West of democratic values like freedom, equality, and tolerance. These emerged in discontinuous pockets of political thought and political institutions from the ancient Greeks to the modern era—interrupted by long periods of absolutism and religious intolerance; compromised by slavery, racism, and male political dominance; and contested throughout the twentieth century by fascism and dictatorship. "The roots of modern democratic and liberal ideas can be sought in terms of constitutive elements, rather than as a whole." Conversely, he challenges the standard anti-ethnocentric view that such ideas are merely Western by showing, with respect to the religious, literary, and political traditions of the Indian subcontinent, that Indian history likewise contains a rich, discontinuous heritage—Hindu and Muslim—of ideas and experiments in democratic values, a wellspring no less ancient or nourishing than the origins of Western democracy. Cf. Amartya Sen, "Human Rights and Asian Values," *The New Republic*, July 14 & 21, 1997, pp. 33–40.

16. Stendhal, *The Red and the Black*, trans. Lloyd C. Parks (New York: Signet, 1970), p. 178. *Le Rouge et le Noir* (Paris: Garnier, 1960), p. 172.

17. "An Answer to the Question: 'What is Enlightenment?'" *Kant's Political Writings*, ed. Hans Reiss and trans. H. B. Nisbet (New York: Cambridge University Press, 1970), p. 54.

18. Robert F. Reid-Pharr, "Speaking through Anti-Semitism: The Nation of Islam and the Poetics of Black Counter-Modernity," W. E. B. Du Bois Distinguished Visiting Lecturer Series (The Graduate School and University Center of The City University of New York, 1995), p. 7.

19. Zygmunt Bauman, *Modernity and Ambivalence* (Ithaca: Cornell University Press, 1991), p. 7. Quoted in Reid-Pharr, p. 11.

20. Reid-Pharr, p. 12.

21. *Ibid.*, pp. 11, 13.

22. *Ibid.*, p. 19.

23. *Ibid.*, pp. 19, 16.

24. Judith Butler, *Excitable Speech: A Politics of the Performative* (New York: Routledge, 1997), pp. 1–41.

25. Hannah Arendt, "Tradition and the Modern Age," *op. cit.*, pp. 22–23.

26. Habermas devoted an important essay to Arendt in the midst of working out his own communicative theory of democratic institutions. He shows that Arendt conceived of power as communicative action. "Power," she writes in *On Violence*, "corresponds to the human ability not just to act but to act in concert." Using the distinctions I have drawn regarding the different frameworks of modern democratic thought and practice—liberal, republican, social-democratic—I see Habermas as attempting to translate, or transfer, Arendt's civic-humanist conception into the social-democratic framework of the impersonal, procedurally grounded deliberation required by modern bureaucracies, parliaments, and courts. However, something is lost in the translation. While Arendt insists on the historical relevance of the discontinuous heritage of republicanism, Habermas attempts to locate the norm of "coercion-free" or "undistorted" communication needed to sustain modern social democracy in the pragmatics and logic of communication itself. In the German context, where republicanism has had little historical actuality, Habermas's efforts to ground democratic commitment in a kind of philosophy of language is understandable. But, in addition to the theoretical problems this endeavor encounters, it also tends to deplete the historical experience of self-rule and participatory democracy of its symbolic and practical resonance. Cf. Jürgen Habermas, "Hannah Arendt: On the Concept of Power," *Philosophical-Political Profiles*, trans. Frederick G. Lawrence (Cambridge, MA: MIT, 1983), pp. 171–187.

MICHAEL BÉRUBÉ

5

THE RETURN OF REALISM AND THE FUTURE OF CONTINGENCY

THE QUESTION I ADDRESS in this essay is by now a familiar one—the question of whether antifoundationalist theoretical commitments undermine progressive politics. Until recently, antifoundationalist progressives found this question fairly easy to answer; we woke up each morning, asked the mirror on the wall whether the world contained people like ourselves, and then, having confirmed our existence, walked the earth contentedly the rest of the day. In the past few years, however, it has become increasingly common to hear voices on the left calling for an end to counterproductive poststructuralist theorizing and for a return to the values and certainties of the Enlightenment, such that your local neighborhood antifoundationalist progressive is now required, at minimum, to establish the possibility of her existence—and the plausibility of her politics—by reference to something other than the household mirror. The most immediate and important audience to whom the antifoundationalist progressive has to appeal, I submit, is the broad constituency of left intellectuals, journalists, and activists that has been so alarmed and threatened by varieties of poststructuralism currently circulating among varieties of the academic left; it is primarily for this constituency that I write, in the hopes of establishing more productive terms of debate between the so-called "two lefts" of U.S. politics, and a clearer understanding of what kind of "grounding" a left politics does and does not need.

Since 1996 it has become nearly impossible to broach these issues in public debate without reference to the array of interventions undertaken by physicist Alan Sokal, who, having successfully pulled off his *Social Text* hoax, followed it with an essay in *Lingua Franca* in which he blamed postmodern literary theory for the intellectual decline of the American left, and explained that he had concocted his hoax not, primarily, to embarrass the academy—or even *Social Text* itself—but to restore the left to its realist heritage:

> For most of the past two centuries, the Left has been identified with science and against obscurantism; we have believed that rational thought and the fearless analysis of objective reality (both natural and social) are incisive tools for combating the mystifications promoted by the powerful—not to mention being desirable human ends in their own right. The recent turn of many "progressive" or "leftist" academic humanists and social scientists toward one or another form of epistemic relativism betrays this worthy heritage and undermines the already fragile prospects for progressive social critique. (63)

There are many "problems" with this passage, at least as it would be read by an antifoundationalist progressive like myself, such as the equation of antifoundationalism with "epistemic relativism" and the bald assertion that the left has simply been "identified with science." But the problem I want to focus on is the elision of two forms of "objective reality (both natural and social)," which, I think, begs every important question in dispute—both in science studies and in political theory.

I do not want or intend, therefore, to revisit the hoax itself, nor do I want to follow Sokal's post-hoax trajectory, in which he has extended his argument to cover both a wide range of science studies and a wider range of French intellectuals—particularly those French intellectuals who have combined a form of poststructuralist psychoanalysis with some truly ludicrous and uninformed proclamations about science and math.[1] And even though much of the first half of this essay will route its argument by way of my own past exchanges with Sokal, I want to insist that Sokal himself is not the "object" of this argument so much as its conduit, just as he has been an important conduit for arguments mounted against the antifoundationalist/academic left even by people who do not share his commitment to epistemic realism. The reason that Sokal is not the point, in other words, is simply that the firestorm he unleashed can no longer be traced back to a single point of origin; on the contrary, the current political landscape is such that every recent defense—or mere invocation—of the Enlightenment (as that intellectual legacy which the academic left has betrayed) necessarily partakes in a project one goal of which is to decouple antifoundationalist thought from progressive cultural analysis and policymaking. For people like myself who want to still want to acknowledge antifoundationalism's powerful reproaches to foundationalist and realist hubris (however hubristically these reproaches may have been announced in the past), this state of affairs has produced a dizzying paradox: there seems to be emerging on one wing of the left, however fitfully and unevenly, something like a consensus that human consensus alone is an insufficient ground for thought and action. If I'm right about this, then antifoundationalist progressives may find themselves in the intolerable position of either (a) believing that social deliberation is the basis for beliefs about social reality even though they seem to be repudiated by a vast majority of the people doing the deliberating, who believe instead that something *else*-God, natural law, moral certitudes—must serve as the basis for both social deliberation and beliefs about social reality, or (b) insisting in the face of (a) that critics of antifoundationalism (left or right) are simply *wrong*, in a foundationalist sense, about the necessity of a noncontingent ground for thought and action, and that antifoundationalism simply *is true* regardless of anyone's espousal or denial of it.

It is in this confusing context, then, that I want to investigate anew the philosophical and political status of antifoundationalism (or, to use another term I will take as a problematic and partial synonym for the remainder of the essay, "social constructionism") with regard to human rights. For I believe the debate as it has so far unfolded has regrettably conflated two theoretical avenues of inquiry, one pertaining to the understanding of human identities, the other pertaining to the means by which we might justify and adjudicate human rights claims.

It is worth remarking, first, that insofar as this discussion is necessary, social constructionism has apparently had some social consequences it wasn't supposed to have. From the work of Stanley Fish especially, we are familiar with the claim that antifoundationalism in itself changes nothing, since no social structure falls simply because people start realizing that it's socially constructed. In *Essentially Speaking*, likewise, Diana Fuss contends that even if you show that patriarchy is historical and not natural, you haven't necessarily created the conditions for gender equity: all you've done is displace the argument from the biological onto the cultural, so that anti-feminists can still say there's no biological reason for patriarchy, but culturally it's good for the family anyway. And yet if biological determinism, in whatever form, is understood to underwrite moral foundationalism, as it often is, then there *is* an important consequence of social constructionism after all—namely, that it prevents its advocates from claiming that their vision of the world is self-evidently true or right. Hence the antifoundationalist rebuke to intellectual hubris. In the social-constructionist universe, of course, nothing is self-evident, and every moral and political premise has to be argued anew precisely because we believe that there are no transhistorical, noncontingent grounds for those premises. For significant segments of the contemporary left, this possibility is evidently so alarming as to amount to a constitutional crisis. It would seem, then, that denaturalization, like defamiliarization (to which it is close kin), has the potential to renew perception, to make the stone stony, and to provoke moral panics and media scandals.

This is one of the conundra with which the Sokal/*Social Text* Affair has left us—the realization that antifoundationalism simultaneously does and does not have political consequences. And in order to explore the conundrum further, I need first to tell the story of my extended encounter with Alan Sokal, which occurred when I agreed to debate him before what turned out to be a standing-room-only audience of roughly nine hundred people at the University of Illinois in late January of 1997. The title of the event, unfortunately, was "Fraternizing Across the Culture War Trenches: Alan Sokal and Michael Bérubé

Search for Common Ground." Although Sokal had kindly asked whether he could debate me rather than simply deliver a stump speech, since we had exchanged some lengthy e-mails in the summer of 1996, at no point had he or I claimed that we would search for common ground, and I was especially uncomfortable with the idea of fraternizing, which implied either a homosocial bonding in the no-man's land between the trenches (intimate sharing of cigarettes and complaints about our respective supply lines) or outright treason. I was justly afraid that this forum had been convened as a space in which Sokal and I were supposed to conclude by agreeing with one another. More specifically, I feared that because Sokal had already declared himself to be a leftist and a feminist, the encounter would degenerate into a collective dismissal of recondite theoretical problems, such that Sokal and I would be understood as saying *what the hell, foundations or no foundations, we're both in favor of single-payer health care.* You say difference and I say *différance*, let's call the whole thing off. At one point during the proceedings, in fact, I stopped and said explicitly that even though Sokal and I professed to share similar political aspirations at the end of the day, it would be a mistake for us to turn this debate into an academic version of the Clinton/Dole or Gore/Kemp nondebates to which we had been subjected during the fall of 1996. You can imagine my dismay, then, when I read and heard post-mortem accounts of the debate in which Sokal and I were likened to Clinton and Dole, and attendees bemoaned the fact that—as one memorable bemoaner remarked to me—there wasn't any blood on the floor at the end.

Nor was that the least of my failures. In the weeks following the debate I found that despite my impression that I had made a fairly cogent and intelligible case for antifoundationalist politics, many of my listeners apparently left with the impression that I was in fact the kind of cartoon relativist Sokal had attacked in his original essay: that I had no account, for example, of why the Holocaust might have been wrong or why some theories might be better than others in terms of their predictive value. And since the debate had turned precisely on the status of antifoundationalism in social theory as opposed to the sciences, I found the post-debate spin even more depressing and discouraging than the pre-debate spin.

My response to Sokal had taken the form of an argument that gave ground only to reclaim it, and it went something like this. I always assume that the phenomenal world exists, that terms such as "deoxyribonucleic acid" or "cosmic microwave background radiation" describe phenomena that exist independently of human observation. I make this assumption only with the caveat that it is a heuristic concession, made chiefly in order to get things done, just as I concede some kind of working relationship with realism whenever I am looking for my keys; should any of my interlocutors actually demand *proof* of this "real world," however, I refer them to the history of philosophy and wish them the best of luck.[2] Having thus generously conceded Sokal the existence of the phenomenal world, I then proceeded to take up John Searle's book *The Construction of Social Reality*, which describes two kinds of "real world"—one of which, Searle claims, is susceptible to social construction and therefore fair game for speech act theory, and the other of which is not. The first he calls "social fact," one crucial subset of which is called "institutional fact," and it concerns phenomena like touchdowns and twenty-dollar bills—items whose existence and meaning are obviously dependent entirely on human construction, insofar as their properties could be redefined tomorrow by human fiat. The second he calls "brute fact," and it concerns phenomena like Neptune, DNA, and the cosmic background radiation.

So far as ordinary language is concerned, I largely agree with this division of labor, again on pragmatist grounds. It makes little sense to say that we are constructing Neptune by looking at it; that kind of language will not answer to the need to understand Neptune as an entity whose existence precedes that of any conscious observer. However, following the argument Martin Heidegger develops at the end of the first section of *Being and Time*, we could also say that the discovery of Neptune in 1846 could plausibly be described, *from a strictly human vantage point*, as the "invention" of Neptune. (For up to that point, the planet "Neptune" did not exist in human consciousness, just as "gravity" had never meant "a universal force of nature" until Newton invented—or discovered—it.)[3] But clearly, the basic physical processes of the universe precede us; they have literally *constructed* us; they do not depend on our understanding or belief. To maintain any other position is to live in the world of that Monty Python housing project in which tenants are required to believe in the buildings they inhabit—and when their belief in the building falters, or they begin to think they would do better to live elsewhere, the building topples over. In that sense, then, brute fact is unquestionably prior to social fact, both in a chronological and a logical sense.

Having granted the priority of brute fact to social fact, however, I then proceeded to invert the terms, arguing that there's a compelling sense in which social fact is prior to and even constitutive of brute fact. Because I knew this proposition would sound counterintuitive to much of my audience, I tried to illustrate what it looks like as part of an intellectual exchange and as a guideline for public policy. Fortunately, since John Searle himself had visited the University of Illinois in the spring of 1996, I was able to dramatize "intellectual exchange" with him by means of a telling anecdote: over the course of delivering an entertaining fifty-minute talk about twenty-dollar bills and performative utterances, Searle explained and expanded on the social fact / brute fact distinction for a large general audience. I had not planned on giving Searle a hard time when I showed up at his talk, but he sounded (to some listeners) so much like the soul of sense, and (to other listeners) so much like a social constructionist, that I thought I should ask him the $64,000 question right off the bat—namely, is the distinction between social facts and brute facts *itself* a social fact, or is it a brute fact?

In my naïveté, I figured I had him here. If Searle had replied by saying that the distinction between the two is *itself* a brute fact, we would be entitled to ask him, in return, where the distinction lies exactly, and how he might know this. If, by contrast, he had replied by saying that the distinction is a social fact, then he would have effectively admitted that social fact is the thing that determines how we draw the distinction. In that sense social facts would actually be philosophically prior to, and certainly more immediately important to us humans than, the world of brute fact (although there would still be lively commerce between the two domains, especially at that indeterminable border between them). And had Searle given this answer, the history of science would have borne him out strongly, since the difference between the ancient (or, for that matter, the "creation science") understanding of the universe and most modern scientific views is largely a difference concerning where that line gets drawn. It is simply the case, and has been ever since hominids first started talking to each other, that we are always and everywhere debating where social fact ends and brute fact begins, and that alone suggests that the realm of brute fact, *as we understand it*, depends on the workings of complex social processes, some of which happen to go by the name of "scientific investigation."

It is because Searle is relatively alive to such difficulties that I thought he would be a good post-lecture interlocutor; he is also, of course, justly famed for his wit. In *The Construction of Social Reality*, he leans considerably further to the side of social constructionism than do many of his critics in the realist tradition, not to mention many scholars in the life sciences. The reason for this is that Searle assigns to "social fact" any and all attributions of *function*, on the grounds that "functions are never intrinsic to the physics of any phenomenon but are assigned from outside by conscious observers and users. *Functions, in short, are never intrinsic but are always observer relative*" (14; emphasis in original). Thus, to take Searle's favorite example, it is a brute fact that the heart pumps blood, but when we start talking about whether the heart has a *purpose*, we are speaking from within the realm of social fact, constructed social reality:

> when, in addition to saying "The heart pumps blood" we say "The *function* of the heart is to pump blood," we are doing something more than recording these intrinsic facts. We are situating these facts relative to a system of values that we hold. It is intrinsic to us that we hold these values, but the attribution of these values to nature independent of us is observer relative.... If we thought the most important value in the world was to glorify God by making thumping noises, then the function of the heart would be to make a thumping noise, and the noisier heart would be the better heart. (14-15; emphasis in original)

For most examples that come down the pike, therefore, Searle sounds more like a social constructionist than like the kind of realist who insists that natural objects have natural functions. For that reason, the metaquestion about the distinction between social fact and brute fact

seems altogether relevant to Searle's work. Likewise, Searle acknowledges that many phenomena, such as color, have been assigned both to
the category of objects intrinsic to the natural world and the category
of objects that exist only from the perspective of conscious observers—
and he judiciously refrains from deciding the status of color as either
brute or social fact (11).

Searle replied to my question, however, by saying that the distinction between social fact and brute fact was neither a social fact nor a
brute fact; it is merely, said he, a procedural question, a matter of logic.
It was at once a deft answer—it won over a good deal of his audience—
and a glib one. For the question Searle begged, of course, is the question of whether human intelligence (and its epiphenomena, like
"logic") is a social fact or a brute fact, and that question in turn opens
onto the questions of whether human behavior is to be explained
genetically, and whether genetic phenomena are beyond our control or
susceptible to one interesting form of "social construction," namely,
genetic therapy and modification.[4] It is my sense that these questions
may be of some relevance to the unfolding of the twenty-first century.
But even if I turn out to be wrong on this one, there's still an important epistemological and political issue at stake here. How do we know
that the phenomenon we're discovering or observing is not, in fact, susceptible to human construction? In asking this question I'm not thinking of something as arcane and as limited in its application as the
Heisenberg Uncertainty Principle or as trivial and as undecidable as
color; I'm thinking about something much closer to home.

My second child, Jamie, was born with Down syndrome in 1991. His
chromosomal abnormality is a brute fact, and if we don't understand it
as such, then we open the door to a number of unsavory political conclusions, one of which is that it becomes possible to "blame" parents of
children with Down syndrome for having done something wrong during pregnancy. Astonishingly, as late as 1959, Down syndrome was still
thought to originate during fetal development, perhaps in the eighth
gestational week. (We have to recall here that Down syndrome was not
understood as resulting from a chromosomal nondisjunction during
meiosis until Jerome Lejeune established this in 1959; we should also

recall that transfer-RNA was not isolated until 1961—that, in other words, it was eight years after the discovery of DNA that scientists finally began to understand the specific transcription mechanism by which DNA base-pair sequences code for the production of amino acids.) But even though it is purely and clearly a genetic phenomenon, Down syndrome is also a profoundly social phenomenon. In fact, thanks to the early-intervention policies and federal legal initiatives of the 1970s, whereby children with Down syndrome in the United States are constructed as being entitled to physical, occupational, and speech therapy from birth, it is now beginning to look as if many of the mental and behavioral characteristics long attributed to children with Down syndrome are the result of pre-1970 social policies of institutionalization rather than to the molecular biochemistry of trisomy-21.

That understanding—the contemporary understanding of Down syndrome—was not won easily. It involves much of the history of genetics since Watson and Crick, and, even more vividly, much of the history of disability policy since the heyday of eugenics in the early decades of this century and the landmark Supreme Court case of *Buck v. Bell* in 1927, which legalized involuntary sterilization and helped pave the way for two decades of Nazi "science." The lack of clarity in the historical record is quite clear: genetics, disability, and intelligence have proven to be three crucial areas of human inquiry in which we are *constitutionally* unsure of how to draw the line between social fact and brute fact. But I can say this much and say it clearly: for James Bérubé, and for every other human with Down syndrome, social facts will be crucial to the brute facts of their lives both politically and physically, and it is likewise by means of those social facts that we will understand what's a brute fact and what's not—about Down syndrome and about everything else. It is for this reason, then, though not for this reason alone, that I am compelled continually to defend the theoretical projects launched by social constructionism, without which life as we know it would not be possible.

This is not a merely local point about my child, about developmental disability, or even about genetic anomaly in general. Rather, it goes to the heart of why we on the left have done well to entertain a healthy skepticism about discourses of biological determinism. For the past hundred years or so, it seems that every time politically powerful humans have tried to extrapolate to the social realm what they thought they understood of genetics, the impulse behind and the results of the extrapolation have been politically reactionary in the extreme. From Social Darwinism to falsified twin studies to *The Bell Curve*, the biochemical template has been misread time and again as the sanction for the naturalization of the social. Genetics has in this sense served as the vehicle for ideology *as such*, the mystification of contingent and historically bounded social formations as the expressions of "natural" constraints and "natural" forces. And every time we hear that infidelity is "in our genes," every time we hear a Newt Gingrich declaim on how the menstrual cycle prevents women from serving in combat duty, we are right to defend the proposition that although humans may not be *infinitely* malleable, still, human variety and human plasticity can in principle and in practice exceed any specific form of human social organization. It should be no surprise, then, that contemporary left theorists are skeptical about every kind of genetic determinism, in however mild or mediated a form: when we hear the word "genome," we reach for our social-constructionist guns.

Nonetheless, I want to argue that left intellectuals have mistakenly defended two forms of "social constructionism" as if their linkage were necessary, when in fact it is not. There is no necessary connection between genetic foundationalism and moral foundationalism, and the sooner the theoretical left manages to decouple the one from the other, the better off we will be—theoretically *and* politically. Let me put this another way: if it were proven tomorrow that every politically significant form of human variation from race to gender to sexual orientation to *political* orientation were somehow indelibly inscribed in our double-stranded genetic fibers, it would not affect my social-constructionist approach to human rights in the least. At present, what we have is an intellectual dispensation in which every time a conservative suggests a biological subtext to the human script, he or she thinks that the social-constructionist basis for claims to egalitarian social justice has been dealt a mortal blow: aha! sickle-cell anemia! this proves the left is wrong and that we can now eliminate affirmative action and Head Start! (Lest this sound like too reductive a caricature, see Francis

Fukuyama's *Commentary* essay, "Is It All in Our Genes?", which links the "findings" of evolutionary psychology to the existence of the "free" market). In other words, in the present climate it looks as if every narrative that concedes ground to evolutionary theory is perforce a narrative that delivers us into the hands of the Social Darwinist oppressor, and that therefore in order to defend a social-constructionist account of human moral action we need to defend at all costs a fully social-constructionist account of what it means to be human.

My argument is that this need not be the case. To return to the realm of brute fact as best I can: James Bérubé is genetically Other. The meanings of Down syndrome, and the life prospects of persons with Down syndrome, differ widely from culture to culture, but the chromosomal nondisjunction is the same across every human culture. In a case like this, can we allow ourselves to tie human rights to a social constructionist account of Down syndrome? I want to claim that James is as human as any of you, and that as your fellow human he has a right to shelter, sustenance, health care, education, political participation and representation, reciprocal recognition, and respect. I believe that this claim is contingent, and that it depends for its realization on specific forms of social organization we have only lately begun to realize; but its contingency as a rights claim has no necessary relation to our understanding of Down syndrome as either a brute fact or a social fact.

By no means am I suggesting that we should stop asking what's fungible in the human condition; certainly, any dreams of political possibility should contain some faith in human possibility. But more crucially, we should insist on the distinction between reading the genome and reading the social text—a distinction dutifully observed by Richard Dawkins in the closing pages of *The Selfish Gene* but, in the past decade, most often honored in the breach by sociobiologists working in Dawkins' wake. I want to insist on this position, this decoupling, for two reasons: first, because the biochemical or social status of crucial human traits, like "intelligence," is not likely to be resolved in our lifetime or any other, and second, because the determination of basic human rights, *whatever we consider these rights to be*, should not be predicated on the biochemical or social status of crucial human traits. Innatist theories can and should be debated on their scientific merits, but in no case should they be taken as the basis for crafting social policy; what matters for a democratic political praxis is the creation of social spaces for noncoercive public deliberation, not (for example) the potential neurobiological bases of linguistic communication. And thus, as I argued in the conclusion of *Life As We Know It*, we should conceive of social justice in strictly social constructionist terms regardless of the biochemical status of individual humans or individual human properties.

What astonishes me about the Sokal/*Social Text* Affair, then, is not that so many progressive thinkers want to hold on to an understanding of brute fact as noncontingent; in the qualified terms I've laid out so far, that's an argument I'm quite willing to concede. (I'm also willing to regard various elements of human behavior, from aggression to language use, as lying at the interstice of social and brute fact.) Rather, what's astonishing is that that so many progressive thinkers seem to want an ironclad, noncontingent account of the bases for social justice. One voluble Chomskian at Illinois, in fact, went so far as to insist to me, in the question/answer session after Sokal and I had made our remarks, that the left must entertain the possibility that there are moral imperatives the content of which we do not yet know, for to believe anything else is to open the door to fascism. My reply was that the door to fascism will be closed only when no one on the planet conceives of fascism as a possible thing, and that in the meantime, the belief that there are moral imperatives the content of which we do not yet know leaves that door as wide open as anything does.

Yet I have to add that this whole line of argument angers me greatly. You would think, from listening to antifoundationalism's antagonists, that the Crusades, the Spanish Inquisition, the extermination of the native populations of the Americas, the massacre of the Armenians, the Stalinist purges and the Jewish catastrophe are all to be laid at the feet of a handful of jejune postmodern latte-drinking relativists. I find it outrageous, frankly, that foundationalists proceed in this debate as if their side, the side that appeals to objective facts and secure moral grounds, has nothing to answer for in the world's long and sorry history of civil butchery. I also find it outrageous that the theoretical left now has to start from the defensive when speaking about the social goals of science studies, as if no one but a credentialed scientist should inquire into the convoluted processes that gave us Tuskegee, Thalidomide, and plutonium experiments on unsuspecting citizens and even mental patients. But I did not answer the neo-Chomskyian position angrily; I merely said to the questioner and to Alan Sokal, "Let me put it this way. I have good news and bad news for you. If you want noncontingent, transhistorical grounds for social justice, the bad news is that you can't have them—and the good news is that you don't need them." This reply then provoked another question: if that's really what I think, then if I were the only person on earth who believed in the human rights of my son James, would he still have those rights after I died?[5]

At the time, I said simply that it would do James a fat lot of good if he "had" rights that no one on earth recognized. But of course, I had to admit, I would like to believe otherwise; I would like to believe that my little boy's humanity is somehow independent of any form of social recognition. I thought of the almost poignant moment at the end of Rorty's introduction to *Consequences of Pragmatism*, where he writes that it is "morally humiliating" to be an antifoundationalist:

> Suppose that Socrates was wrong, that we have *not* once seen the Truth, and so will not, intuitively, recognize it when we see it again. This means that when the secret police come, when the torturers violate the innocent, there is nothing to be said to them of the form "There is something within you that you are betraying. Though you embody the practices of a totalitarian society which will endure forever, there is something beyond those practices which condemns you." This thought is hard to live with, as is Sartre's remark: "Tomorrow, after my death, certain people may decide to establish fascism, and the others may be cowardly or miserable enough to let them get away with it. At that moment, fascism will be the truth of man, and so much the worse for us. In reality, things will be much as man has decided they are." (xlii)

Crucially, Rorty does not claim that his vision of post-philosophical culture expresses at last the real truth of humankind; he asks us merely to entertain the notion of a world in which no one makes appeals to the Truth with a capital T, and to decide whether such a notion is true in the pragmatist sense, that is, good in the way of belief.[6] Yet for many of us mortals, it appears that the answer is simply no: when the secret police arrive, these people want to be able to tell them that fascism is wrong, and they want to be able to point to something more authoritative on the subject than *Consequences of Pragmatism*—just as I sometimes want to believe, despite my theoretical commitments, that my child has "intrinsic" value whatever the world might think.

Naming this desire, I have found, is dangerous. It invites realists and their friends to say, aha, you see, this Bérubé has been to graduate school and has been indoctrinated by Richard Rorty, and yet down deep, in his heart, he wants to have an objective, noncontingent moral philosophy after all. But this is just a realist's version of wishful thinking. I do not have one desire that resides more deeply than another; I have lots of desires, one of which entails the vain hope that someday we will no longer need to make the case for the human rights of every human born. Yet another of my desires runs directly contrary to that one, for it entails the imperative to keep arguing with moral foundationalists, to try to convince them somehow that it is the sheerest folly—politically and theoretically—to think that such an argument about human rights can ever be "won" once and for all, in such a way that no one need ever worry about fascism or eugenics again. Still another of my desires entails the recognition that no argument about the impermanence of argument can ever be won once and for all, either, and that therefore I should walk this earth with great patience and an antifoundationalist's sense that I just can't always be right about everything, despite my many other desires to be just that.

And naming all *these* conflicting desires takes me to my concluding point, as well as to the basis for my title, both of which have to do with a fascinating passage in the final chapter of Barbara Herrnstein Smith's *Contingencies of Value*. I think it is becoming clear, a decade after the book's publication, that *Contingencies of Value* occupies a crucial place in the recent intellectual history of the academic left, simultaneously looking back over the debates about canons and representation, and forward to debates over relativism, strategic essentialism, and the disjunctions between interpretive theory and political practice. The question at hand in this passage is a practical and recursive one: if "truth" is understood as "what it is best to believe," then what if it's best for us to believe in a noncontingent basis for moral action, in order to mobilize important political constituencies, form coalitions, and get things done? Smith writes:

> It is sometimes objected . . . that one cannot live as a nonobjectivist because, in the real world of real peasants, politicians, and police, one must deal with people for whom only objectivist-type considerations and justifications—appeals to "fundamental rights" and "objective facts," not just to contingent conditions—will be acceptable and effective. Two replies may be made here. One is that it would be no more logically inconsistent for a nonobjectivist to speak, under some conditions, of fundamental rights and objective facts than for a Hungarian ordering his lunch in Paris to speak French. . . . The other and equally important reply, however, is that the power, richness, subtlety, flexibility, and communicative effectiveness of a *nonobjectivist idiom*—for example, forceful recommendations that do *not* cite intrinsic value, or justifications, accepted as such, that *do* cite contingent conditions and likely outcomes rather than fundamental rights and objective facts—are characteristically underestimated by those who have never learned to speak it or tried to use it in interactions with, among others, real policemen, peasants, and politicians. (158)

Here, one answer suggests that when we're among objectivists we should temporarily talk objectivist; the other suggests that we should try talking nonobjectivist first, and that we shouldn't knock it until we've tried it. This formulation has the advantage of putting the nonobjectivist in a position where she can never be wrong, but it leaves the uneasy impression that the objectivist idiom is a language of last resort, to be employed only if nonobjectivist language does not (literally) pay its way.[7] I want to suggest that recent schisms in the left have strained the tension in this passage to the breaking point. What, indeed, should we do when claims to contingency fail to persuade policemen, peasants, politicians—and the press? Do we simply mumble an apology and order dinner in French? Does this passage even earn its analogy between national languages and ethical discourses of justification?[8]

What this passage invites, in retrospect, is what Amanda Anderson calls the "double gesture"—a theoretical conviction that antifoundationalism does in fact describe the truth of human affairs but foundationalist claims will get us what we want and need in the meantime. And here the double gesture leads us to a bizarre impasse. After Sokal and I had finished debating, one listener pointed out that we had seemed to exchange places: the self-professed realist, Sokal, was arguing pragmatically that science seems to get things done and therefore serves as a good model for distinguishing fact from mere belief, and the self-professed pragmatist, Bérubé, was arguing quite emphatically, in the realist tradition, that we did not have access to noncontingent, transhistorical grounds for social justice because they simply did not exist. All I could say was that I was trying my best to persuade people to adopt my position in this debate, and that I hoped to convince my listeners that the world would be a better place, all around, if fewer humans were sure that their beliefs and actions were objectively and transcendentally *right*. Yet could I honestly have said anything else? I believe it's true that we don't have recourse to objective grounds for action unless we practice specific kinds of religious faith—and to say otherwise, I believe, is not just to order in French when in Paris but to pretend to convictions I do not have. At which point I ask myself, with a Wittgensteinian surmise, what it would be like to have deep convictions but only for a moment. If, then, I have no honest recourse but to believe that rhetorical strategies of persuasion, and nothing else, are the bases for human moral codes, then it is incumbent upon me to devise rhetorical strategies of persuasion that will convince people of the usefulness of this proposition. That means that the future of contingency is itself contingent: contingent, in this case, on forms of human agreement that antifoundationalist progressives urgently need to discover—or invent.

NOTES

1. I have written elsewhere on Sokal's post-hoax trajectory, however. See "Of Fine Clothes and Naked Emperors," *Tikkun* (March/April 1999), pp. 73-76, a review essay on Sokal and Jean Bricmont's *Fashionable Nonsense: Postmodern Intellectuals'*

Abuse of Science (Picador, 1998), originally published in France as *Impostures Intellectuelles*.

2. Here I'm thinking particularly of the passage in *Being and Time* in which Heidegger writes, "The 'scandal of philosophy' is not that this proof has yet to be given, but that *such proofs are expected and attempted again and again*. Such expectations, aims, and demands arise from an ontologically inadequate way of starting with *something* of such a character that independently *of it* and 'outside' *of it* a 'world' is to be proved as present-at-hand. It is not that the proofs are inadequate, but that the kind of Being of the entity which does the proving and makes requests for proofs has *not been made definite enough*" (I.6 ¶ 43(a), 249; emphasis in original).

3. See *Being and Time* I.6 ¶ 44(c): "Newton's laws, the principle of contradiction, any truth watever—these are true only so long as Dasein is. Before there was any Dasein, there was no truth; nor will there be any after Dasein is no more. . . . To say that before Newton his laws were neither true nor false, cannot signify that before him there were no such entities as have been uncovered and pointed out by those laws. Through Newton the laws became true; and with them, entities became accessible in themselves to Dasein. Once entities have been uncovered, they show themselves precisely as entities which beforehand already were" (269; emphasis in original).

4 I concede that deliberate genetic modification (as opposed to random mutation) is not usually considered a form of "social constructionism," at least not in the same sense that twenty-dollar bills and zoning laws are socially constructed. I intend this argument simply to indicate that the genetic is not necessarily a "ground," that it cannot be mapped (so to speak) onto a nature/ culture opposition so neatly as is generally assumed.

5. There are more problems with this question than I can discuss here, and many of them were called out immediately when I delivered this paper at the English Institute in 1997. First, there is the question of what "human rights" means in this context; second, the question presumes an absurdly monolithic model of humans who are never internally inconsistent, who never change their minds, or who could never be compelled by Jamie himself to rethink their understanding of human rights; third, it suggests that an account of human rights could be sustained merely by one person's belief. Though all these caveats have merit, I still think of the question as a variation on Sartre's vision of fascism being established "tomorrow, after my death" (hence my segue to this passage in the body of the essay), and take it as a thought-experiment challenge in the same vein. Under that heading, the specific content of "human rights" matters less than the mere existence of rights claims in the world; that is, whether health care is included as such a right is immaterial to the question of whether, in general, Jamie will continue to possess "rights" that only I recognize as valid. Nevertheless, in the world we inhabit, where such thought-experiments are, for now, nothing more than philosophical brain teasers, it does matter what kind of rights I imagine Jamie to possess—namely, not only the rights enumerated in the 1948 UN Declaration, but also the rights vouchsafed in the U.S. Individuals with Disabilities Education Act

(revised 1997) and the 1990 Americans with Disabilities Act. These latter rights verge on what Amartya Sen calls "capability rights," in that they seek to secure for individuals with disabilities the very broad right to be accorded the social services that foster their independence and autonomy to the greatest extent possible—in other words, the right to be given the opportunity to make the most of other rights (to food, housing, health care, and employment). The fine interplay between the ideal of individuals' independence and the manifest dependence of such individuals on the apparatus of the state is worth scrutiny here, as is the attempt to establish political mechanisms that will enable persons with disabilities to advocate for their own conceptions of human rights. This, indeed, may be the most fundamental meta-right I can imagine proposing as a contingent universal—to invoke yet another famously problematic phrase.

6. "The question of whether the pragmatist view of truth—that it is not a profitable topic—is itself *true* is thus a question about whether a post-Philosophical culture is a good thing to try for. It is not a question about what the word 'true' means, nor about the requirements of an adequate philosophy of language, nor about whether the world exists 'independently of our minds,' nor about whether the intuitions of our culture are captured in the pragmatists' slogans" (xliii; emphasis in original).

7. My thanks here to Amanda Anderson, Joe Valente, Idelber Avelar, Peter Garrett, Simon Joyce, and Stephanie Foote, who participated in a Unit for Criticism and Interpretive Theory seminar on "theories of value" (organized by Valente, Joyce, and Foote) in the spring of 1996. It was this seminar's discussion of *Contingencies of Value* that foregrounded the tensions in Herrnstein Smith's text in such a way as to impel me to the argument with which I close this essay.

8. My own answer to this is no: there is a profound assymetry in the implied proposition that nonobjectivism is to Hungarian as objectivism is to French (though these languages come from thoroughly different linguistic roots, I know of no study that suggests French is less contingent than Hungarian). Curiously, Searle's *The Construction of Social Reality* opens with an extended meditation on ordering a beer in a Paris café, an event whose "metaphysical complexity," as Searle rightly remarks, "is truly staggering" (3). I do not know whether, in order to order in Paris, one needs to subscribe to Searle's modified philosophical realism or Herrnstein Smith's skeptical nonobjectivism; my antifoundationalist impulses tell me that the latter will do just fine. But I do gather, having never been to Paris myself, that ordering in French must be a major preoccupation of intellectuals seeking to calibrate the relation between language and action.

WORKS CITED

Anderson, Amanda. "Cryptonormativism and Double Gestures: Reconceiving Post-structuralist Social Theory." *Cultural Critique* 21 (1992): 63–95.

Bérubé, Michael. *Life as We Know It: A Father, A Family, and an Exceptional Child.* New York: Vintage, 1998.

——. "Of Fine Clothes and Naked Emperors." *Tikkun* (March/April 1999): 73–76.

Dawkins, Richard. *The Selfish Gene.* London: Oxford UP, 1976. 2d ed. 1989.

Fukuyama, Francis. "Is It All in the Genes?" *Commentary* 104.3 (September 1997): 30–35.

Fuss, Diana. *Essentially Speaking: Feminism, Nature, and Difference.* New York: Routledge, 1990.

Heidegger, Martin. *Being and Time.* Trans. John Macquarrie and Edward Robinson. New York: Harper, 1962.

Rorty, Richard. *Consequences of Pragmatism: Essays, 1972–80.* Minneapolis: U of Minnesota P, 1985.

Searle, John. *The Construction of Social Reality.* New York: Free Press, 1995.

Smith, Barbara Herrnstein. *Contingencies of Value: Alternate Perspectives for Critical Theory.* Cambridge: Harvard UP, 1988.

Sokal, Alan. "A Physicist Experiments with Cultural Studies." *Lingua Franca* 6.4 (May/June 1996): 62–64.

Sokal, Alan, and Jean Bricmont. *Fashionable Nonsense: Postmodern Intellectuals' Abuse of Science* (Picador, 1998). Originally published as *Impostures Intellectuelles.* Paris: Éditions Odile Jacob, 1997.

WILLIAM E. CONNOLLY

6

THE MODUS VIVENDI
OF SECULARISM

THE HISTORICAL MODUS VIVENDI
called secularism is coming apart at the
seams. Secularism, in its Euro-American forms, was a shifting, unsettled, and
yet reasonably efficacious organization
of public space that opened up new possibilities of freedom and action. In so
doing it shuffled some of its own pre-
conditions of being into a newly crafted
space of private religion, faith, and ritual. It requires cautious reconfiguration
now when religious, metaphysical, ethnic, gender, and sexual differences both
exceed those previously legitimate
within European Christendom and
challenge the immodest conceptions of
ethics, public space, and theory secularism carved out of Christendom. I do
not suggest that a common religion
needs to be reinstated in public life or
that separation of church and state in

REFASHIONING

THE

SECULAR

some sense of that phrase needs to be reversed. Such attempts would
intensify cultural wars already in motion. Secularism needs to be refashioned, not eliminated.

The secular modus vivendi ignores or devalues some dimensions of
being that need to be engaged more actively. On one level, the secular
is more bound up with generic characteristics of Christian culture than
its most enthusiastic proponents acknowledge. On another, the partial
success of secularism in pushing specific Christian sects into private life

has had the secondary effect of consolidating flat conceptions of theory, ethics, and public life.

Secularism, in its dominant expression, combines a distinctive organization of public space with a generic understanding of how discourse and ethical judgment proceed on that space. The historical narrative many secularists offer in support of this modus vivendi goes something like this:

> Once the universal Catholic Church was challenged and dispersed by various Protestant sects, a unified public authority grounded in a common faith was drawn into a series of sectarian conflicts and wars. Since the sovereign's support of the right way to eternal life was said to hang in the balance, these conflicts were often horribly destructive and intractable. The best hope for a peaceful and just world under these new circumstances was the institution of a public life in which the final meaning of life, the proper route to life after death, and the divine source of morality were pulled out of the public realm and deposited into private life. The secularization of public life is thus crucial to private freedom, pluralistic democracy, individual rights, public reason and the primacy of the state. The key to its success is the separation of church and state and the general acceptance of a conception of public reason (or some surrogate) through which to reach public agreement on non-religious issues.

This is not the only story that could be told about the origins of secularism. You could tell one about the needs of capital and commercial society to increase the range and scope of monetary exchange in social relations. Here Adam Smith, Montesquieu, and Adam Ferguson would take on great salience.[1] Or you could concentrate on the challenge that nominalism posed within Christianity to enchanted conceptions of the world in the medieval era, showing how the nominalist intensification of faith in an omnipotent God presiding over a contingent world (rather than one obeying the dictates of a teleological order) ironically opened the door to secularist conceptions of mastery over a disenchanted nature.[2] Or you could treat secularism as the loss of organic connections that can only be sustained by general participation in a common Christian faith. Or play up the role of princely statecraft in

supporting secular forces in order to strengthen itself.[3] I want to suggest, however, that the story summarized above has become the dominant self-representation by secularists in several Western states. This
story prevails largely because it paints the picture of a self-sufficient
public realm fostering freedom and governance without recourse to a
specific religious faith.

Evidence of the dominance of the first story can be found in the
OED. According to it, *Seculere* in Christian Latin means "the world,"
as opposed to the One Church or Heaven. The early (Christian)
Church treated the secular as a necessary but residual domain of life. It
was, the *OED* says, mostly "a negative term." A sense of how it could
be both lowly and necessary is revealed in this statement by a priest in
1593 (quoted in the *OED*): "the tongue is the Judge; the rest of our
organs but the secular executioners of his sentence." As you go down
the list of *OED* meanings and up the list of temporal references the secular becomes a more positive and independent domain. Thus Benjamin Franklin is moved to say, ironically, that he speaks as "a mere
secular man" in expressing his opinions. By the modern period, secularism, as a distinctive political perspective and social movement, is
represented positively as "the doctrine that morality should be based
solely in regard to the well-being of mankind in the present life to the
exclusion of all considerations drawn from the belief in God or in a
future state." Note, for later consideration, the reference to "the belief
in God," in which both a personal God and beliefs about it are treated
as definitive of the religious practice. And now to "secularize" is to "dis-
sociate (say art or educational studies) from religion or spiritual concerns." This language of "solely," "exclusion," "dissociation," conceals
the subterranean flow between the Christian sacred, which now
becomes lodged in something called the private domain, and secular
discourse, which now becomes associated with public authority, common sense, rational argument, justice, tolerance, the public interest,
publicity, and the like. The *OED* story, in fact, soon becomes a partisan secular history of the sacred/secular division in the West, adopting
as neutral terms of analysis several concepts and themes that became
authoritative only through the hegemony of secularism.

John Rawls, too, participates in the dominant story. In *Political Liberalism,* he says that "Catholics and Protestants in the sixteenth century"

lacked the ability or willingness to disconnect their divergent religious views from contending conceptions of public life. He distills a cardinal point from these presecular regimes. "Both faiths held that it was the duty of the ruler to uphold the true religion and to repress the spread of heresy and false doctrines." Under such intense conditions either tolerance emerged as a precarious modus vivendi between contending groups or one side suppressed the others in the interests of truth or justice. Finally, Rawls insists upon the sanctity of an authoritative line of division between religion in private life and public political discourse, even while joining a list of modern predecessors in trying to redefine that line:

> We appeal (instead) to a political conception of justice to distinguish between those questions that can be reasonably removed from the political agenda and those that cannot.... To illustrate: from within a political conception of justice let us suppose we can account both for equal liberty of conscience, which takes the truths of religion off the agenda, and the equal political and civil liberties, which by ruling out serfdom and slavery take the possibility of those institutions off the agenda. But controversial issues remain: for example, how, more exactly, to draw the boundaries of the basic liberties when they conflict (where to set the 'wall between church and state'); how to interpret requirements of distributive justice even when there is considerable agreement on general principles.... But by avoiding comprehensive doctrines [i.e., basic religious and metaphysical systems] we try to bypass religion and philosophy's profoundest controversies so as to have some hope of uncovering a basis for a stable, overlapping consensus.[4]

So secularism takes metaphysics out of politics . . . but notice how fragile the specific discrimination between the secular public realm and private life amid insistence that such a line of discrimination provides way to regulate religious disputes in public life: "Let us suppose"; "avoiding"; "We try to bypass"; "so as to have some hope of uncovering a basis for a stable, overlapping consensus." The word "avoid" is revealing because it mediates effortlessly between a demarcation established by some philosophical means and one commended because its political acceptance of a philosophy of justice would reduce the intensity of cultural conflict. You also encounter in these lines a paradigmatic secular tactic for taming conflict: the idea is to dredge out of public life as much cultural density and depth as possible so that muddy "metaphysical" and "religious" differences don't flow into the pure water of public reason, procedure, and justice. Finally, the word religion now becomes treated as a universal term, as if could always be distilled from a variety of cultures in a variety of times rather than representing a specific fashioning of spiritual life engendered by the secular public space carved out of Christendom.

The first quandary of secularism, then, is that its inability to draw a firm line between private life and public discourse creates opportunities for some Christian enthusiasts to call for the return to a theologically centered state, while the increasingly transparent favoritism of its "neutral" public space opens a window of opportunity for critics to accuse secularists of moral hypocrisy. Thus, in an issue of *First Things: A Journal of Religion and Public Life*, the editors assert that the American courts have lost cultural legitimacy because their secular stands on abortion, homosexuality, and the right to die disenfranchise religious Americans.

> Almost all Americans claim adherence to an ethic and morality that transcends human invention, and for all but a relatively small minority, that adherence is expressed in terms of biblical religion. By the strange doctrine promulgated by the courts, Christians, Jews and others who adhere to a transcendent morality would, to the extent that their action as citizens are influenced by that morality, be effectively disenfranchised. . . . It is a doctrine that ends up casting religious Americans, traditionally the most loyal of citizens, into the role of enemies of the public order.[5]

Secularism, its (primarily) Christian critics contend, lacks the ability to come to terms with the sources of morality most citizens endorse; therefore, secularism itself drifts toward public orientations that challenge the moral sensibilities of many of its citizens. Many such theological critics call upon secularists to return to the nineteenth-century vision of public life registered by Tocqueville.

Consider two quotations from Tocqueville. The first deals with a network of internal relations between religion, mores, reason, and morals in the American civilization:

> In the United States it is not only mores that are controlled by religion, but its sway extends over reason.... Among Anglo-Americans there are some who profess Christian dogmas because they believe them and others who do so because they are afraid to look as though they did not believe them. So Christianity reigns without obstacles, by universal consent; consequently . . . everything in the moral field is certain and fixed, although the world of politics seems given over to argument and experimentation.[6]

You might read this to say that while politics is located in the secular realm, that realm remains safe for Christianity because it is already inscribed in the prediscursive dispositions and cultural instincts of the civilization. Tocqueville defends a religiously contained secularism, while secularism supports secular containment of religion. Tocqueville proceeds by invoking a conception of mores eventually pushed out or debased by most secular self-representations. But why, then, bother to support separation of church and state at all? Here is part of the answer, for Tocqueville at least:

> There is an innumerable multitude of sects in the United States. . . . Each sect worships God in its own fashion, but all preach the same morality in the name of God.... America is still the place where the Christian religion has kept the greatest power over men's souls; and nothing better demonstrates how useful and natural it is to man, since the country where it now has widest sway is both the most enlightened and freest.[7]

Separation of church and state softens sectarian divisions between Christian sects while retaining the civilizational hegemony of Christianity. This is so because the instinctive register of intersubjective judgment to which Tocqueville appeals both embodies Christian culture and regulates public argumentation. Most contemporary secularists, unlike Tocqueville, either ignore this register of being or locate it beneath public deliberation. And most religious critics of secularism who do recognize the visceral register invoke it to deepen the quest for unity or community in public life. My suspicion, contrary to one element in each view, is that enactment of an expansive pluralism appropriate to contemporary life involves cultural investments in the visceral

register of subjectivity and intersubjectivity. We must press Tocqueville's appreciation of mores beyond his colonization of them by a
civilization of Christian containment. And we must press the (under-
developed) secular appreciation of diversity into layers of being it
reserves to "religion."

VISCERAL JUDGMENT AND REPRESENTED BELIEFS

Talal Asad, an anthropologist of Islamic heritage, has explored long-
term shifts in the Christian experience of ritual, symbol, belief, faith,
and doctrine. It is not simply that dominant Christian beliefs have
changed over the centuries, as, say, the doctrine of Original Sin gives
ground to that of individual choice. But the operative meanings of ritual and symbol have shifted too. With the emergence of secularism and
Protestantism, a symbol, in its dominant valence, becomes the representation of an inner state of belief that precedes it; and ritual is now
understood to be the primitive enactment of beliefs that could also be
displayed through cognitive representation. Even sophisticated anthro-
pologists such as Clifford Geertz, says Asad, tend to adopt these historically specific meanings of symbol and ritual as if they were pertinent to
the universal experience of "religion." But in medieval Christianity,
Asad asserts, a symbol was bound up with enactment or perfection of
inner states and meanings it also represented; and ritual was practiced as
a means of educating and constituting appropriate dispositions of
appraisal and aptitudes of performance. In medieval monastic life,

> The liturgy is not a species of enacted symbolism to be classified
> separately from activities defined as technical but is a practice
> among others essential to the acquisition of Christian virtues....
> Each thing done was not only to be done aptly in itself, but done
> in order to make the self approximate more and more to a pre-
> defined model of excellence. The things prescribed, including litur-
> gical services, had a place in the overall scheme of training the
> Christian self. In this conception there could be no radical dis-
> junction between outer behavior and inner motive, between
> social rituals and individual sentiments, between activities that are
> expressive and those that are technical.[8]

Asad draws upon Mauss's exploration of *habitus* as "embodied aptitude" to sharpen the sense of how intersubjective dispositions, instincts, and virtues can be constituted through ritual performance.

If Asad is right, then secular understandings of discourse, analysis, and argument capture merely one dimension of thinking, intersubjective judgment, and doctrinal commitment in public life. You might say, then, that intersubjectivity operates on several registers (with significant subjective variations) and that each register exerts effects upon the organization of the others.

I would augment Asad modestly. First, as my reading of Kant will suggest, to draw a sharp line between presecular and secular understandings is an exaggeration. Some of these practices persist in Christian Protestantism as well as in some secular orientations to education and training in citizenship. Secularists sometimes address these practices, but seldom in ways that affect profoundly their presentations of how an ethos is to be fostered in public life. So Asad seems right in suggesting that the extent and significance of such practices in contemporary life is underappreciated in secular discourse. Second, and connected to the above, it may be important to underline how representational discourse itself, including the public expression and defense of fundamental beliefs, affects and is affected by the visceral register of intersubjectivity. Public discourses do operate within dense linguistic fields that specify how beliefs are to be articulated and tested and how ethical claims are to be redeemed. But repetitions and defenses of these articulations also write scripts upon prerepresentational sites of appraisal. Although secular presentations of public reason and moral discourse remain tone deaf to this second register of intersubjectivity, they nonetheless depend upon it to stabilize those practices.

Most pertinent for my purposes, however, is that in addition to the appreciation of this register by many theological thinkers, several non-secular, a-theistic thinkers pay attention to it as well. This correspondence opens a line of potential communication between theistic and non-secular, a-theistic agents deflected historically by the secular division between private faith and secular public argument. Indeed, as we shall soon see more closely, secularism as an authoritative model of public life is predicated upon a two-fold strategy of containment: in order to secure the public realm as it construes it, it is almost as important to quarantine certain nontheistic patterns of thinking and technique as it is to monitor ecclesiastical intrusions into public life.

Consider, then, how Nietzsche makes contact with Christian practices of training and thinking. In *The AntiChrist*, he distinguishes between Christian doctrines of Original Sin, Free Will, Heaven, and damnation, which he attributes to Paul, and pre-Pauline practices of character formation, which he attributes to Jesus. He finds the latter infinitely preferable to the former:

> It is false to the point of absurdity to see in a "belief," perchance the belief in redemption through Christ, the distinguishing characteristic of the Christian: only Christian *practice*, a life such as he who died on the Cross *lived*, is Christian. . . . Not a belief but a doing, above all, a not doing of many things, a different *being*. . . . States of consciousness, beliefs of any kind, holding something to be true, for example—every psychologist knows this—are a matter of complete indifference and of fifth rank compared to the value of the instincts. . . . "Faith" has been at all times, with Luther for instance, only a cloak, a pretext, a *screen*, behind which the instincts played their game—a shrewd blindness to the dominance of *certain* instincts. . . .⁹

If you attend to what Nietzsche says elsewhere about the relations between culture, instinct, thinking, and language, it becomes apparent that instinct is more than a brutish, biologically fixed force. Instincts are proto-thoughts situated in culturally formed moods, affects, and situations. They are not even entirely reducible to implicit thoughts or tacit judgments. For the latter imply thoughts and judgments like those in explicit discourse that have not been raised to its level. In such a view, a dialectical logic of rendering explicit what was implicit would be sufficient to the case, fitting the new entry into an emergent, coherent whole. But for Nietzsche, thinking bounces in magical bumps and charges across several registers of thought. Proto-thoughts undergo significant modification and refinement when bumped into a complex linguistic network of contrasts. Moreover, these visceral modes of appraisal are often very intense, carrying considerable energy and fervency with them into the other registers of being. This "invisible" set of intensive appraisals forms (as I will call it) an infrasensible subtext from which conscious thoughts, feelings, and discursive judgments draw part of their sustenance. Moreover, instincts that are culturally formed can sometimes be modified by cultural strategies applied by groups to themselves and by the individual to itself by arts of the self. Hence, Nietzsche's durable interest in polytheistic and monotheistic rituals and festivals, and the "misuses" to which Christianity has subjected them.

So Nietzsche says things like, "our true experiences are not garrulous" and "even one's thoughts one cannot reduce entirely to words" and "our invisible moral qualities follow their own course—probably a wholly different course; and they might give pleasure to a god with a divine microscope." He says these things because instincts are thought-imbued intensities moving below language, consciousness, and reflective judgment as well as within them.[10]

What Nietzsche shares with the medieval Christian perspective explored by Asad is the idea that thinking and intersubjectivity operate on more than one register and that to work on the instinctive register of intersubjective judgment can also be to introduce new possibilities of thinking and being into life. What the medieval and Nietzschean orientations have in common is an appreciation of the significant role the visceral register of intersubjectivity plays in moral and political life and a desire to do some of their ethical work on that register. Where they may differ is in the goals they set for such work, though it is not at all clear that such differences can be read off simply by knowing whether a thinker is a theist or a nontheist. Bertrand Russell and Nietzsche were both atheists, but they diverged significantly in their orientations to ethics and the registers of being they acknowledged.

When Nietzsche, again, speaks of "thoughts behind your thoughts and thoughts behind those thoughts" he is speaking of "concealed gardens and plantings" below the threshold of reflective surveillance.[11] Now, ecclesiastical practices of ritual are translated by Nietzsche and Foucault into experimental arts of the self and by Deleuze into an experimental micropolitics of intersubjectivity. Each tries to shift ethical practices which impinge on the visceral register from their uses, say, in the Augustinian confessional or in state practices of discipline, but each also strives to make investments in this domain that exceed the scope of secular self-representations. Such strategies are experimental because they work on thought-imbued intensities behind conscious

thoughts not themselves subject to conscious purview; they are important to thinking and theory because such work can sometimes untie
knots in one's thinking; they are important to politics because such
work can pave the way for new movement in the politics of becoming;
and they are pertinent to the ethos of a pluralist culture because such
work can help to install generosity and forbearance into ethical sensibilities in a world of multidimensional pluralism. To change an intersubjective ethos significantly is also to modify the instinctive
subjectivities and intersubjectivities in which it is set. But this may
sound like mumbo-jumbo to many secularists.

The recent work by Joseph LeDoux, a neurophysiologist who maps
complex intersections between the several human brains involved in
the thought-imbued emotional life of human beings, may be pertinent
here. His study not only confounds behaviorist and computer models
of thinking, it may also expose insufficiencies in linguistic models of
thought and discourse. Let us focus on the relation between the amygdala, a small almond-shaped brain located at the base of the cortex, and
the prefrontal cortex, the large brain developed more extensively in
humans than in other animals. The amygdala and the prefrontal cortex can receive messages from the same sources, but each registers them
in different ways. When receiving a sign it has stored as an indication
of danger, the amygdala reacts quickly, relatively crudely, and with
intense energy. Exposure to signs that resemble a past trauma, panic,
or disturbance "pass like greased lightning over the potentiated path-
ways to the amygdala, unleashing the fear reaction."[12] The prefrontal
cortex receives its version of the danger message more slowly, process-
ing it through a sophisticated linguistic network in a more refined way
and forming a more complex judgment. In a situation of stress, the
amygdala also transmits its interpretation and much of its intensity to
the prefontal cortex; and

> the amygdala has a greater influence on the cortex than the cor-
> tex has on the amygdala, allowing emotional arousal to dominate
> and control thinking.... Although thoughts can easily trigger emo-
> tions (by activating the amygdala), we are not very effective at
> willfully turning off emotions (by deactivating the amygdala).[13]

The amygdala is a site of thought-imbued intensities that do not in themselves take the form either of conscious feelings or representations. The amygdala is, then, literally one of the "concealed gardens and plantings" of which Nietzsche speaks, implicated in a set of relays with other more open gardens. LeDoux suggests that it is for the most part a good thing the amygdala is wired to the cortex. For it imparts energy and intensity to that center needed for the latter's formation of representations and practical decisions. And, we may suggest, those gaps and dissonances between it and the cortex, and between it and the hippocampus (the site of complex memories), create some of the frictions from which creativity in thinking and judgment arises. How, though, can the amygdala be educated? It is under variable degrees of control by the cortex, depending on the context. But, also, since its specific organization is shaped to an uncertain degree by previous intensities of cultural experience and performance, either it or, more likely, the network of relays in which it is set may be susceptible to modest influence by rituals and intersubjective arts thematized by religions of the Book and Nietzscheans respectively.

So, if the first quandary of secularism is bound up with uncertainties in the line of demarcation it pursues between private and public life, the second is that its forgetting or depreciation of an entire register of thought-imbued intensities in which it is set requires it to misrecognize itself and encourages it to advance dismissive interpretations of any culture or ethical practice that engages the visceral register of being actively. The secular understanding of symbol and ritual reviewed by Asad provides one index of this combination. A whole litany of dismissive misinterpretations of Nietzschean and Foucauldian arts of the self provides a second.[14]

THE SECULAR PUBLIC SPHERE

We now need to draw this preliminary engagement with secular accounts of thinking and discourse into coordination with a conception of public space that has become hegemonic within Euro-American secularism. For to engage its presentation of public life is to go some way toward explaining how the plurality of secular self-interpretations we noted earlier becomes organized into a hierarchy. And it helps to set the table for another conception of public life that more actively appreciates the visceral register, that engages the role of micropolitics, and that embraces a more expansive and generous model of public discourses. Let's begin with Kant. Kant struggled to give "universal philosophy" primacy over ecclesiastical (Christian) theology in a way that has become authoritative for secularism. And his passage from an account of the proper organization of the university to the proper organization of public discourse is also exemplary.[15] Card-carrying secularists are typically university academics as well as citizens of a state. And they often seek the same degree of authority in each domain. Most pertinently, the way in which they imagine the contour of one institution regularly infiltrates into the mode of governance they project into the other.

In *The Conflict of the Faculties*, Kant's immediate objective is to curtail the authority of the faculty of ecclesiastical theology within the German university and the larger political culture.[16] His concern is that since (Christian) ecclesiastical theology is governed by texts and practices located in the medium of history and sensibility, the claim by each ecclesiastical "sect" to moral supremacy is likely to meet with an equal and opposite claim by others. The object is to cleanse the university and public life of the adverse effects of sectarianism. This is to be accomplished by elevating universal philosophy, also known as "rational religion," to the authoritative position previously reserved for Christian theology. For

> a division into sects can never occur in matters of pure religious belief. Wherever sectarianism is to be found, it arises from a mistake on the part of ecclesiastical faith: the mistake of regarding its statutes (even if they are divine revelations) for essential parts of religion.... But since, in contingent doctrines, there can be all sort of conflicting articles or interpretations . . . , we can readily see that mere dogma will be a prolific source of innumerable sects in matters of faith unless it is rectified by pure religious faith.[17]

Kantian philosophy is then wheeled out to fill the place of ecclesiastical authority just vacated by his simulation. But, as we now know from repeated experience after Kant, the claim of an upstart to occupy the authoritative place of a teetering authority succeeds best if the upstart plays up the arbitrariness and divisiveness of the resources its predecessor drew upon while sanctifying and purifying the source from which it draws. Kant imagines himself to be up to the task. He elevates a generic Christianity called "rational religion" above sectarian faith, anchoring the former in a metaphysic of the supersensible that, so the story goes, is necessarily presupposed by any agent of morality. In the process, he degrades ritual and arts of the self without eliminating them altogether. For these arts work on the lower sensibility rather than drawing moral obligation from the supersensible realm as practical reason does. The point is to deploy them just enough to render crude sensibilities better equipped to accept the moral law derived from practical reason. Secularists later carry this Kantian project of degradation a step or two further.

To secure the authority of philosophy over theology Kant then reduces sound thinking to reason alone; for reason enables thought to achieve its true rigor uncontaminated by the visceral and variable effects of the sensible. The program of anointing one discipline by degrading the other is pursued in the following formulation:

> For unless the supersensible (the thought of which is essential to anything called religion) is anchored to determinate concepts of reason, such as those of morality, fantasy inevitably gets lost in the transcendent, where religious matters are concerned, and leads to an illuminism in which everyone has his own private, inner revelations, and there is no longer any public touchstone of truth.[18]

Kant anchors rational religion in the law of morality rather than anchoring morality in ecclesiastical faith. That is, he retains the command model of morality from Augustinian Christianity, but shifts the proximate point of command from the Christian God to the moral subject itself. This, with significant variations, becomes a key move in later secular models of public life. But it also engenders a legacy of uncertainty and instability that still haunts the secular problematic. For authoritative moral philosophy and/or rational religion are now only as secure as the source of morality upon which they draw. And morality as law now itself becomes anchored only in the "apodictic" recognition by ordinary human beings of its binding authority. To tie this knot of recognition tightly Kant must continue his attack on the relative difficulties ecclesiastical theology faces in anchoring morality directly in the commands of God:

> Now a code of God's *statutory* (and so revealed) will, not derived from human reason but harmonizing perfectly with morally prac-tical reason toward the final end—in other words the Bible—would be the most effective organ for guiding men and citizens to their temporary and eternal well being, if only it could be accred-ited as the word of God and its authenticity could be proved by documents. But there are many difficulties in the way of validat-ing it. . . . For if God would really speak to man, man could still never *know* it was God speaking. . . . But in some cases man can be sure that the voice he hears is *not* God's; for if the voice com-mands him to do something contrary to the moral law, then no matter how majestic the apparition may be . . . , he must consider it an illusion. . . . And . . . we must regard the credentials of the Bible as drawn from the pure spring of universal rational religion dwelling in every ordinary man; and it is this very simplicity that accounts for the Bible's extremely widespread and powerful influ-ence on the hearts of the people.[19]

While it is a significant move to give morality priority over ecclesiology, Kant's rational religion shares much structurally with the "dogmatic" ecclesiology it seeks to displace. First, it places singular conceptions of rea-son and command morality above question. Second, it sets up (Kantian) philosophy as the highest potential authority in adjudicating questions in these two domains and in guiding the people toward eventual enlighten-ment. Third, it defines the most dangerous danger to public morality as sectarianism within Christianity. Fourth, in the process of defrocking ecclesiastical theology and crowning philosophy as judge in the last instance, it also delegitimizes a place for several non-Kantian, nontheis-tic perspectives in public life. Thus, as Kantian philosophy is elevated to public preeminence, the pre-Kantian philosophies of Epicureanism, Spin-ozism, and Humeanism are devalued because of the priority they give to sensible life and the ethics of cultivation respectively over the supersensible and a morality of command. Moreover, a series of post-Kantian philoso-phies such as Nietzscheanism, Bergsonism, Foucauldianism, and

Deleuzianism are depreciated in advance on similar grounds. For denigration of these latter perspectives sets a crucial condition of possibility for authoritative regulation of religious sects in public life by universal philosophy.

Neo-Kantian simulations of secularism, then, consist of a series of attempts to secure these four effects without open recourse to the Kantian metaphysic of the supersensible. Secularism, in its dominant Western forms, is this Kantian fourfold-without-metaphysical portfolio. The slogans "political not metaphysical," "postmetaphysical," "beyond metaphysics," and even "pragmatic" often provide signals of this attempt, although they occasionally set the stage for attempts to refigure secularism. My sense is, as I will argue later, that the latter attempts to be postmetaphysical complement secularism by depreciating the secular register of intersubjectivity pursuing too much purity in politics. At any rate, the third quandary of contemporary secularism is that its advocates often disavow dependence upon a metaphysic of the supersensible to fend off sectarian religious struggles in the public realm while they then invoke authoritative conceptions of thinking, reason, and discourse against non-Kantian, postsecular orientations that themselves have depended historically on the Kantian metaphysic of the supersensible. Secularism thereby opens itself to critical forays by religious representatives into its own underpinnings. It functions most effectively politically when its criticisms of Christian theology are insulated from its corollary disparagements of nontheistic, non-Kantian philosophies.

The Kantian achievement, however, is cast from fragile crystal. For what if one contends, as Gilles Deleuze does, that the recognition by ordinary people upon which Kantian morality is now grounded in the first instance is actually a secondary formation reflecting the predominant Christian culture in which it is set, rather than the apodictic source Kant represents it to be? Now the same objections Kant brought against the arbitrary authority of ecclesiology haunt the critic. And this difficulty returns to haunt every attempt to secure secular authority in the public realm after Kant—even in the case of secularists who eschew reference to the Kantian supersensible. The return of Kantian charges to haunt the philosophy that issued them against others leads one to wonder whether every attempt to occupy such an authoritative place re-enacts the plot of Greek tragedy in which each party promising to resolve an obdurate conflict in the same old way soon finds itself succumbing to it.

Kant introduces defining elements into the logic of secularism. But he himself does not construct a complete philosophy of secularism. His obsequious deference to the Prince, his explicit dependence on the supersensible, his hope that a natural teleology of public life will promote rationality in the public sphere by automatic means, and his hesitancy to include most subjects within the realm of public discourse render him a forerunner rather than a partisan of secularism.[20] Nonetheless, most contemporary secularists attempt to secure the Kantian effect by Kantian and/or non-Kantian means. This implicates them, though to varying degrees, in a cluster of protectionist strategies against: (a) the intrusion of ecclesiastical theology into public life, (b) the academic and public legitimacy of nontheistic, non-Kantian philosophies, (c) the exploration of visceral registers of thinking and intersubjectivity, (d) the admiration of creativity in thinking, (e) the related appreciation of the politics of becoming by which the new comes into being from below the operative register of justice and representational discourse, and (f) productive involvement for ethical reasons with experimental practices of micropolitics and self-artistry. These intercoded interventions are pursued in the name of protecting the authority of deliberative argument in the secular public sphere, that is, of securing the Kantian effect.

Let's look at how one effort to secure the Kantian effect by non-Kantian means unfolds in the early work of Jürgen Habermas, when he is tracing the emergence and decline of "the public sphere" in modern Western societies. In *The Structural Transformation of the Public Sphere*, Habermas draws sustenance from Kant without endorsing the metaphysic of the supersensible. According to Habermas, a small, vibrant public sphere shone brilliantly for a brief time in eighteenth-century Europe. Here salons, coffee houses, and weekly periodicals coalesced to foster a public that received ideas disinterestedly and debated them in a way that allowed "the authority of the better argument" to prevail. Early theorists who catalogued this sphere, including Kant, eternalized the historically contingent conditions that rendered it possible. But this historical practice of publicity, critical reason, and pursuit of a free public consensus set a model for public life transcending its immediate place of approximation. Unlike most secularists, the early Habermas finds this moment to be short-lived. One element in his account of its fall from grace, however, may express a more pervasive proclivity in secular conceptions of public discourse.

By the middle of the twentieth century, according to Habermas, under pressure from an expanding welfare state, the sophisticated capacities of corporate and political manipulation, and so on, the authentic public sphere gave way to a false copy. Consider some summary formulations from Habermas to capture the character of this decline:

> Put bluntly, you had to pay for books, theater, concert, and museum, but not for the conversation about what you had read, heard, and seen and what you might completely absorb only through this conversation. Today the conversation itself is administered. Professional dialogues from the podium, panel discussions and round table shows—the rational debate of private people becomes one of the production numbers of stars . . . ; it assumes commodity form even at "conferences" where anyone can "participate."[21]

> The sounding board of an educated stratum tutored in the public use of reason has been shattered; the public is split apart into minorities of specialists who put their reason to use nonpublicly and the great mass of consumers whose receptiveness is public but uncritical. Consequently it completely lacks the form of communication specific to a public.[22]

> The consensus developed in rational political public debate has yielded to compromise fought out or simply imposed nonpublicly.[23]

> A process of public communication evolving in the medium of the parties . . . obviously stands in an inverse relation to the staged and manipulative effectiveness of a publicity aimed at rendering the broad population . . . infectiously ready for acclamation.[24]

> The collapse of ideology ... seems to be only one side of the
> process.... The other side is that ideology ... fulfills, on a deeper
> level of consciousness, its old function.... This false consciousness
> no longer consists of an internally harmonized nexus of ideas ...,
> but of a nexus of modes of behavior.[25]

I do not object, of course, to exploration of how the contours of public
discourse shift with changes in their technological and economic context. Nor to how structural binds created by the expansion of capitalism
squeeze the space in which public discourse appears. But the early
Habermas—for his position, as we shall see, changes later—inflects the
account of this history in a particular direction. Interpreted through the
perspective advanced here, the early Habermasian formulations first
extract a desiccated model of discourse from early modern salon conversations and then re-present the elements purged from those representations as potent modes of destructive effectivity concentrated in the
present. On the line of elevated extractions you find rational argument,
true publicity, public opinion, collective consensus, and political action;
on the remaindered line of correspondences you find management,
manipulative effectiveness, staging, interest compromise, unstable settlement, behavior, and infectious acclamation. Indeed, the early Habermasian projection of a past and future model of public life in which the
visceral element is contained depends upon playing up the negative
potency of that very element in the present. For if the visceral element
were treated as both inappropriate and ineffective the most powerful
impediments to actualization of the model of rational public consensus
would disappear too. It would become more difficult to explain why the
present is so degraded. The postulated potency of this dimension, then,
might tempt you to think that a reworked version of it should be folded
into the ideal of discourse itself. But if the degraded element were
reworked and incorporated into the model, the Habermasian imagination of sufficient and authoritative argument would be jeopardized. The
early Habermasian contempt for existing public opinion is determined
in part, then, by his infectious insistence upon an authoritative model of
discourse from which the visceral element is subtracted. The sufficiency
of the secular model itself fades once the element it can neither eliminate
nor manage is folded back into it.

How might emendation of the secular be pursued? Such an attempt seems to require a series of revisions in secular simulations of public argumentation. In place of the Habermasian ideal of a consensus between rational agents who rise above their interests and sensibilities you might substitute that of ethically sensitive, negotiated settlements between chastened partisans who proceed from contending and overlapping presumptions while jointly coming to appreciate the unlikelihood of reaching rational agreement on several basic issues; in place of a reduction of public discourse to pure argument you might appreciate positive possibilities in the visceral register of thinking and discourse too, exploring how this dimension of subjectivity and intersubjectivity is indispensable to creativity in thinking, to the introduction of new identities onto the cultural register of legitimacy, and to the possibility of contingent settlements in public life; in response to the quest for rational purity in moral motivation, judgment, and authority you might explore an ethic of cultivation in which a variety of constituencies work on themselves to attenuate that amygdalic panic that often arises when you encounter gender, sensual, or religious identities that call the naturalness, rationality, or sanctity of your own identities into question, and in which each constituency works to cultivate generosity and critical responsiveness in its negotiations with alter identities that help it to be what is; and in response to the secular demand to leave controversial religious and metaphysical judgments at home so as to hone a single public practice of reason or justice, you might pursue a generous ethos of engagement between a plurality of constituencies inhabiting the same territory and honoring different moral sources. And so on.[26]

I sense that amygdalic pressures working on secularists may push some to ignore the next point: but nothing in the above carries the implication of eliminating argument, rationality, language, or conscious thought from public discourse. It merely insists that these media are always accompanied and informed to variable degrees by visceral modes of thinking, prejudgment, and sensibility not eliminable *as such* from private or public life. To participate in a multi-track model of subjectivity and intersubjective discourse, then, is to work on each of these fronts in relation to the others, seeking to infuse an ethos of care for the plurovocity of being into partisan modes of thinking, discourse, and judgment. It is not even, as I will address shortly, that everyone would have to endorse this practice of care (for care can come from multiple sources) to participate in the pluralized public life endorsed here. It is however, that most would come to appreciate the profound element of contestability in the practice they do endorse. And they would incorporate that recognition positively into the way they engage other visions of public discourse in actual public life. That cardinal virtue is yet to be folded into most models of secular discourse with which I am familiar. Indeed, the Kantian inspiration of much of modern secularism, in its ambition to enable (Kantian) philosophy to wrest public moral authority from ecclesiastical theology, militates against it. Neither Kantian philosophy, nor the secularism that follows it, is alone responsible for this effect. It also involves pressure from ecclesiastical forces upon secular practices. But once it is understood that secularism is a political settlement rather than an uncontestable dictate of public discourse itself, the possibility of reworking that settlement under new conditions of being takes on new significance.

PLURALIZING THE SECULAR

By the mid-1980s, the Habermasian version of secularism had become chastened and moved closer to the Rawlsian model. While Rawls now seeks to ground secular justice at least partly in an overlapping cultural consensus without invoking "controversial" religious and metaphysical conceptions, Habermas has moved more actively to a postmetaphysical stance. One can understand the pressures pushing each in that direction. While each had expected the fervor of religious controversies to abate as the years rolled by, they have, in fact, intensified. By eschewing reference to controversial metaphysical assumptions in their own forays into public life, secularists hope to discourage a variety of enthusiastic Christians from doing so in their turn. Sometimes, indeed, such a stance folds the admirable virtue of forbearance into public debate. But the cost of elevating this disposition to restraint into the cardinal virtue of metaphysical denial is also high. First, such a stance makes it difficult for its partisans to engage a number of issues of the day, such as varieties of sexual orientations, the construction of gender, the moral dimensions of doctor-assisted death, the ethics of abortion, and the extent to which a uniform set of public virtues is needed. Academic secularists are almost the only partisans today who consistently purport to leave their religious and metaphysical baggage at home. So, the claim to be post-metaphysical opens you to charges of hypocrisy or false consciousness: "you secularists quietly bring a lot of metaphysical baggage into public discourse even as you tell the rest of us to leave ours in the closet." Finally, metaphysical abstinence increases the pressure on secularists to pretend that actually operative reason, in one form or another, is suffi-cient to the issues at hand, even in the face of their own insights into how cultural specificities, contingent elements, and artificial closures help to set the actual conditions for actual practices of discourse and judgment. Habermas, for instance, after eschewing the transcendental status of the Kantian supersensible, first underlines uncertainties and contingencies that rejection implies for his perspective and then tries to recapture the Archimedean point he has just let go:

> Transcendental thinking once concerned itself with a stable stock of forms for which there were no recognizable alternatives. Today, in contrast, the experience of contingency is a whirlpool into which everything is pulled: everything could also be otherwise, the categories of the understanding, the principles of socialization and morals, the constitution of subjectivity, the foundation of rationality itself. There are good reasons for this. Communicative reason, too, treats almost everything as contingent, even the con-ditions for the emergence of its own linguistic medium. But for everything that claims validity *within* linguistically structured forms of life, the structures of possible mutual understanding in language constitute something that cannot be gotten around.[27]

Habermas now acknowledges more actively the role of sensibility in reflection and the role of contingency in the formation of sensibility. But he still tries to preserve the Kantian effect by non-Kantian means, substituting the presumption of rational decidability built into the logic of linguistic performance for the necessary presupposition of the supersensible. But, it is now fair enough to ask, Why is that condition of discourse the only one treated as if it "cannot be gotten around"? What about visceral and contingent elements within thinking and discourse? Can they be gotten around? Or that problematic relation between the unthought (which only a contestable metaphysical assumption could assure you is already preshaped like thought) and its translation into thought? If you were to say that all three of these characteristics form constitutive conditions of thinking and discourse, and if you then acknowledged, as Habermas now does, the ideal of rational agreement to be a counterfactual never actually realized in practice, you would already have the makings of a more robust, ambiguous, multivalent model of discourse. Its ambiguity would reside in the need to push on one dimension of discourse (say, hidden contingencies folded into an operative presumption of universality) just after you had played out another (say, the presumption of possible accord). Now a New Habermas could say: "It is impossible to participate in discourse without projecting the counterfactual possibility of consensus; but, since each attempt to interpret the actual import of that counterfactuality in any concrete setting is also problematical and contestable, this stricture does not rule out in advance religious or nontheistic metaphysical perspectives that exceed the terms of the postmetaphysical alternative that my younger self endorsed as necessary."

What, then, is the thought behind the thought that drives the actually existing Habermas to give singular primacy to one dimension of discourse over all others? Perhaps, at a visceral level, it is reiteration of the Kantian/Christian demand to occupy the authoritative place previously reserved for ecclesiastical theology. The imperative to occupy that place of authority may be bolstered by another preliminary drive, that is, the political sense that a non-Kantian, religiously pluralized world would fall either into disorder or religious tyranny if its participants did not endorse a single standard of rational authority, regardless of the extent to which such a standard can, in fact, be secured transcendentally.

In an age of globalization and the accentuation of speed in so many domains of life, a cultural pluralism appropriate to the times is unlikely to be housed in an austere postmetaphysical partisanship that purports to place itself above the fray. The need today, rather, is to rewrite secularism to pursue an ethos of engagement in public life between a plurality of controversial metaphysical perspectives, including, for starters, Christian, other monotheistic perspectives, secular thought, and refashioned secular perspectives. A new modus vivendi is needed to replace the Kantian achievement in which a few fundamental differences *within* Christianity were relegated to the private realm in the name of a generic rational religion or a generic reason. Here pluralism would not be grounded in one austere moral source adopted by everyone (say, a universal conception of rational religion, or discourse, or persons, or justice). It would be grounded in an ethos of engagement between multiple constituencies honoring a variety of moral sources and metaphysical orientations. Such an ethos between interdependent partisans provides an existential basis for democratic politics if and when many partisans affirm without deep resentment the contestable character of the fundamental faith they honor most. Such a general affirmation amidst variety in faith and belief enables mutual forbearance in public debate and the assembly of majority alliances across several lines of difference. On this rendering, then, political judgment of the types of sensibility it takes to foster action in concert in a world of metaphysical plurality precedes and informs development of an ethos of engagement. There are significant currents already operative in contemporary life that point toward the possible consolidation of such an ethos, even as intense constituencies mobilize against that very possibility.

Let us simulate modifications in the secular model of discourse. We draw Kantian philosophy, Habermasian thought, post-Nietzschean thought, and one form of Christian theology into engagement during a time in which Habermas circumscribes such engagements and Rawls doubts their desirability. We proceed, of course, in a partisan way, while simultaneously seeking to open up the terms of conversation with others.

In a recent essay entitled "Postmetaphysical Thinking," Habermas identifies metaphysics with the attempt to "secure the precedence of identity over difference and that of ideas over matter."[28] Such a definition places Plato under the rubric of metaphysics, as it does Christian philosophers such as Augustine, Aquinas, Kant, and Hegel. But what does it say about diverse non-Platonic and non-Christian perspectives in the history of the West represented by such names as Epicurus, Lucretius, Spinoza, Hume, Nietzsche, Bergson, Freud, Levinas, Butler, and Deleuze? Are they metaphysical or postmetaphysical? Each conveys a set of fundamentals that differ from the set christened as metaphysical by Habermas, yet none, in the most obvious sense of these phrases, gives precedence to "identity over difference and . . . ideas over matter." Once you encounter these perspectives, and also keep in mind how each fundamental reading of the world is bound up with particular orientations to ethics, identity, and politics, the Habermasian constitution of metaphysics begins to feel provincial. And the pretense to be postmetaphysical now gives off a hollow sound.

Consider a Deleuzian metaphysic. It invokes a non-Kantian transcendental field of (as I call it) the infrasensible. The infrasensible, like the supersensible it tracks and challenges, does not exist in the world of appearance. As a virtual field made up of elements too small to be perceptible and/or too fast to be actual, it insists below and within culturally organized registers of sensibility, appearance, discourse, justice, and identity. The amygdala, for instance, subsists on this register, projecting effects into the world of conscious thinking, feeling, and judgment. Thinking, for Deleuze (and Epicurus, Spinoza, Bergson, Freud, and Nietzsche too), operates on more than one level; it moves on the level of the virtual (which is real in its effectivity but not actual in its availability) and that of the actual (which is available to representation, but not self-sufficient). Infrasensible energies of proto-thinking, for instance, provide a reservoir from which surprise sometimes unsettles fixed explanations, new pressures periodically swell up to disrupt existing practices of rationality, and new drives to identity occasionally surge up to modify the register of justice and legitimacy upon which established identities are placed. Again, this is so because the swarm of intensities emanating from the infrasensible are too multiple, finely meshed, and fast to be captured entirely in the coarse nets of explicit identity, conscious representation, and public appearance.

How does Habermas relate to such a perspective? Unlike most Rawlsians he does take note of its type. But he then delegitimizes it through his typification of it. He subsumes it under the labels "irrationalism" and "negative metaphysics." Here Habermas recapitulates

Kant beautifully, binding one attempt to defang Christian ecclesiastical metaphysics to another to push nontheistic/a-Kantian metaphysical orientations below the field of intellectual eligibility.

How does Habermas make this move? First, he equates such an orientation with a loss of bearings essential to political and ethical life. It is received as inherently pessimistic and despairing, even though its partisans seldom present it in that light.[29] Second, he projects onto it a claim to secure the certainty of its own stance that is operative in other metaphysical doctrines and in the Habermasian perspective. Thus, "Every comprehensive, closed, and final system of statements must be formulated in a language that requires no commentary and allows of no interpretations, improvements, or innovations that might be placed at a distance."[30]

Habermas, then, is "postmetaphysical" in that he places none of his basic assumptions—except one—above the possibility of modification or reconfiguration. But Deleuze and Nietzsche, whom I call metaphysical, take this perspective a step further. As I read them, they first treat their basic presumptions to be contestable suppositions and then strive to interpret and act through them. For, first, these fundamentals are anti-systematic. They carry within them the expectation that no theoretical system will ever be complete, that every explanation will periodically meet with surprise, that each identity is to a considerable extent an entrenched, contingent formation situated at the tense nexus between the self-identification of its participants and modes of recognition institutionally bestowed upon it, that a formation typically contains internal resistances or remainders, and that it might become otherwise if some of these balances shift. Second, the Deleuzian metaphysic reconfigures the standing of the Kantian transcendental field until his non-lawful transcendental is itself presented as a contestable interpretation. It is transcendental in residing above or below appearance, but not in being unquestionable or in providing a command morality. This, then, is metaphysics without the claim to certainty, a combination that eludes the Habermasian division between metaphysics and postmetaphysical thought.

Put this way, a couple of potential points of contact now emerge between these two different perspectives. Habermas plays up elements of contingency and uncertainty in a doctrine that transcendentalizes the linguistic presupposition of a possible consensus. And Deleuze acknowledges the need for rules and norms for discourse to proceed while thinking that surprising changes might unfold in rules now presumed by Habermas to be fixed. Yet, this line of potential communication across significant difference—a line enlarging the field of discourse rather than curtailing it—cannot be pursued until the definitive barrier Habermas poses to it has been addressed. For, at precisely this point of possible connection between two opposing perspectives Habermas pulls out the hangman's noose of critical philosophy and lowers it around the neck of the Deleuzian: "all such attempts to detranscendentalize reason continue to get entangled in the prior conceptual decisions of transcendental philosophy, decisions in which they remain trapped."[31] "Negative metaphysics" has now been rendered null and void.

But is the noose tied that tightly? Most of those on the block already acknowledge how often they become entangled in the coils of paradox. Deleuze, for instance, insists upon it. But he also reads the anxious imperative to avoid paradox at all costs as a sign that the philosopher in question still treats Kantian models of recognition, common sense, and the upright character of thought as if they were apodictic. For only if they were apodictic would the encounter with self-referential contradictions and paradoxes necessarily show thinking to have gone awry. Does the Habermasian noose, then, muffle those who call into question the upright character of thought? For Deleuze, the encounter with paradox is sometimes a sign of the limit of thought and an indication of a reservoir of fugitive elements below and within thinking that might inspire creativity in thinking itself. This is the Deleuzian "field of immanence" upon which thinking is located but which is not itself exhausted by a logic of thought. Deleuze, like Nietzsche, seeks to alter the mood or sensibility within which the encounter with paradox occurs. He welcomes the encounter in a way that both recalls one side of Kant and confounds the Habermasian attempt to secure the Kantian effect.

> Philosophy is revealed not by good sense but by paradox. Paradox is the pathos or the passion of philosophy. There are several kinds . . . , all of which are opposed to . . . good sense and common sense. Subjectively, paradox breaks up the common exercise

of the faculties and places each before its own limit. . . . At the same time, however, paradox communicates to the broken faculties . . . , aligning them along a volcanic line which allows one to ignite the other, leaping from one limit to the next. Objectively, paradox displays the element that cannot be totalized within a common element, along with the difference that cannot be equalized or cancelled at the direction of good sense. It is correct to say that the only refutation of paradoxes lies in good sense and common sense themselves, but on condition that they are already allowed everything: the role of judge as well as that of party to the case. . . .[32]

Once these different responses to the occasion of paradox become clear, Habermas can criticize and resist a Deleuzian metaphysic, but he may not be able to produce a postmetaphysical rationale to rule it definitively out of public discourse. If that is so, it now seems imperative, on Habermasian terms, to enter into dialogue with it, to pursue a critical dialogue in which neither party insists upon being the final judge above the fray as well as party to the case. Because Deleuze requires rules of discourse to proceed and Habermas increasingly acknowledges contingent elements in the conditions of discourse, a new avenue of communication opens up across difference. Each party, certainly, may press the other to clarify itself and, perhaps, to revise itself. The Habermasian charge of performative contradiction, for instance, presses Deleuzians to clarify their orientation to paradox.[33]

We can, then, simulate discourse in one direction beyond the parameters of Habermasian permissibility. But what about public engagements between those who bring religious faith with them into public debates and those who eschew reference to a personal god or rational religion? "Communicative reason," Habermas says, is treated by "negative metaphysics" as "the colorless negative of a religion that provides consolation." But Habermasian reason neither shrieks out heroic slogans against a universe without consolation nor offers religious solace. It

neither announces the absence of consolation in a world forsaken by God nor does it take it upon itself to provide any consolation.... As long as no better words for what religion can say are found in the medium of rational discourse, it will even coexist abstemiously with the former, neither supporting it nor combatting it.[34]

This seems to announce that while communicative reason would purge public discourse of post-Nietzschean perspectives (in the name of coherence) it would practice respectful co-existence with powerful institutions of religious consolation. That is a fairly good reproduction of the Kantian effect. But surely there is a less self-effacing way to engage theistic perspectives in public life. Only a colorless demand to be postmetaphysical could stop you from exploring them.

In *Difference and Repetition*, Deleuze finds a way to engage Kantian and Kierkegaardian orientations to religious faith. There is a dramatic moment, he says, when Kant is poised between a critique of ecclesiastical theology and the defense of rational theology. In that fissure other non-theological alternatives flash by for a second, only to be forgotten through insistent Kantian presentations of recognition and common sense. To pursue one of those nontheistic paths would be to open a public dialogue with Kantian religion. But the Rawlsian and Habermasian versions of secularism refuse to walk through that door.

Let us address the Deleuzian engagement with Kierkegaard. Kierkegaard represents a phase in high Christianity after the necessity (but not the option) of Kantian rational religion has been called into question. In Kierkegaard, faith relinquishes its mooring in a Kantian postulate of reason. It then seeks to make up that deficit with an increase in intensity. "Kierkegaard and Peguy are the culmination of Kant, they realize Kant by entrusting to faith the task of overcoming the speculative death of God and healing the wound in the self." Faith unavoidably changes its character in their hands. The experience of faith now becomes ambiguous: it is "no more than a condition by default, one lost in sin which must be recovered in Christ."[35]

This means, I take it, that the divine object of devotion is treated *as if* it were once there to faith in its fullness, so that the faithful can hold themselves responsible for its loss and pursue an imagined future of its recovery. Faith now becomes ironized so that it can also be intensified. Such a movement backward and forward, the faithful disclose, makes a profound difference in your general bearing, your ethical conduct, and the rich horizon of being toward which you are opened. This is repetition with spiral effects, rather than bare repetition.[36] Kierkegaardian faith, however, repeatedly bumps into gaps or feelings of estrangement between repetitions, when traces of faithlessness intervene inadvertently and unintentionally. Perhaps such an effect is bound up with the very ground of Kierkegaardian faith, giving it its impetus to intense practices of faithfulness. Deleuze, the a-theist, pounces upon this trace of faithlessness between repetitions. I would do so too, not to purge faith from the faithful or disenfranchise expressions of faith from public life, but to open a window within theistic representations of faith for appreciation of recurrent moments of difference in faith from itself. Now, alongside the difference between two practices of representation another more volatile difference is forming, a difference that also has the potential to connect the contending parties. Each practice of faith (theistic and nontheistic) may contain an element of difference within itself from itself that tends to be blurred or obscured by the representations it makes of itself.

This difference between faith and its representation explains why two devout believers "cannot observe each other without laughing." Such laughter testifies to breaches that unavoidably occur within the house of faith.[37] For

> there is an adventure of faith according to which one is always the clown of one's own faith, the comedian of one's own ideal. . . . Eventually faith reflects upon itself and discovers by experiment that its condition can only be given to it as "recovered" and that it is not only separated from that condition but doubled in it.[38]

Deleuze deploys this ambiguity to give more room to the nonbeliever. "We have too often been invited to judge the atheist from the viewpoint of the belief or faith that we suppose still drives him . . . not to be tempted by the inverse operation—to judge the believer by the violent atheist by which he is inhabited, the Antichrist eternally given 'once and for all' within grace."[39] But we can add, now a space also emerges to inform the dialogue between some representatives of theistic faith and some representatives of nontheistic gratitude for life. For if the true believer is a simulacrum of himself, in what relation does the nonbeliever stand to herself? Does the nonbeliever who, say, affirms a Deleuzian nontheistic transcendental, often inadvertently project life forward as if it might perpetuate itself eternally? Epicurus, at least, thought so. This pre-Christian spiritualist who treated the gods as if they were unconcerned with human life, counseled his followers to resist that recurrent moment when life projects its continuation after death so that they might overcome existential resentment against the contingency of life. Epicurus thus testifies to a visceral tendency to project life after death even before the advent of the Christian Heaven. Do such projectionist tendencies reveal that we who represent ourselves as nontheistic are comedians of ourselves too, harboring truant moments of forgetful faith that belie the steadfastness we present to Christians and other monotheists whenever they press hard upon us? We, too, may exist in a condition that can "only be given . . . as 'recovered' and it is not only separated from the condition but doubled in it." Is it possible, then, for believers and nonbelievers from a variety of faiths to double over in laughter together on occasion across the space of difference? On principle? Doing so partly because each party harbors in itself an ineliminable element of difference from itself?[40] And partly because the dominant self-representation of each party contains within it an element of faith that is likely to remain contestable?

Yes, those differences within that support connections between tempt many to close off discourse in exactly this domain. But, still, the other possibility returns, to counter such a temptation. Even if to pursue it we have to fashion reciprocal modifications in the very sensibilities in which theistic faiths and nontheistic faiths are set.[41] And even if the boundaries of secularism must be stretched to incorporate such discourses into public life.

The step to which each party gives priority does have a distinctive effect on the type of character developed, the character of the ethic supported, the sources it draws sustenance from, and the political priorities supported, though none of these can be read from bare knowledge of the official stance. Repetition, in its spiral pattern, makes an important difference to the registers of belief, identity, and self-representation even while it does not erase all difference within these appearances. My discussion of the multiple registers of intersubjectivity has already suggested this.

By placing a Deleuzian sensibility into conversations with Habermas, Kant, and Kierkegaard, we expand and pluralize secular practice. We also join Kant, Rawls, and Habermas in acknowledging the connection between models of academic discourse and conceptions of public life. We simply pursue that connection differently, stretching the parameters of secular discourse in a couple of directions without claiming the right to be final judge of each dispute as well as fervent party to the case.

NOTES

1. An excellent version of this story is told by Albert Hirschman in *The Passions and the Interests: Political Arguments for Capitalism before Its Triumph* (Princeton: Princeton University Press, 1977).

2. For an engaging version of this story, see Hans Blumenberg, *The Legitimacy of the Modern Age*, trans. Robert Wallace (Cambridge, MA: MIT Press, 1983). This is an indispensable element in any story I would endorse. One of its effects is to call into question those stories of secularism as a loss of Christian community engendered by the forces of science, capital, and secular morality alone. For movements within Christianity itself also helped to pave the way for this possibility. I pursue some of these themes in *Political Theory and Modernity* (Oxford: Blackwell, 1988) 2nd ed. with new Epilogue (Ithaca: Cornell University Press, 1993). Others will be addressed shortly.

3 Such a reading is discernible in Foucault's essay "Governmentality," in Graham Burchell, Colin Gordon, and Peter Miller, eds., *The Foucault Effect* (Chicago: University of Chicago Press, 1991), pp. 87–105. A thoughtful exploration of Foucault's work by Thomas Dumm, *Michel Foucault and the Politics of Freedom* (Thousand Oaks: Sage Press, 1996), provides several elements in that interpretation.

4. John Rawls, *Political Liberalism* (Cambridge, MA: Harvard University Press, 1993), pp. 151–52. The quotes in the previous paragraph are from page 148.

5 Editorial, *First Things* (January 1997), p. 27.

6. Alexis de Tocqueville, *Democracy in America*, 2 vols., trans. George Lawrence (New York: Harper & Row, 1969), p. 292.

7. *Ibid.*, pp. 290–91.

8 Talal Asad, *Genealogies of Religion* (Baltimore: Johns Hopkins University Press, 1993), p. 63.

9 Nietzsche, *The Antichrist*, trans. by R. J. Hollingdale (New York: Vintage Press, 1968), p. 151.

10. See *Twilight of the Idols*, trans. R. J. Hollingdale (New York: Vintage, 1968), p. 82; *The Gay Science*, trans. Walter Kaufman (New York: Vintage, 1974), p. 274, #8. Drawing inspiration from Gilles Deleuze, Brian Massumi probes "The Autonomy of Affect" in *Deleuze: A Critical Reader*, ed. Paul Patton (Oxford: Blackwell, 1996). Massumi's rich essay correlates nicely with the above quotations from Nietzsche, and it also gains support from LeDoux's work on the complex circuits connecting the multiple brains within each individual.

11. *The Gay Science*, #9.

12. Joseph LeDoux, *The Emotional Brain: The Mysterious Underpinnings of Emotional Life* (New York: Simon and Schuster, 1996), p. 258.

13. *Ibid.*, p. 303.

14. For a review of how several neo-Kantian secularists reduce "the aestheticization of ethics" to a caricature and a set of thoughtful corrections to these misrepresentations, see Jane Bennett, "How is it, then, that we still remain barbarians: Schiller, Foucault and the Aestheticization of Ethics," *Political Theory* (November 1996).

15. I concentrate here on the implications of the Kantian account of the university for the organization of public life. Kant himself pursues such implications as he proceeds. For an excellent account that focuses on the university, see Barry Hindess, "Great Expectations: Freedom and Authority in the Idea of a Modern University," in *The Oxford Literary Review* (1995), pp. 29–51.

16. An excellent account of Kant's *Conflict of the Faculties* can be found in Ian Hunter, "Conflicting Enlightenments: Kant's True Rational Religion," *Political Theory Newsletter* (December 1995), pp. 20–35. Ian Hunter gave an earlier version of this paper at Johns Hopkins in 1994, and it became clear to me then that I would need to engage this text. Hunter's essay explores Kant's ambivalence about disciplines of the sensuous self in a subtle way. He also is very clear about the role of rational religion in Kant's version of enlightenment. Finally, Hunter suggests that Thomasius offered a better model from which secularism could draw than that presented by Kant and followed by many contemporary secularists.

17. Immanuel Kant, *The Conflict of the Faculties*, trans. Mary J. Gregor (Lincoln: University of Nebraska Press, 1979), p. 89.

18. *Ibid.*, p. 81.

19. *Ibid.*, pp. 115–17, my emphasis.

20. The engagement by Jürgen Habermas with Kant's conception of public life is very insightful on these issues. While I take issue with the Habermasian conception of the public sphere in *The Structural Transformation of the Public Sphere*, trans. Thomas Burger and Frederick Lawrence (Cambridge, MA: MIT Press, 1989), this book, originally published in 1962, has several admirable traits, including an engagement with Kant that addresses thoughtfully the tension between Kant's conception of moral life and his projected teleology of progress by automatic means in public life.

21. *The Structural Transformation of the Public Sphere*, p. 164.

22. *Ibid.*, p. 175.

23. *Ibid.*, p. 179.

24. *Ibid.*, p. 210.

25. *Ibid.*, p. 215.

26. To pursue the spatial conditions of an ethos of engagement is beyond the terms of this essay. I begin such an effort in chapter 5 of *The Ethos of Pluralization* (Minneapolis: University of Minnesota, 1995) entitled "Democracy and Territoriality." That essay attends in particular to how the production of cross-national, non-statist movements beyond the parameters of any state can place states under new pressures and break the monopoly that state-identification has over citizen action. Thomas Dumm, in *Michel Foucault and the Politics of Freedom*, pursues closely and sensitively the relation between freedom and the organization of political space. See particularly chapter 2, "Freedom and Space."

27. Jürgen Habermas, *Postmetaphysical Thinking*, trans. William M. Hohengarten (Cambridge, MA: MIT Press, 1992), pp. 139–40.

28. *Ibid.*, p. 32.

29. Habermas makes this move easier for himself by tending to equate all such perspectives with the thought of Theodore Adorno. He sees pessimism built right into Adorno's "negative metaphysics," while I see much of Adorno's pessimism to flow from the awful particulars of life under Nazism in a world where even most opponents of Nazism were unable or unwilling to rise above "identitarian thinking." But that is another story. Romand Coles paves the way for it in *Rethinking Generosity: Critical Theory and the Politics of Caritas* (Ithaca: Cornell University Press, 1997).

30. Habermas, *Postmetaphysical Thinking*, p. 36.

31. *Ibid.*, p. 41.

32. Gilles Deleuze, *Difference and Repetition*, trans. Paul Patton (New York: Columbia University Press, 1994), pp. 227–28.

33. Further clarifications, responses, and challenges are possible. For example, Barbara Herrnstein Smith, in *Belief and Resistance: Dynamics of Contemporary Intellectual Controversy* (Cambridge, MA: Harvard University Press, 1997) argues that the trap of the performative contradiction is often set by subtle redefinitions of key terms by the critic, pulling discussants away from the multiple, culturally informed uses by those about to be entrapped. It is this translation below the level of critical attentiveness that does the job, if it remains unnoticed or unchallenged by others.

34. Habermas, *Postmetaphysical Thinking*, p. 145.

35. Deleuze, *Difference and Repetition*, p. 95.

36. For a discussion of the difference see Jane Bennett, "The Enchantments of Modernity: Paracelsus, Kant and Deleuze," *Cultural Values* (Winter 1997).

37. Kierkegaard: "Or there is the man who says he has faith, but now he wants to make his faith clear to himself; he wants to understand himself in faith. Now the

comedy begins again. . . . On the contrary, he has learned to know something different about faith than he believed and has learned to know that he no longer has faith, since he almost knows, as good as knows, to a high degree and exceedingly knows." *Concluding Unscientific Postscript to Philosophical Fragments*, ed. and trans. Howard Hong and Edna Hong (Princeton: Princeton University Press, 1992), p. 211.

38. Deleuze, *Difference and Repetition*, p. 95.

39. *Ibid.*, p. 96.

40. My reading, augmentation, and consequent endorsement of Deleuze on this point seems to me to parallel compelling points Judith Butler makes about Foucault on identity in *The Psychic Life of Power* (Stanford: Stanford University Press, 1997), chapter 3. She is talking about identity, and I am discussing theistic faith or its denial, but the two logics are close. "For Foucault, the symbolic produces the possibility of its own subversions, and these subversions are unanticipated effects of symbolic interpellations" (p. 98). (I address these similar issues under the headings of the visceral and the infrasensible.) According to Foucault (and me) the subject does not reside simply in the symbolic, or merely at those moments of subversion within it, though these are extremely important. The most productive and fateful sites are those points of intersection between the symbolic and tactics or disciplines not entirely reducible to the symbolic. It is at such intersections where disciplinary power operates and where arts of the self do their best work. When Althusser's cop hails a pedestrian, the interpellation is accompanied by the possibility, and sometimes the actuality, of being handcuffed or beaten with a night stick. It is partly because the latter happens often enough that it enters into your imagination when you are hailed. When a "straight" steps into a gay rights march for the first time, one part of the anxiety may involve the fear of being identified under that label and another part may be bound up with the imagination of becoming an object of violence. To participate may thus be to do some work on the visceral register of subjectivity as well as to support a cause with which you identify.

41. The prefix "theistic" in front of faith and faithlessness is significant. For I do not claim that atheism is without an element of faith. It just does not inflect that faith as theistic. That issue is discussed in my *Identity\Difference: Democratic Negotiations of Political Paradox* (Ithaca: Cornell University Press, 1991).

7

PICTURING

PLEASURE:

SOME

POEMS

BY

ELIZABETH

BISHOP

"To be confused about what is different and
what is not, is to be confused about
everything."

David Bohm,
Wholeness and the Implicate Order

"I believe it is when a way of looking
encounters those objects it should least be
able to think about that it shows its true
strength, which is never distinct from its
pathos."

T. J. Clark, quoted from
manuscript version of
"Freud's Cézanne," in *Representations*

"The nature of theory…is to undo, through
a contesting of premises and postulates,
what you thought you knew.... [It is an]
attempt to learn more about those aspects
of literature and criticism that attracted you
to it in the first place and to investigate the
premises of the modes of study in which you
have some experience."

Jonathan Culler, "Literary Theory," in
*Introduction to Modern Languages
and Literatures*

I

THIS ESSAY HAS TWO PARTS, AN ACCOUNT of my coming to
read Elizabeth Bishop and an account of her poetry. I use the genres of
map, itinerary, and anecdote to organize the first part; in the second, I
offer a reading and a move in the direction of gender theory. The way
that these parts and genres depend on each other can be taken as an
answer—a formal or procedural answer—to the question posed as this
year's conference topic: "What's left of theory?"

MAP

My title does not, on the face of it, speak to our conference question. Indeed, both the title and topics of this paper emerged in a happenstance way. "Picturing Pleasure" was my on-the-spot reply to John Guillory's plea to help him satisfy the English Institute's urgent request for early program copy. When the phone rang, I was reading Elizabeth Bishop, getting ready for next day's class. I had never taught Bishop before and was doing so now only because pressed into service by the graduate students. In order to get my bearings on a poetry I knew only casually, I had paired Bishop with Wordsworth, a poet who, for me (and it would seem for Bishop too) sets the standard for modern lyric. I defended the move by citing Bishop's ironic but revealing self-characterization as a "minor, female Wordsworth."[1]

At the time I conceived the course, I was far less interested in Bishop than in what was left of Wordsworth once you subtracted *major* and *male*, a question I had taken up in other contexts.[2] Yet all through the Bishop half of the term, I had been noticing two new sensations: first, a kind of pleasure that I didn't remember from other textual encounters, and second, a conscious resistance to *reading* the poetry, in the sense of critically reconstructing it. Both the pleasure and the reluctance to give that pleasure a knowledge form were intense when the phone rang with John Guillory on the other end. Thus, "Picturing Pleasure: Some Poems by Elizabeth Bishop."

I do not tell this story to deny either my stake in that title or its exact intentionality. In fact, my title's mode of emergence authenticates it for me, for I am still an unregenerate believer in the truth of the unconscious. I *am* unhappy, though, about the disrespect my title seems to show for the etiquettes of this conference. I refer not just to the narrowly literary, textual emphasis (that is, "Some Poems . . ."), but to what is to my own ears a very strange participle: *picturing*.

When "picturing" does not reference picture theory, W. J. T. Mitchell's term for those cultural studies that link visuality to visibility, or phenomenologies of seeing to the social and technological construction of objects of sight, it implies a pre-critical mode of encounter.[3] Thus do we indicate spontaneous reproduction of the textual object as *given*, that is, given without reference to the social processes that historically *gave* the object (and continue to deliver it, at different moments of its reception history) in some determinately organized form or as some particular play of aspects.

The one exception to this rule is a usage sometimes observed among British art historians; in that idiom, *picturing*, as a description of painterly work, shares with *representing* a constructivist emphasis and an insistence on the motivated and problem-solving nature of the construction. But whereas the latter term, *representing*, tends to invoke the realm of the social and ideological—the perceived reality principle—as its governing orientation, *picturing* leans more toward the phantasmatic plane, governed by the pleasure principle. In line with this difference, *representing* is as apt a description of critical and as it were "scientific" work as it is of the imaginative or literary, the domain of "primary" creativity. *Picturing*, however, describes *only* that realm of primary creativity—the work and implied inner workings of the artist. (Whereas one *would* say, "this account *represents* the action or argument of the poem," probably not "this account *pictures* the action or argument.") *Picturing* locates itself as easily in the realm of the mental as the social. By contrast, when the *representation* we intend to signify is exclusively inward, we must add the adjective, *mental*.

Of course, *picturing* also gains considerable resonance by its implied rejection of the term *painting*—in the disciplinary idiom, located at the high-cultural end of the spectrum, the place where we find original works of art and their "aura." The word, *picture*, calls up images that invite or emerge through a process of mechanical reproduction. The epistemic and class connotations come together most dramatically when we reflect on the way that *representing* brings to mind an act of reduction in the interest of analytic clarity and scientific truth or accuracy; *picturing*, however, implies elaboration, expansion, material addition to or proliferation of the Real. If we *were* to count *picturing* as a scientific exercise or method, it would fall under the rubric of thought experiment (something closer to a search for variables than constants). "Picture this," we say, meaning: "Given this hypothesis—this counterintuitive or empirically inconsistent or simply not yet observed state of affairs—what would follow, both *in light of* our governing logical and causal relations and *to* those relations."

So, while saying one plans to "*picture* pleasure" seems another way of saying one will not be trying to *know* it (e.g., historicize, theorize, in short, *read* it), it can also mean *knowing* attempted with the keenest awareness of the issues driving this conference. Although my title arose in the ad hoc manner I sketched above, I have come to see it as directly engaging our conference question, when both the political connotations of *left* and the idea of the remainder are in play. Having refined the corrosive operations that reveal the unfreedom mixed in with (and enabling) the liberatory effects of art, we can hone the constructive skills that allow us to give form to the pictured presences within the work of a more or differently human life. Or, whereas materialist analysis has tended to focus on the *work* that the artwork effects (its ideological functions: typically, for the artworks of modernity, resolving at an emotional and/or verbal level contradictions that cannot be resolved through more directly social or economic practices), it may now want to investigate the *pleasure* that the artwork yields (at different moments of its reception, and/or to differently positioned subjects), both so as to gain a better knowledge of the object and so as to illuminate pleasure itself, conceived as a more complex experience than the problem-solving or anxiety-reducing dividends released by the ideological functions of the artwork.

This brings me to another feature of my title, namely, the ambiguous grammatical subject and function of *picturing*. Although I will be speaking about Elizabeth Bishop's representation of pleasure and about the pleasure-seeking impulse driving Bishop's picturing poetic, it is also about *my* pleasure in picturing her poetry. I trouble to state the obvious because a picturing pleasure, on the part of a critic, would seem to rule out theory, whereas in this paper, theory in one of its most doctrinaire and potentially reductive manifestations (namely, the discourse of psychoanalysis) plays an important role. In what follows, I will try to present my "doing" of theory (and of this *particular* theory) as something other than a denial of the legitimation crisis we were called to address.

For the past six years, I have been struggling with my version of the question we entertain today, a version that substitutes *critique* for the term, *theory*.[4] My grappling with critique has taken two forms. First, I have reviewed the commitments that historically define critique in the light of economic, social, and institutional conditions currently in play.

I conceive of the practice that descends to us from Kant and Hegel as a simultaneously reflexive and objective hermeneutic. Bound on the one hand to demystification, or sociohistorical narratives of becoming, critique also attaches itself to transfigurative goals. It wants to release from its own inevitably rationalizing, normalizing stories something exceeding that reason.

This idea of critique as a bootstrapping, self-surpassing process depends on a more basic idea, the idea of the *negative* as that which exists within but in an oppositional, subversive, or non-logical relation to the identity principles defining the Real for a particular group or society. The composition of objects within that cultural domain is taken to mirror the unique ratio of negative to affirmative elements defining the culture at large. The origin of this magical negative is not the past but the future, in the sense that the negative marks out where, within the present order of things, the peculiar resolution of the contradictions that structure the present has already taken root.[5] The names that go with this dialectical futurism (in a rigorous sense, a revisionist theory of history) are familiar: Walter Benjamin, Theodor Adorno, Marc Bloch, Herbert Marcuse.[6]

I will use a familiar shorthand to reference what it is about present-day conditions that changes the redemptive workings of the negative. I feel I can take this shortcut not just because the thing is too big to argue but because most of us—*us* meaning persons willing to question the end of theory—probably give it some degree of assent. While the most searching studies of aesthetic modernism argue a continuity between the expedient negativity of the nineteenth-century avant-garde and that of postmodern culture, there is also a case to be made for the way that quantity changes quality. It is one thing for distance and difference to participate in the normalizing work of high culture; in fact, the clichéd nature of the phrase "distance and difference" makes that case all by itself. Things look rather different, however, when oppositional gestures become part of the business-as-usual of business itself (or, when the gestures of the early avant-garde recur in a context where base-superstructure distinctions have eroded altogether). This recuperation of the negative has not happened by design, of course, nor even as a result of inexorable internal pressures. Instead, it is usually understood as a kind of systems effect or emergent global property. Theory-types call it *overdetermination, totalization,* or *structural causality*; a more sociological, empirical idiom might invoke the terms *postindustrial capitalism* or *information society.* It is hard to see how the via negativa of critique can survive in this environment as anything but parody or simulacrum: or, to use a phrase I propose in the essay cited above, *posthumous critique* (see note 4).

That view does not imply, however, that one should or even *can* abandon theory or critique. In the essay I mention, for example, although I set my writing under the sign of rhetoric, formal invention, and tactical rather than strategic objectives, I have no illusions about genre control over individual readings much less over modes of circulation. Further, I know that I undermine my postfoundationalism from within, for by performing both the necessity and impossibility of such work I end up investing it with all the spiritual prestige one would expect from a lapsed Romanticist—the purest form of our breed.

I have come to be a little less hard on myself; or, to take account of an order of things that stands between the global conditions I just mentioned and my personal identification with Romanticism. My introduction to this order came via Paul Mann, author of *Theory-Death of the Avant-Garde* and more recently, *Masocriticism.*[7] With that title, Mann defines a critical practice that "endlessly postulates its own torment" and he shows how normative this practice has come to be. Mann traces this irresistibly absorptive and infectious genre to the early avant-garde, showing how that movement was and is *repeatedly* killed by the "crushing embrace" of the dominant (which includes even its most determinedly marginal voices, like Mann's own), only to be thus launched into an afterlife of infinite reproduction. "Theory"—twin-born with the avant-garde—is part of that afterlife and a means of its ghostlier demarcations. Emulating the anti-mimetic and oppositional thrust of the modern arts, theory *articulates* that negativity, valorizes it, and in so doing, becomes the agent of the recuperation it opposes.

It is not just the legitimation status of theory that evacuates theory's subject and object of their working difference. Within a cultural economy powered by the circulation of signs, discourse itself is living death. In other words, this conference is the best possible way to ensure the continued production and emptiness (though not the ineffectuality, for good and ill) of theory.

And so, naturally, is Paul Mann's own critique, which, as he is the first to say, is the best example of its argument for the way that critical endgames prolong the prolific agony. Nothing can save them from this fate, but what seems in Mann's case to hold off this absorption (which I no doubt hasten with every word I write) is its indifference to failure (and thus, to success as well). His genre is that of serious sophistry; it blurs the distinction between art and critique, pleasure and knowledge, beauty and truth, drawing its energy, which is enormous, strictly from its own operation. It both demystifies and exemplifies Flaubert's desideratum, the "book about nothing." *Masocriticism* is performance art that erases the critic-as-hero performer, substituting for that normatively human and originary intelligence a strictly working, as it were task-oriented intelligence. Mann's writing is an exercise in scholarly domination, but because the mastery is so sustained and impersonal—so disinterested—one submits to it and to one's own passivity in an access of textual pleasure. Moreover, the exposition is so deadpan and so perfect in its observance of scholarly convention that you cannot help suspecting you are being had: John Cleese doing *Negative Dialectics*. In other words, all the critical "places" from which we are accustomed to read are bracketed rather than negated; thus are they made unavailable even for oppositional purposes. Judgment is not an option.

My initial response to the Nietzschean gaiety of Mann's writing was a mix of envy and curiosity. How is it that he, a Romantic(ist) like myself, can confront the absorption of the negative—which is to say, the end of dialectics and of the meaningful because integral differences that construct for us a future we *want* to inhabit because immanent in it we recognize an altered past—and do it with such verve? How can a person have so hopeless a vision and at the same time feel sufficiently motivated to *write* that vision, and to do so with infinite delight in the process and product? Or, reversing the query, how can a person (a person like myself, for example) affirm every twist and turn of Mann's logic, take the keenest pleasure in the spectacle of his danse macabre, and yet find herself constitutionally unable to engender work of that kind? What bars it from serving to model her own writing? Or, what bars *her* from internalizing it?

My reading of Mann and my work on Bishop lead me to frame the problem in terms of libidinal stake and to relate *that* to the kind of identification obtaining between the critic and her discourse (both the one she writes and the one she writes about). By *identification*, I mean a certain set toward the object that in turn implies a set toward the body, preexisting any actual intellectual engagement.

Above, I named Mann a Romantic(ist); I used that affected style of notation to suggest that we are alike not just in our professional formation but in the idealist cast of our notion of criticism. (It is only a logical contradiction—not a practical one—for materialist critique to arise from the feeling or wish or metaphysical belief that knowledge *will* set you free. Marx himself is a good proof of that.) There is, however, a difference in our notions of knowledge and I believe it is that which explains how the end of dialectics can be for Mann an enabling fact and for me so disabling. Both the ideas and methods of my study of literature can be traced to a single equation: knowledge is sorrow. Or, to switch from the language of Romanticism to a poststructuralist idiom, figuring is disfiguring, meaning is truncation in being, writing is the remedy that kills what it cures, eviscerates what it supplements. This epistemic scene plays out in some of the grandest metaphysical theaters of our culture; among the best-known scholarly directors of these dramas, Meyer Abrams, Harold Bloom, Geoffrey Hartman, Paul de Man, Earl Wasserman—and, behind them, Marx, Freud, Nietzsche, Hegel, Kant, and Wordsworth.

As I look back on my work, I see why it is that, as I said earlier, Wordsworth is the poet who gives me my bearings. Long ago, I named that strain in Wordsworth's poetry which embraces rather than denies the negativity of history as "the Jewish Wordsworth," a phrase I took from Lionel Trilling (another name to add to the list above). Ever since, I have thought of those critics and philosophers I just listed as "Jewish readers" (might this offer a clue to the active anti-Semitism tainting nearly half the names on that list?). What "Jewish" means in this context is rejection of the false closures and unities engendered by and as the very law of representation. It means iconophobia or fear of graven images: fear of the positivity, the narcissism of "picturing," a representational mode said to be incapable of negating. I take "Jewish" to mean a horror of "the despotism of the eye."[8]

You see more clearly now just how alien *picturing* is to my critical paradigms. *Pleasure* runs a close second in strangeness, its binary relation to *knowledge* and its long association with affirmative culture (that is, pleasure as acquiescence to culturally prescribed needs) a linkage that a dialectical critic would not want to take on board. But strangest of all in my mouth is the name Elizabeth Bishop—the name of a woman poet. I do not say that to launch a conversion narrative. In fact, much of what I have been and will be saying about my coming to read Bishop is by way of rejecting the teleology of that genre. I capture my sense of the journey through a figure from Wordsworth; in one of the *Essays on Epitaphs*, he describes the movement of consciousness as a "subtle progress by which . . . qualities pass insensibly into their contraries, and things revolve upon each other."

ITINERARY

My answer to the question of how I come to be writing about pictures, pleasure, and a woman takes the form of a history, one that is, following the Wordsworth metaphor just quoted, "revolutionary," where it is the obsolete and physical meaning of the adjective that obtains. My six-year struggle to relate theory's historical commitments to its current conditions of production has included another kind of inquiry: a search through backroads and byways for a new picture of what being in the world and practicing an identity might look like, or, a new way of linking up matter, making, and value. Unlike the pictures and stories that had prompted my readiest identifications, the view I was seeking would not hinge on absence and presence, loss and recovery, division and integration, fall and redemption. The narrower aim was to teach myself a method of knowing and of representing knowing that could not be troped as a prolific cut into the otherwise indifferent—mute and unmeaning—materiality of the text, nor could it be seen as a critico-historical reactivation (i.e., a resurrection) of its buried life.[9] My quest for a way of imagining knowledge and its objects as some kind of differentiated unity—the differences a function of complexity and aggregation, not structural or even relational definition—and of picturing consciousness as a fully embodied state began with Spinoza, a reasonable jumping-off point for a Romanticist who felt she had seen the limits of a Hegelian Romanticism. It was not, however, either Coleridge or Shelley who introduced me to Spinoza, but rather Althusser's *Essay in Self-Criticism*, where he struggles to explicate his own concept of structural causality by way of the immanentism and pantheism of Spinoza's thought and writing. Althusser's Spinoza led me down several paths. I acquainted myself with the critical literature on Spinoza, with Deleuze's attempt to adapt to his own purposes Spinoza's method and insights, and with the work of Levinas, a direct though somewhat reactive successor to Spinoza (that is, a philosophy of suffering rather than joy). I studied the writings of Aarne Naess and others in the deep-ecology movement, which finds its ancestor in Spinoza's anti-objectal view of nature. I read various works of mind-body philosophy and scientific realism thinking to find there an account of knowledge and objects that would offer an "out" from praxis as well as mimesis, or an "in" to a less anthropocentric concept of consciousness.[10] I moved back chronologically through Hegel's chapter on Spinoza in the *Lectures on Philosophy* to readings in Aristotelian hylozoism, thence to accounts of the pre-Socratic materialisms. The nonlogical relationship (or is it an identity?) between the Spinozistic "attributes," thought and extension, or mind and matter—the central mystery of "Deus sive natura," where *sive*, "or," expresses identity *and* difference—takes the name, in Spinoza studies, of *incommensurability*. The word set me on a course of reading in postcolonial thought, and specifically its studies of foreclosural resistance—or modes of opposition incommensurable with their Other (as in passive and imitative resistance).[11] In two critiques of a constructivist materialism, André Gorz's efforts to articulate a post-productivist Marxism and Alfred Schmidt's *Idea of Nature in Marx*, where he tries to conceptualize a non-triumphalist engagement with nature, I recognized a similar effort to detach varieties of individual and collective dynamism from prolific negativity. That exploration of non-oppositional, non-dyadic mind-matter relations brought me to work in the physical and life sciences that theorizes entities and environments through models of aggregation, not division, and that links identity to historical persistence rather than spatially determinate embodiment.[12] I have been re-reading Freud's

"Project Toward a Scientific Psychology," wondering if its barely artic- ulate insistence on embodied neural states represents the road not taken, and I have been doing my best to grasp the principles of mod- ern physics, helped enormously in that by David Bohm's *Causality and Chance in Modern Physics, Wholeness and the Implicate Order,* and *The Undivided Universe: An Ontological Interpretation of Quantum Theory.* Arkady Plotnitsky's work on *complementarity* as a physical principle that parallels the workings of deconstruction became an excellent resource.[13]

While I neither can nor want to overcome my distrust of the holism implied by today's many critiques of enlightenment, I am also desperate to imagine a matter that is not *resistant and thereby instrumental* to the self-fashioning of human beings and their cultures: desperate to imag- ine a humanness not built on injury and reparation, and a history that is not the breeding trace of "what hurts" (Fredric Jameson's phrase, one I have quoted admiringly in many contexts). One very concrete expres- sion of this longing (and one that reinforces my above linking of Jew- ishness, Romanticism, and poststructuralist theory) is a wish to revise my own (Hegelian) reading of the practice of circumcision, so as to see it as something other than a symbol of history's realizing incursions on the indeterminate purity of the organic. The wish is to set aside my iden- tification with a Jewishness conceived as the embrace of what most of us trained in the hermeneutic and critical traditions of the nineteenth and twentieth centuries acknowledge as the irremediable paradoxes of iden- tity. By that I mean a system of double-binds wherein the feature that is above all others central to our understanding and valorization of the human—namely, reflective self-awareness—arises from insults to our narcissism and from the self-representation called forth by that suffering state. The general rubric under which these paradoxes are explored is of course writing and difference, and its symbology includes the knife and the pen, the cut and the cure, the less that is more, grave and graph, verso and recto, the name of the Father.

My word, *desperate,* and my swerve to a scene of phallic injury bring me back to the difference between Paul Mann's work and my own, a difference that hinges on my romanticization of the negative. In the last instance, it is that overcathexis which accounts for the different tonalities of our work and that can be mapped, I believe, onto our different subject-positions and beyond or before that, our genders.

By way of developing that claim, I'll relate another story. Some years ago, I had given a talk on a Wordsworth poem in which I isolated an image of passivity that attracted me because unlike countless similar instances in Wordsworth, this one was not in the least productive. Borrowing from Wordsworth, I described that image as a refusal of the "wise passiveness" that, throughout his major work, serves to promote acts of self-representation.[14] This image chimed with those non-dyadic, non-oppositional models I had been looking for in the diverse pre- and postmodern places I listed above. In my talk, I said I wanted to explore this image of submission as a kind of blueprint for modeling what I called a nonprofit criticism: one that does not by its very form set itself up as a subject to its textual object, (or, as *value* both grounded in and negating the textual *matter*) but neither does it fly off into Deleuzian wishfulness nor fall back into parasitic, self-serving appreciation.

At the end of my talk, Carol Kaye, a person I had never met, asked me if my whole way of seizing my subject might not be occasioned by despair about the failure of revisionist reading (and the strenuous, materialist—I heard, *phallic*—hermeneutics grounding those movements) to change anything in the academic production of knowledge. She saw that the view I had developed via Wordsworth *idealized* failure and depression (calling it unrecompensed loss) and thus brought me to see that this was the only way I could imagine a humanness not predicated on violence toward the self or other, neither sadism nor masochism—i.e., the only way I could think an ego *not* constituted by conflict and repression but also not narcissistic. My choice of Wordsworth's "Old Man Travelling: Animal Tranquillity and Decay, a Sketch" as my study text suggested to me that the only kind of body I could conceptualize as a value-producing, self-realizing body was a body scored by history, and in that picture of woundedness, of "animal tranquillity," of somatic inscription (much like Wordsworth's blind beggar in *The Prelude*, Book 7) I saw a providentially castrated or circumcised body. In other words, I saw in my critical project a reactive idealization of a pre-given picture of the feminine.

For the first time, I understood that my interest in poetry and theory had always been the very basic, I might even say "primitive," one of trying to understand difference and identity. Perhaps because I did my graduate work at the University of Chicago in the mid-seventies, just before the so-called moment of theory, and because I owe so much to that time and place I want to call this interest "formalist." But, whereas a classical, Aristotelian formalism presupposes the human body as a template for invented forms ("[t]ragedy should . . . resemble a living organism in all its unity, and produce the pleasure proper to it"), thereby providing itself an a priori distinction between parts and whole, my work, like so much of my generation's, has taken the *invented* body, the textual as opposed to the organic form, as the founding fact. The project is to re-examine familiarly mapped textual bodies as if de novo, or as if the governing ratios of part to whole were not already known, or perhaps, as if one saw with an infant's eyes.[15]

I had grasped the utopian drive behind this scientific or philosophic (or visionary) project of mine. It was Carol Kaye's comment that made me look behind that drive, or to a moment preceding its emergence. Throughout my life as a reader, and without knowing it, I have been asking formalist questions by way of body images that are also pictures of gendered or becoming-gendered bodies. My first book was about the fragment poems of my period: damaged or aborted or residual texts. I took my task to be that of recuperating those damaged forms: literally, making them whole by the prosthesis of my critical narration. But each chapter ended on a melancholy note, with a sense of regret for having repaired the brokenness that had endeared those bodies to me. Next, I looked at Wordsworth's poetry, and following Bloom and Hartman, I saw a body made heroic by the contradictions it both could and would *undertake* to suffer. Later, with Keats, I saw a culturally wanting body, forced to appropriate the empowering languages of the literary tradition but at the same time, to *signify* that fact, impairing its own legitimacy, its wholeness, as the price of establishing its individuality. I named the breeding dilemma of this poetry "capable self-negation," ringing a change on Keats's more directly idealizing phrase "negative capability." Unlike the classical Wordsworthian *Aufhebung*, where annihilation is also preservation at a higher level and thus a moment in a process of self-transcendence, the Keatsian self, as I cast it, exists only in the moment of its self-cancellation, leaving no remainder and thus requiring endless beginning again and again.[16]

ANECDOTE

I described my critical practice as driven by a primitive interest. I will finish up this part of my talk and make good on my promise to ground my epistemic attractions in an experience of gender by saying how I come to be talking about a particular Bishop poem, "In the Waiting Room." When I first taught this poem, I stopped when I came to the narrator's stunning aside, line 15: "(I could read)." I asked my students to recall their first scene of reading and as I listened to their accounts, I found myself remembering—for the first time, it seemed—my own entry into reading. I saw my mother, with my sister and me on either side of her on the couch, a folio-sized book stretched across our three laps. The book had a smell that I now recognize as a feature of expensively illustrated art-books, having something to do perhaps with the paper and ink of the plates. The book was opened to a photograph of a sculpture, or as I saw it then—without benefit of a developed concept of representation—a tiny body of no particular color. At roughly the center of this greyish form was something that had the same general look as everything else, something that in its substance or medium seemed to belong, but at the same time gave notice of a different kind or category of body altogether. This knot or confusion at the center resembled leaves or grapes or flowers—some feature (or features) from the nonhuman world, and thus, a kind of clothing or decoration, something superadded. But "it" or "they"—this disorganized zone—also had a way of seeming both integral and foregrounded, as if the human form behind it was merely shadow or remainder or ornamental backdrop.

More vivid than the picture-memory, however—that is, the memory of *what* I saw—was a perception-memory: the memory of *how* I saw, or how the seeing felt. As I reviewed my mental image in class that day, a definite anxiety surfaced, but it was not tied to the question of the genitals per se (integral part? add-on? point of origin? vestigial organ?). Instead, it attached to my inability to see what was there on the page and to see it clearly, that is, as an organized form having a determinate relation to its visual context. If I was seeing an occluding or distorting cover, why could I not move that layer aside to look underneath? Or, if what I was seeing was two-dimensional, why couldn't I make sense of it by getting closer to the image or by viewing it from different angles and in better light? How was it that I was seeing an ambiguous object clearly? In a later language, I would say I had encountered the very shape of indeterminacy.

It took me a long time to appreciate the strangeness of this act of remembering. As I said, it sprang up as my immediate association and counterpart to Bishop's "(I could read.")." But in my remembered scene there is nothing about reading nor can I recover any sense of captions or text to that art-history book. *Seeing* is the working theme of that memory. At the same time, however, since I recalled it *as* a scene of reading, and not just "a" scene but a primal scene, that is exactly what it is. Or, instead of characterizing my memory as one of *seeing*, perhaps I should name its subject-matter *not-(or not-yet)-reading*. Making a narrative of this contradiction, I could say that the memory records that moment in my actual history when I learned to read—to swerve from image to text, photograph to caption—so as to avert my gaze from the anxiety-producing picture of a male body (or, when I started learning or wanting to read so as to find out what it was I could not see in that picture of a sculpture: reading, thus, as a technique for seeing more, seeing around, seeing through). Or, on the view that I already knew how to read, the scene might be taken to record the moment in psychic history when reading became a *defense* against seeing, or, against the desire and fear of seeing the father's body. Or again, it might mark a moment when seeing and reading were one—literally, when reading made *sense*, as in, *sensation*: when the written word had the mute because full presence of a material object and when the meaning and value of that object were immanent in it. "There was a time . . ."

II

"In the Waiting Room" enjoys a special status among Bishop readers because of its explanatory value in the corpus. Its place in Bishop's canon is comparable to that of the Immortality Ode in Wordsworth's. Because Bishop's poetry is so elusive (some might say, evasive), one is especially grateful for the aid to reflection. As with Wordsworth's Ode, the story on offer in Bishop's poem is a chronicle of subject formation. Where Bishop's poem differs from Wordsworth's—that is, from the Romantic myth-of-self—is in its failure to include in that story a genealogy of the writing self: that is, the capably self-conscious and reflective self. The formation of *that* subject, defined by his access to language not as an instrumental but as a humanly transformational grammar, redeems the *natural* subject's fall from unity into division. "I love the Brooks which down their channels fret, / Even more than when I tripped lightly as they." The Ode thus tells and shows the new power arising from the disenchantment of nature. In confronting a collection of objects stripped of their physical and metaphysical sanctions, the narrator also comes into possession of a system of words loosed from their referential origins and thus made available for acts of self-fashioning and self-rescue. Bishop codes Wordsworth's transfigurative finale by the device of return in the last stanza of the poem. But the poem neither tells nor shows us the metamorphosis of the subjected narrator into the empowered subject nor does it intimate that identity through a newly integrative and commanding language. Nothing happens to organize much less valorize the difference between before and after, or between the first and the last line of the poem.

I read this omission as an interference effect created by the double genre of "In the Waiting Room" (henceforth IWR). Alongside the myth of self is a drama of interpellation; the narrator, hailed by the cry of her suffering aunt, takes up a cultural position as "woman," a position that is marked in the poem by the epithet "foolish, timid." Bishop's omission of the Wordsworthian payoff—the child's move into the Symbolic—would seem to be no more than the mimetically appropriate short-circuiting that is the child's fate when she happens to be a girl. The poem would thus show that the child's transition from a seeing to a reading self (line 15)—her Alice-like plunge down the rabbit hole between being and meaning—is not remedied by a move into writing because the child is a girl. In literary, intertextual terms, one could say that Bishop uses a contrastive technique so as to reveal and critique the gendering of a prestigious Romantic form. However, if we give the poem that metanarrative dimension, we must also rethink the explanatory and exemplary status of IWR in Bishop's canon. We have to ask what kind of writing (or more narrowly, poetry, or narrower again, lyric) is it that IWR *does* both explain and embody.

From what I have said, you can see that I will treat IWR as a problem poem to help us get at the question to which all of Bishop's poetry is an answer; I hope also to identify the reading subject for whom that poetry constitutes an answer. I have no quarrel with the consensus that finds in IWR an explanation of Bishop's overall project. My point is to show that it offers this explanation less directly than it seems and that this indirection outlines a project of its own. Briefly, I want to look at the poem's formalization of its content, a phrase coined by Herbert Marcuse as a synonym for "the aesthetic dimension." Through this kind of study, I believe we can improve our understanding not just of Bishop's poetry but of the striking interest it has been arousing for the past ten years or so. The MLA Bibliography lists approximately 173 entries for dissertations and journal articles on Bishop from 1988 to 1997. There are even two articles on the phenomenon itself.[17] The emergent textual history of Bishop's work as well as the exigencies and fashions of the academic marketplace are of course important factors in this turn toward Bishop, but they need not rule out more integral and for that reason, interesting explanations. For example, it might be the case that people are seeing in Bishop's poetry some figure, logic, or process that engages problems many of us are interested in—the kind of problems I sketched in the first part of my talk.

Above, I described IWR as an exemplary Bishop text, not just an explanatory one. I need to qualify that statement because on the face of it and in ways I must emphasize since they are so oddly neglected in the criticism, IWR departs sharply from Bishop's stylistic norms. Those departures are important; they point us toward the special way this poem illuminates Bishop's corpus. I call IWR *exemplary* not because of its formal features, since it does not look like the bulk of Bishop's poems, but because its textualized relation to its referent, *National Geographic*, delineates a fantasy structure that does indeed "resemble" those formal features this particular poem does not share with the rest of Bishop's oeuvre. One way to conceive the expressive mode of this poem is to say that it gives access to "the unthought known" of Bishop's poetry. That is Peter Bollas's phrase for the psychic shadow that is cast by an object occurring so early in the child's development as to precede the experience of objects as such, and also, to continue escaping cognitive determinacy.[18]

Let me say how IWR departs from the norm of Bishop's poetry. First, the poem offers a far more rationalized and teleological narrative than anything else in the canon. (Even "The Fish," with its heavily allegorical closure, permits itself breaks from a readerly into a writerly etiquette.) Although Bishop favors highly disciplined poetic forms (e.g., sestina, villanelle), her use of *narrative* genre is typically exploratory, transgressive, and unstable. "The Man-Moth" is a good example of both tendencies. IWR, by contrast, shows a relaxed form and a high degree of content determination. And, whereas the bulk, and I think the best of Bishop's work shows minute attention to the medium, IWR has very little of the verbal reflexivity for which Bishop is so admired. The thinness of the acoustic and iconic self-reference reinforces the poem's mimetic orientation. I think we could fairly describe IWR as a poem driven by story and idea, a poem that works its analogies into causal relations, condensing these relations into developmental and even teleological vectors.

I describe it that way so as to light up another anomalous feature of IWR. In "The Bight," another defining poem for Bishop, Baudelaire's poetics of "correspondence" is invoked as a model for Bishop's own aesthetic. The allusion is as useful for the differences it brings out as it is for the identities. In Baudelaire, a controlling consciousness lodges in the very idiom of the writing: a highly inflected, socially placeable lexicon, tonality, and drift of desire. By contrast, Bishop's correspondences are left to speak for themselves; they are not subjected to a grammar of motive, an atmospheric intelligence, or anything else that might mobilize them in the direction of statement or character. Bishop's free-floating analogies, echoes, and couplings are offered neither as objectively grounded relations, "released" by the mechanisms of the poem or derived from some metaphysical source; nor are they presented as artifacts contrived by an agency that is textualized in the poem. As a rule, resemblance in Bishop acts as an inscrutably first and formal cause, responsible for the narrative movement and conceptual designs that emerge from the poem.

In line with this, *seeing* in Bishop's poetry—and there is a lot of it—remains at a tangent to knowing rather than crystallizing in something like "composition as explanation," much less symbol or proposition. Typically, the seeing has a strongly tactile quality, as if the poem's eyes are at the tips of its fingers. "We can stroke these lovely bays," writes the narrator of "The Map," giving us a figure for a poetics of sensuous tracing, like braille, rather than positional observation. Bishop's way of seeing (that is, of constructing or writing seeing), holds off the surface-depth, presence-absence ratios that always threaten a visual poetics. Just as our fingers, no matter how deep they go, are always touching surfaces, so Bishop's eye moves from texture to texture, never encountering vacancy or blank.

Against this norm, the emphatic perspectivalism of IWR stands out. "I read," "I looked," "I said," "I felt." The poem bristles with prepositions ("beneath," "in," "on," "outside," "inside"), each encoding a propositional content. A self-advertising meaningfulness infuses the poem, traveling through its sight-lines. If IWR could speak, it would say, "I do not have to mean; I am." I cannot think of another place in Bishop's canon where this cliché of lyric is so honored.

Consistent with its fiction of seeing and despite the restraint that is the signature of Bishop's poetry, the writing shows a high proportion of decoration. That is Bishop's own word, and presumably, her way of underscoring the peculiar status of detail in her work: that is, as excess rather than as a particularizing, sensualizing, or synecdochically troping elaboration of the central argument.[19] The leading trait of Bishop's poetry (and I mean that literally: as in iconically "leading" the eye) is its way of drawing out the poetic line beyond the boundaries of the text proper. I want to call these filaments and tendrils *flourishes*, because the term aligns more closely with design than with expressivity. In "The Map," Bishop offers a defining contrast to her own practice of excess. The narrator of that poem, observing how the names of towns run out to sea, ascribes to the printer "the same excitement as when emotion too far exceeds its cause." The next line of the poem, extending farther than any other in the text—or, tracing a peninsula jutting out from the right-hand margin—runs as follows: "These peninsulas take the water between thumb and finger / like women feeling for the smoothness of yard-goods." The content of this reflexive simile could not be quieter or more measured. It could not be *less* a case of "emotion too far exceed[ing] its cause."

If the only Bishop poem you know is IWR, you will find my way of characterizing her poetic norm hard to credit. You see for example that IWR is given through the consciousness of a speaker having coherence, inwardness, and perspectival self-awareness. She tells us where she is in the world and when she falls off it. She neatly breaks down the poetic space into scene of representation (the waiting room), textual space (*National Geographic*), and represented space (somewhere in Africa, Alaska, or the South Seas). (And she does the same thing with time.) The story is told not just in the first-person but as an autobiographically specific discourse, referencing places, dates, and incidents from the life. The discourse is strongly gendered as female, with gender the foregrounded thematic element as well. Yet a review of the rest of Bishop's poetry shows that her personae are either male or gender-neutral. As for gender thematics, Bishop vigorously refused a feminist identification; nowhere in her published poetry and fiction does anything approaching a politics of gender take shape. Bishop was extraordinarily discreet about her private life, which she took to include her sexuality. Her sense of poetic decorum is also highly developed. She is not so ladylike in her language as Marianne Moore but she comes close. I believe that IWR is the only Bishop poem containing direct references to sexual bodies (that is, to sexual *human* bodies; there *are* sexy lizards). This candor extends to the rhetorical stance of the poem. In the child-narrator's demonstration of her access to knowledge through reading—and the narrative's identification of knowledge with cultural demystification—IWR codes a meta-critical blueprint. Of course, this poem is a favorite. For critical readers, it is a goldmine.

I want to look this gift horse in the mouth not just because this kind of candor in so guarded a poet must be tested but because of Bishop's strange insistence on the accuracy of her references. In the poem, she cites the February 1918 *National Geographic* as the source of the images given in the opening. When she learned that only the volcanoes appeared in that issue, Bishop corrected the cite, saying she had taken the "African things" from the March issue. No such images occur there either. In light of Bishop's famous passion for exactitude, my inclination is to assume that there *is* something pictured in the February issue that finds its way into IWR—something central enough to Bishop's understanding of the poem to make her so stubborn about it. When I provide some of the textual history, I think you will agree that we need not limit ourselves to the February *or* the March numbers, for it seems probable that Bishop did not.

IWR was first published in *The New Yorker*, 1970; it recounts an incident from 1918 that is also worked up in Bishop's unpublished story "The Country Mouse," probably written in 1961. In 1967, Bishop sent IWR to Robert Lowell, asking him to tell her

> what's the matter with this poem . . . I really mean it, and say what you think—I'll scrap it, if necessary. I like the idea, but know there's something very wrong and can't seem to tell what it is . . . (It is one of those [poems] I dream [sic]—woke up one morning at Jane's with almost the whole thing done.) It was funny—queer—I actually went to the Library & got out that no. of the N G [*National Geographic*]—and that title, the Valley of 10,000 Smokes—was right, and has been haunting me all my life, apparently.

Brett Millier, who gives us this excerpt, comments that "two and a half years passed before [Bishop] solved her difficulties with the poem and finished it."[20] In other words, Bishop had the means, motive, and opportunity to work out her difficulties by looking at back issues of *National Geographic*. In a little while I will show you some pictures from the February 1918 volume and also some from the October 1919 volume (the source of the Long Pig photo). My general assumption about informal bibliographic cite is that month and year are easily transposed. When, in 1977 (ten years after writing the poem), Bishop jumped from February to March, she might well have intended 1918 to 1919.

The facts to keep in mind are these: 1) Bishop is certain about having seen something *somewhere* in a *National Geographic* issue from sometime at or around February 1918, and *what* she saw has for her the authority of absolute fact. 2) The poem shows no significant link to its alleged mimetic original. I think that in this case, there is a way to trust both the poet and the poem. Drawing on images from

National Geographic, I will argue that the principles driving the poem's formalization of its content are those of condensation and superposition, or, metonymy and metaphor: nothing surprising there. What *is* interesting is the way that this analysis raises up a fantasy—a picture and a story of the body, of gender-identification, and of desire—that casts some light on Bishop's poetry and possibly, on psychosexual development more generally. The stylistic feature of Bishop's poetry most lit up by this fantasy is that peculiar figuring of detail that I mentioned above, and also, what I did not mention, the troping of this textual practice through images of things leaning, hanging, dragging, winding, trailing. Not to make a mystery of my destination, I will be saying that the workings and position of ornament in Bishop's poetry align it *not* with an *écriture feminine*—the standardly gendered reading of detail—but with that part of the male body most resembling the fleshly extravagance, externality, vulnerability, and (here I add even more culturally inflected terms), contingency and asymmetry of the female form. I wish I could call this part the phallus but I am afraid that I must use its everyday name, for it is the penis, not phallus, that corresponds to the style of Bishop's details.

Recently, Mira Schor, an artist and critic, has observed of some postmodern picturing that "if the penis is represented then the phallus may become unveiled in the process."[21] Schor's juxtaposition alerts us to the demystifying effect of Bishop's use of detail in IWR. It also encourages us to apply what we learn through Bishop's practice to the classic Freudian account of fetishism. For the fetishist (always male for Freud), any one part or attribute of the woman (e.g., breast, shoe) metonymically figures her whole body. Further, that female body, grasped as a whole or integral form, metaphorically or substitutively figures the phallus (when we signify by that term the symbolic, idealized, ultimately inalienable representation of the anatomical body part). The child's discovery of the horrifying absence of the penis from the mother's body is said to drive these displacements. As we proceed, I hope to show how, through the highly "decorated" style of her writing, Bishop offers a wonderfully literal version of the phantasmatic endpoint of this logic. In the general context of Bishop's themes and narratives, the overwrought, baroque quality of her writing takes on a special significance. In effect, it sutures Freud's penis-woman—that is, his structural analysis of the fetish (the signifying penis, or penis-turned-phallus)—back onto the male body. As a result, instead of seeing the penis as that which most sharply distinguishes the sexes, we are led to see it as the epitome of feminine detail, excess, and ornament. (Translated into epistemic terms, we see it not as the hard truth of masculine difference, or of truth as a function of sharper and sharper analytic distinctions, but as the soft beauty of sameness, adjacency, aggregation.) This mental picture generates another droll turn; if for Freud's male fetishist the woman's body is a giant penis, then for the phallophilic or heterosexual woman, the penis must also be a tiny woman, and we are all gay.

Bishop's style is not only a wicked and witty deconstruction of patriarchal binarism, it also re-opens the Freudian account of female heterosexuality in a serious way. Instead of seeing the girl's turn to the father as the only possible donor of what she lacks, one might see it as a defensive swerve from the dangerous falling together of identity and desire in same-sex love. (I take this up below in my reading of the play of orality in IWR.) (p. 222).

Superposition and condensation are not just the standard mechanisms of dream representation, they also organize what psychoanalysis calls "screen memory." Freud notes the paradox that "whereas important things are not retained, apparently insignificant memories sometimes are (and they are characterized by unusual sharpness). [Often], the subject himself is surprised that they should have survived." Freud makes grand claims for these screen-memories; he says that they retain "not only some but *all* of what is essential from childhood. They represent the forgotten years of childhood as adequately as the manifest content of the dream represents the dream thoughts. It is simply a question of knowing how to extract it out of them by analysis."[22] With Freud, "extraction" does not mean searching for what lies *behind* the manifest content; it means studying the processes by which that content came to achieve a certain form. It is the form that discloses the nature of the compromise between the defenses and whatever they are seeking to repress.

Lee Edelman has characterized Bishop's *National Geographic* as an "imagined periodical" used in the poem as an "exemplary text to instruct the young Elizabeth and us in the difficulty of reading."[23] My view is a bit more literal than Edelman's; not only do I see Bishop's dream-magazine as an *actual* composite, made up of pieces of several issues, I also see her *representation* of that magazine as a hybrid, a screen memory. Let me note here that I want my reading of IWR to be seen as a complement to Edelman's definitive and beautiful account. His is not just the first major reading, but, I believe, the only one to turn our attention from "the central event" of the poem to the "doubts about that event" and to see that the poem does not just suffer some incidental and bibliographical confusion, it "*insist*[*s*] on confusion" (my emphasis). Edelman's focus is on "the difficulty of reading." I will be casting reading as a defense against seeing, when seeing is attended by wishes and fears that exceed because they *precede* representation. That is to say, I take IWR to be more about the difficulty of seeing than of reading. Like Edelman, I treat confusion as a motivated feature and thematics in IWR; I will show that confusion is the way that sexual doubleness, or perhaps oneness (the better word might be *interchangeability*) and the pleasure that goes with it, get expressed.

To model the form of IWR on the screen memory is to foreground for analysis the action of remembering and to see if it introduces materials that do not belong to the manifest content. My look at the intra- and intertextuality of the poem is not meant to challenge the poem's self-understanding as a story of fall into division that is also a coming to consciousness of the self as such, as an individual (as in "you are an *I,* / you are an *Elizabeth*"). I will, however, try to show that because IWR is also about an earlier fall, or *falling together*, coming to consciousness will not take the form familiar to us from the long history of both Cartesian and German philosophies of the subject, "where the subject makes itself subject by constructing itself objectively to itself." Further, the writing that embodies that coming to consciousness will not figure as the dividend of a self-enriching alienation.

I say *falling together*, echoing the narrator's phrase for the mixed-up identity of aunt and child, to bring out the way that the shaping moment in IWR is not equated with separation but convergence, or again, to use Edelman's good term, confusion. I see the developmentally later crisis—crisis of desire and individuation—as mapping onto an earlier one: namely, the formation of the ego as a mental image of the body's surface. The poem certainly emphasizes division. Line 66, for example, presents such cardinal coordinates as "trousers and skirts and boots and different pairs of hands"; the final passage is a web of positional contrasts ("in it," "on," "outside") and the closing War reference thematizes and even gives a mythic form to difference. But these emphases can just as well signify a functional embrace of difference as a suffering of it. Why couldn't difference operate as a defense against a frightening wish for incorporation, comparable to the way that the child-narrator uses linguistic splitting—"I said to myself," line 34—as protection from her vertigo? My word, "incorporation," shifts the focus from the six-year-old's crisis to the crisis of the earlier, so-called pre-Oedipal moment—crisis of identification, not separation and reappropriation. The early question is not "*who* am I and what or whom do I want?"; it is "*what* and *where* am I?" This early phase is organized by the logic of resemblance, not difference, and of incorporation not acquisition; perhaps one could also describe it by way of need, in distinction to the desire that characterizes Oedipal dynamics. And whereas the theater of the Oedipal phase is genital, the scene of the earlier moment is oral. Now you see exactly why I want to look IWR—this critical gift horse—in the mouth.

IWR opens in the comforting manner of a children's story: it so much as says, "I am the one who occupies this well-defined place within this concentrically organized nest of time- and space-zones." The movement is from the relatively large and abstract (Worcester, Massachusetts) to the smaller and more concrete (the dentist's waiting room), and this pattern repeats in the companion sentences that follow ("It was winter. It got dark early"). The next sentence does the same thing, using the line break (line 8) and a syntax of apposition as a hinge; on one side, the text establishes the abstract, conceptual, and categorical (grown-up people), and on the other, the realm of concrete particulars (arctics, overcoats, lamps, and magazines, that is, what is actually seen). The theme is one of *fit*. Bishop moves this theme around various levels so as to raise the related but harder question of identity. For instance, the poem asks how exactly *is* knowledge (say, "it was winter") the same as experience ("it got dark early"); and it asks, how exactly *are* "grown-up people"—that categorical mystery—the same as the world which is their giant form, as Blake might say: the world of magazines and dentists.

The next passage works at this question in a temporal (and Humean) key; how exactly is the first picture of a volcano, its inside black and full of ashes, the same as the next picture where I see slopes running with fire. How do I know that one identity having constancy over time contains both states? The mildly counterintuitive sequence of the language—from ashes to fire—throws some doubt on the natural development that we take to be inscribed in the pictures, and that would certainly be clear from the caption. Elizabeth, nearly 7, tells us she can read—that is, she has just *learned* to read. The caption identifying the two images as one volcano at different times might still be a doubtful medium of information for her—less self-evident, certainly, than the pictures.

That kernel of doubt starts sprouting in the following section, clearly, the centerpiece of IWR. Whereas the poem opens in a cosy, taxonomic way—a Noah's ark coupling of arctics and overcoats, lamps and magazines—the mention of Osa and Martin Johnson not only specifies the gender-curiosity that drives the two-by-two phrasing, it also shifts the discourse into the mode of inquiry rather than exposition. Or, it shows that what looked like descriptive statement was inquiry all along. That is, do men and women "belong" together in the manner of arctics and overcoats, or perhaps as inside the volcano fits with outside? Edelman tracks the picture-reference to Osa Johnson's autobiography, *I Married Adventure*. There, Osa tells how she put off her Edwardian dresses, shifting to the trousers and field gear necessary for her new life as an ethnologist and naturalist. She uses the trope in a conventional way to mark the transition from confinement to freedom. In keeping with this, the accompanying photograph shows Osa alone. In adding Martin to the picture, Bishop again poses the "difference" question, but since the topic here is gender, the question broadens. Looking at the narrator looking at this picture, we know she is asking how, or by what principle, different things combine, and what do they then become or produce. In other words, the textual sequence frames the classic primal-scene question: what do my parents do when I am not around? And what *did* they do to *bring* me around? (Those questions, by the way, are premised on the prior existence of an "I," an event that, in the chronology that interests me, has not yet taken place. What I am doing here is spelling out the poem's offered narrative.) The couple's matching clothes iconically frame that question as "Does resemblance *explain* why things are linked (are these people together because they dress alike?), or, do people look alike because they are together"? In other words, is resemblance the way we come to perceive culturally linked things?

Before continuing with gender matters, I want to say quickly how the passage under discussion entertains various principles of identity and belonging. Is it, for example, proximity, or containment in a bounded space that makes for a shared identity: as with the patients in the waiting room? Is it a common function that makes things alike: so that a man soon to be roasted is the same as a pig, or protective arctics (boots) the same as overcoats? Here are some other textual possibilities: position in space (man on a pole=pig), family/tribe/group/or nation (all clearly referenced in the poem); constancy of mass, behavior, location over time (the volcano). Or, is identity a function of what lies *on* the body—covering, hanging from, wrapping around it—as opposed to what is *in* the body? When you look at the particulars used to instance these principles, you see that the ethnographic questions broaden into anthropological ones. Quite systematically, the passage presents a series of cultural binaries for review: human vs animal, organic vs. inorganic, dead vs. living, children vs. adults, black vs. white, male vs. female. Conceptualizing the list, you could say that humanness is interrogated both as a function of differences *internal* to a system (say, black/white, man/woman) and as a function of *external* or boundary relations (animate/inanimate).

I frame these questions as either-or's so as to follow the dyadic lead of the poem. But you can also see that the poem's visual logic is combinatory, not exclusionary. Respecting this, I would say that the text's answer to the identity question it poses is that it is position in cultural space *and* the positioning of cultural space on the body, in the form of ornaments, accessories, clothing etc., that determines both human and gender identity. For instance, we might answer the question, when is a man not a man?, by saying, when his position in cultural space is that of a pig: or, when he is slung on a pole. Or, when is a woman not a woman?: when she is wearing breeches, boots, and a helmet. Or, when her neck and head, verbally equated with the babies' elongated heads (both "wound round and round" with string or wire), looks like a lightbulb, or a penis; or, when her breasts hang so loosely from her body that they have the semi-detached, appendage-like, decorative rather than integral appearance of a man's genitals.

These are, to me, shocking things to say and I can barely believe these are my words in my mouth. But it is just as weird to think that the self-evident and, it would seem, causally or functionally or temporally organized differences arrayed in the passage—lamps, magazines, men, women, adults, babies—are, in fact, given as positions on a continuum. And not abstract positions, like map coordinates, but concrete and particularized forms, as in a topographical relief map. IWR is the map that answers the question "what is Geography?"—the question put by the volume epigraph—by reframing it as "what is gender?" Maps always answer questions in the language of space. But in IWR, space is the *content* not just the form of the answer. Where bodies are and what lies on them, what touches what, *this* determines identity (for the developmental correlate, think of the child's certainty that peas touching meat on a plate are not the same thing as peas or meat alone). IWR gives a picture of a whole system of classification—a world— "where everything is only connected by 'and' and 'and.'" Gender (as Bishop says of maps in the epigraph) is both a part of that world and a picture of the whole. I use Foucault's phrase, "system of classification," to summon up his discussion of resemblance in the pre-Classical eras, or episteme (his term). He calls resemblance the "hinge of the whole world," a world that is taken to be an "unbroken tissue of words and signs, accounts and characters, discourse and forms," or, maps and bodies. In such a world, "adjacency is not an exterior relation between things, but the sign of a relationship, obscure though it may be."[24] Thus, correspondence does the connecting work that causality does for a later, mechanistic and Cartesian world. For the second time, this quotation from Bishop's "Over 2,000 Illustrations and a Complete Concordance" is apposite: "Everything only connected by 'and' and 'and.' / Open the book. The gilt rubs off the edges of the pages and pollinates the fingertips."

If resemblance is the "hinge" of the world of IWR, what are we to make of the poem's central trauma, the child's fall into sexual difference at the sight of the hanging breasts? In the textual economy, this is equivalent to the crisis moment of Wordsworth's Ode,

Figure 1 October 1919: "She Wears Her Badge of Sorrow," p. 353.

Figure 2 October 1919: "It Is the Fashion," p. 351.

"—But there's a Tree, of many, one, / A single Field which I have looked upon, / Both of them speak of something that is gone." The analogy is not offered so as to present Wordsworth's loss of his visionary endowment as a castration scene. And by the same token, there is no textual imperative forcing us to construe the Bishop-narrator's sighting of those breasts as her coming to know herself as foolish, timid, and victimized: that is, either essentially or culturally castrated. I *do* read the child's view of those breasts as the poem's turning point, and as Bishop's equivalent to stanza 4 of the Immortality Ode, but again, I would characterize the scene as a hinge rather than a break.

Why must we read the breasts as a sign of injury, weakness, and lack, especially since what seems to be horrifying about them is their physicality and presence: their weight, mass, and definition against the body. Maybe what is scary is that they are *not* a sign (as of, for example, castration, or femininity, or maternity); instead, they are a *thing*. All right: but then why should a "thing" be scary? Why does the language of the poem fail at this sight, falling into the sloppy emotiveness of "horrifying," repeating that failure later on, where "awful" fills in for some more pondered and precise word, a word in keeping with the poem's lexical decorum? I do not propose that the breasts do *not* signify castration, or that Bishop's poem does not know what it is doing. I will say, however, that the poem does not present *all* that it is doing. The poem does not bring under a concept the "all of childhood" that Freud ascribes to the screen-image.

Figure 3 October 1919: "Proof of the Catch," p. 203.

Although the poem does not produce itself as a knowledge, it makes *us* see, through the child's eyes, not just the meaning behind the metaphor—the missing penis behind the breasts—but the materiality of the metaphor itself, the visibility of the sign: the penis that is like, and therefore *is* the breast and vice versa. I say it goes both ways because the dead man slung on a pole, especially when glossed by this picture of a fish on a pole (from the Long Pig issue) [figure 3], makes a visual link between body and body part, and then again, penis and breast. It is in that issue that we find what Bishop called the "African things," i.e., pictures of barebreasted Bayanzi and Congo Tribeswomen [figures 1 and 2]. The issue also features pictures of scarification, where the decoration creates a kind of second-skin, a relief that alters the body contour, or a writing that becomes its own subject.

I still have not answered the question, why horror? Is it just that identity is always more threatening than difference? Or is it something to do with the assumed repellence of flesh when it is unhallowed by bone or muscle, i.e., the grossness of matter uninhabited by the concept? Maybe. Probably. Here for example is an excerpt from H. L. Mencken's *In Defense of Women*, 1918:

> A man, save he be fat, i.e., of womanish contours, usually looks better in uniform than in mufti; the tight lines set off his figure. But a woman is at once given away: she looks like a dumb-bell run over by an express train. Below the neck by the bow and below

the waist astern there are two masses that simply refuse to fit into a balanced composition. Viewed from the side, she presents an exaggerated S bisected by an imperfect straight line, and so she inevitably suggests a drunken dollar-mark. . . . Compared to the clumsily distributed masses of the female form, the average milkjug or cuspidor is a thing of beauty.[25]

Mencken has no trouble writing his horror of what hangs on the female body. Of course, it is harder to be a self-hating woman than a male misogynist, but that kind of answer to the question of the narrator's horror does not get us very far, abstracted as it is from the workings of the poem and from Bishop's lesbianism. Closer to the verbal mark is the visual link between a woman's breasts and a man's genitals; if the latter, by that similitude, cease to be a marker of masculinity, of difference itself, and also of presence, then the classical binaries that structure the mind-set of modernity start to give way, and so does the gendering that has accompanied those Cartesian binaries and helped ensure their intellectual prestige. There is an up-side to that development. To picture the penis-breast-phallus as a continuum or as indifferent instances of phenomenal particularism is to put the Symbolic philosopher's stone of our culture into the hands of women as well as men, an advance from oligarchy to democracy. Then too, if you see the resemblance moving in the other direction, toward a desublimation, or a feminization of the phallus, the advantage definitely accrues to the woman. In other words, the narrator's horror remains to be explained.

One feature of IWR I have not considered is its orality. The narrator is after all in a *dentist's* waiting room. The cry from the aunt is prompted by something alien in the mouth and the cry is said by the narrator to be "in my mouth," as the family voice is "in my throat." The image of the hanging breasts comes in the same sentence as the baby reference, as if to imply the effects of breastfeeding. In both the poem and the October 1919 *National Geographic*, the inscription of cannibalism (Long Pig) is highly sanitized. In the magazine, the scene is labeled as a simulation, and that is just how it looks [figure 4]. But in the issue Bishop *said* she consulted—the February number—this weirdly apposite picture appears [figure 5]. "Pig clubs" were a wartime home-effort to provide food for the troops, and much touted in the

Figure 4 October 1919: "A Scene Posed by Marquesan Natives … and 'Long Pig'."

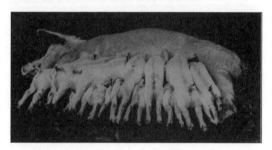

Figure 5
February 1918: "A Double-Decker," p. 182.

long article on the subject in the February issue, an issue largely devoted to the war. I counted more than eight pictures of pigs, suckling, being fed by bottles, slung under a farmer's arm, and massed for market [figures 6 and 7].

I think we can say that *this*, the photograph of nursing pigs [figure 5], is Bishop's picture of cannibalism—specifically, matricide—and of hanging breasts and other elongated structures in the poem (conehead children, lightbulb women). Through this visual thickening, the horror offers itself to our reading as a defense against the desire: to eat the mother. Let me point out as well this picture of a python disgorging a pig, also from the 1919 issue [figure 8].

Figures 6 (above) and 7 February 1918: "Their Full Dinner-Pail," p. 181; "Being Brought Up on the Bottle," p. 173. In this context, let me also call attention to a great many pictures in the March 1918 issue of uniformed soldiers massed in ceremonial and training formations (March, pp. 222, 225, 228, 229) and in the September issue, pictures of indistinguishable factory workers, "America's Industrial Army," involved in the war effort. The  visual analogy between the crowds of animals eating and about to be eaten, and the crowds of soldiers and workers to be consumed by the War matches the thematics of orality and violence that I have been tracing.

The screen memory encodes in its formal structure an earlier narrative; or, IWR, over and above being a poem about sexual difference is also about the *in*difference of what later comes to be imagined, for defensive reasons, as anatomical distinction. The poem presents itself as a transitioning from latency to adolescence, that resurgence of Oedipal issues, resolved (so we are told) when the girl agrees to substitute desire for identification: that is, when she accepts having a man, or his penis or baby—whatever—for the obviously better deal of being one herself. But Bishop's way of telling this story codes another, earlier story, this one about the coming into being of the mind's picture of the body: the ego. For mainstream Freudian theory, this occurs through a mental mirroring of the body-surface as plotted by its erotogenic

Figure 8 October 1919: "A Python Being Made to Disgorge Its Dinner—A Full-Grown Pig," p. 368.

zones; we psychically map ourselves by means of the differing intensities of pleasure and pain surrounding the body openings. Melanie Klein offers a more dynamic account; for her, the shaping processes are introjection and projection, organized by what I will call—for want of a non-anachronistic term—self-other relations. The work accomplished by this mental taking-in and spitting-out is the transition from the body experienced as reversibly permeable to the body as a bounding line or sealed container. The impulse driving this process which yields up the ego—picture of a self-contained body—is the wish to take in the mother so as to protect this all-important presence from damage or loss. But, of course, eating the mother also *ensures* her annihilation, as well as the triumph of the "aggressive" over what Klein calls the "depressive position." For Klein, the ego is the trace that marks the truce between greed and guilt.

Above, I proposed that we read the style of Bishop's poetry as the answer to a question. Now that we have gotten at the mystery of the child's horror, we may inquire more closely into the special pleasure afforded by the fantasized resemblance between penis and breast. Fantasies are not, of course, just repetitions of pleasure in a finer tone. They solve problems. Specifically, they assuage the anxiety that accompanies the sought-after pleasure. To learn what that pleasure and anxiety might be, I will go first to a picture and then to a comment on it, and finally, back to Bishop's poetry where I will end.

Earlier, I cited Lee Edelman's observation that the "critics' certainties distort IWRs'" insistence on confusion." Here, in language remarkably like, is T. J. Clark's comment on the Barnes Museum version of Cézanne's *The Bathers*:

> the unfinishedness [of the picture] is its definitiveness. It states what the conditions of depicting the body in the world amounted to.... It is as if the picture wants to offer us ... [a] figure of complete knowledge of things, of power over them, of totalization— as just part of the picture itself, an orientation inscribed onto its surface.[26]

Clark reads that "figure of complete knowledge" as the phallic mother: an "ultimate sexual material—for Cézanne, that is—which could only gradually be dragged into the light of day." Clark notes that in the 1904 photo of the canvas, the woman's body is "more flaccid, less pneumatic . . . and the penis-head is as yet no such thing." In other words, Clark shows us how Cézanne revised in the direction of a very literal picture of the uncanny, a phenomenon described by Freud as the repressed memory of home: that is, of the mother's body as a site of castration, and layered within that vision, the earlier imaginary of the mother's phallus. But Clark also shows how, in Cézanne, the vertiginous sighting is not just of the uncastrated mother but of an *erect* ("pneumatic") penis: it is that condition which inscribes "power over [things]" or "totalization."

IWR *tells* us it is a poem of the uncanny: "I knew that nothing stranger/had ever happened, that nothing/stranger *could* ever happen . . ." "How—I didn't know any/word for it—how 'unlikely' . . ." You recall that in the letter to Lowell excerpted above, Bishop says of IWR: "I know there's something very wrong and can't seem to tell what it is." In a 1970 interview with George Starbuck, she says "Something's wrong about that poem and I thought perhaps that no one would ever know.

But of course they find out everything." Bishop is talking about the *National Geographic* mis-cite but her language is not only overwrought and sexualized, it is consistent with the language of her letter to Lowell, where the anxiety is about the poem itself.

Clark's caution that the sexual material in *The Bathers* is ultimate "for Cézanne" is well taken. For in IWR, Bishop reaches back to an even earlier sighting, or perhaps, to the girl's as distinct from the boy's fantasy: a picturing of the phallus as penis and as interchangeable with the breast. The fantasy at play in *The Bathers* offers reassurance as to the body's integrity, addressing the boy's worry about castration. It is likeness—the imagined identity of men's and women's bodies—that reassures. But what kind of fantasy is on offer in Bishop's poem, or for the anxiety a girl might feel if her first *Gestalt* looks less like a wounded, differentiated body than a doubled one, or, a *mise-en-abîme*? Or again, what is it about the resemblance between the mother's breast and the father's genitals that makes it a solution to the dilemma inscribed in that picture: picture of the child who wants to eat the mother but also not to destroy her? In the same spirit, we might ask of Klein: *why* does the girl "want the penis as an object of oral satisfaction, not an attribute of masculinity," when she can have the breast?[27]

This question returns us to some unfinished business, where I earlier traced out some implications of the Freudian account of the fetish. Figurally, IWR allows us to see heterosexuality for women not as the choice of a donor who has what we lack but as love for a special kind of mother—a male mother—whom we cannot devour because the penis both is and is not the breast. By virtue of that yes/no signifying status, the penis thus represents an object that will serve the child as a defense against the (aggressive) reaches of her own desire. (By most psychoanalytic accounts of child development, the breast just *is* the mother; consuming the breast [that is, imagining consuming] means losing the mother. But both culturally and developmentally, the penis—reinscribed as phallus—operates more like a metaphor than metonym or synecdoche: not so much a *part* of the man's body, it rather *resembles* in miniature the erect posture and axial cultural position of that body.) In theory terms, IWR wonders aloud, or in pictures, whether phallocentrism—a way of seeing governed by center-periphery, mass-detail, necessity-excess relations—might be the girl's defense against her wish both to have and be the mother. Perhaps some of us idealize penis as phallus (or, consent to the notion of a phallic/Symbolic) so as to avail ourselves of a chain of substitutions that will leave the body of our primary love object intact. Thus do we safeguard the mother from our consuming desire.

So, let us say that we have arrived at the strategic, problem-solving dimension of IWR's poetics of gender "correspondence." But where is the *positive* pleasure to the fantasy? Or, to revisit my first two questions: what remains of Wordsworth when you subtract major and male, and of lyric without the structure and movement of dialectics? Further, if the fall in IWR is not into a world of division, and if writing is not presented as compensation, remedy, prosthesis—that is, antidote to that fragmentation—what kind of writing *does* the poem explain and embody?

By way of an answer, here again is T. J. Clark:

> Cézanne's paintings offer a picture of what a materialist account of the world would be like, if it were pursued to the point where the world we knew began to come apart in representation: they show us what sorts of order and intensity might be on offer when that point was reached . . . [and] whether the account would be able to admit, maybe even to relish, the vertigo it then induced[:] the impossible objects, the tenuousness of edges and orientations, a whole world without hierarchy. Or, . . . would [the picture] be bound to . . . insist on the object quand même . . .

IWR does *not* insist on "the object quand même"; as Edelman says, it insists on confusion. As with *The Bathers*, IWR makes "a tremendous effort . . . to have the existence of the body in phantasy be literalized: Not nude but naked—the body coming in or coming back as it really was." Like the painting, the poem allows itself to wonder if it might be resemblance, incorporation, and equilibrium that organize identity, rather than difference, separation, and longing. It searches for a thinking of identity as something other than a relation to difference, conceived either as a boundary or interior phenomenon.

In "The Fish," Bishop gives a succinct verbal equivalent to Cézanne's picturing: the poem is *her* attempt, one might say, "to imagine what the imagining of bodies would be like in a fully and simply physical world." "The Fish" struggles to describe an object causing the same kind of speechlessness as the "awful hanging breasts" in IWR; the fish is "terrible," "tremendous." In one of the narrator's victories over the aphasia induced by this Leviathan sublime, we find reference to "his frightening gills," "fresh and crisp with blood, / that can cut so badly." The blood is on the inside of the fish's body, crisping and sharpening the gills, but the verbal arrangement of the line insists that the blood *also* belong the person handling the fish, cut by those rigid gills. When we think about the function of the gills, organs of oxygen exchange, we realize that Bishop is imagining the structure or place where what we take to be antithetical worlds—water and air, fish and mammal—intermingle. The verbal construction of the gills establishes them as genitals, but which kind, or whose? Changing shape and turgor with blood flow, they resemble a penis. But, comprised of folds, textually linked to layered flesh, like feathers, and acting as portals, the gills take on a feminine character, reinforced in the image directly following. The narrator, seeing the gills, imagines the "pink swim-bladder" inside this five-star general of a grunting He-fish. An occulted uterus in this old man of the sea? Or, Bishop adds to the mix of sea and air, fish and mammal, another binary: male and female.

Bishop condenses this doubleness or indeterminacy in the wording of her summary simile, a very flowery, feminine one: "the pink swim-bladder / like a big peony." A *peony*? In the context of all the genital doubling, this is funny, of course, but it also strikes me as brave. Despite its rationalized surface and readerly style, IWR gives notice of the dangers this writer risks, the defenses she agrees to abandon, in deciding to take what is "like" and not "unlikely" for her object of both identification *and* desire.

In Freud's view, intellectual curiosity is a displacement of the very young child's wish to fathom the mystery of his parents' sexuality and thus of his own origins. On this view, our scientific and speculative urges reflect the wish to see as a means to know and control. Perhaps an earlier impulse, toward seeing that is *not* instrumental in that egoistic way, gets expressed in the curiosity of Bishop's writing and in the curiosity so many of us have about it. Perhaps Bishop experiments with seeing as the way we knew *before* there were objects to know or subjects of knowing—before even the Imaginary in which "I was the world in which I walked, and what I saw / Or heard or felt came not but from myself; / And there I found myself more truly and more strange."[28] Perhaps she calls back for us the kind of seeing we did before we knew how to read: before a concept of representation had emerged. What I called the sensuous tracing that defines Bishop's visual poetics recapitulates an earlier work of the soul: that of building the body in the mind—the body not as a house in which to dwell as a ghost might in a machine, but a house *as* which to dwell. "The monument's an object, yet those decorations, / carelessly nailed, looking like nothing at all, / give it away as having life, and wishing." "It is an artifact / of wood"—of *would* ("The Monument").

IN THE WAITING ROOM

In Worcester, Massachusetts,
I went with Aunt Consuelo
to keep her dentist's appointment
and sat and waited for her
in the dentist's waiting room.
It was winter. It got dark
early. The waiting room
was full of grown-up people,
arctics and overcoats,
lamps and magazines.
My aunt was inside
what seemed like a long time
and while I waited I read
the *National Geographic*
(I could read) and carefully
studied the photographs:
the inside of a volcano,
black, and full of ashes;
then it was spilling over
in rivulets of fire.
Osa and Martin Johnson
dressed in riding breeches,
laced boots, and pith helmets.
A dead man slung on a pole
—"Long Pig," the caption said.
Babies with pointed heads
wound round and round with string;
black, naked women with necks
wound round and round with wire
like the necks of light bulbs.
Their breasts were horrifying.
I read it right straight through.
I was too shy to stop.
And then I looked at the cover:
the yellow margins, the date.

Suddenly, from inside,
came an *oh!* of pain
—Aunt Consuelo's voice—
not very loud or long.
I wasn't at all surprised;
even then I knew she was
a foolish, timid woman.
I might have been embarrassed,
but wasn't. What took me
completely by surprise
was that it was *me*:
my voice, in my mouth.
Without thinking at all
I was my foolish aunt,
I—we—were falling, falling,
our eyes glued to the cover
of the *National Geographic,*
February, 1918.

I said to myself: three days
and you'll be seven years old.
I was saying it to stop
the sensation of falling off
the round, turning world
into cold, blue-black space.
But I felt: you are an *I,*
you are an *Elizabeth,*
you are one of *them.*
Why should you be one, too?
I scarcely dared to look
to see what it was I was.
I gave a sidelong glance
—I couldn't look any higher—
at shadowy gray knees,
trousers and skirts and boots
and different pairs of hands
lying under the lamps.

I knew that nothing stranger
had ever happened, that nothing
stranger could ever happen.
Why should I be my aunt,
or me, or anyone?
What similarities—
boots, hands, the family voice
I felt in my throat, or even
the *National Geographic*
and those awful hanging breasts—
held us all together
or made us all just one?
How—I didn't know any
word for it—how "unlikely". . .
How had I come to be here,
like them, and overhear
a cry of pain that could have
got loud and worse but hadn't?

The waiting room was bright
and too hot. It was sliding
beneath a big black wave,
another, and another.

Then I was back in it.
The War was on. Outside,
in Worcester, Massachusetts,
were night and slush and cold,
and it was still the fifth
of February, 1918.

> (from *Elizabeth Bishop: The Complete Poems*
> *1927–1979* [Farrar, Straus and Giroux, 1983],
> pp. 159–61)

NOTES

I thank Professor Susan Rosenbaum, Loyola University, for encouraging me to write about Bishop and for setting such a fine example with her own study of Bishop and Frank O'Hara.

All Bishop texts cited from: Elizabeth Bishop, *The Collected Prose* (Farrar, Straus, and Giroux, 1984).

Elizabeth Bishop, *The Complete Poems 1927–1979* (Farrar, Straus and Giroux, 1983).

1. Letter from Elizabeth Bishop to Robert Lowell, July 1951 ("On reading over what I've got on hand I find I'm really a minor female Wordsworth—at least, I don't know anyone else who seems to be such a Nature Lover"); quoted from *Elizabeth Bishop: One Art, Letters,* ed. Robert Giroux (Farrar, Straus and Giroux, 1994), p. 222.

2. Levinson, "Romantic Poetry: The State of the Art," *MLQ* 54.2 (June 1993), pp. 183–214; "Pre- and Post-Dialectical Materialisms; Modeling Praxis without Subjects and Objects," *Cultural Critique* #31, (fall 1995), pp. 111–128.

3. W. J. T. Mitchell, *Picture Theory: Essays on Verbal and Visual Representation* (U. of Chicago, 1994).

I had originally planned to revise this talk so as to engage directly with this discourse. Below, I offer a short bibliography of the work I found most helpful in this effort. However, my readings in the theory and historicity of seeing made me aware that the interests driving this paper belong to a different frame of reference, one that studies seeing in terms of theory and historicity of the mind. My general topic in this talk is the formation of mental representations of objects at early stages of cognitive and affective development and under the social and technological conditions of modernity.

I am not sure how to name this topic that cuts across several disciplines, but *object-relations theory* might serve. This would cover both classic and recent work by Kleinian, middle-school, and ego-psychologists (much of it from a feminist position) as well as studies in philosophy, and in the neuro- and cognitive-sciences that investigate mind-body relations at the level of representation. Or, to give titles that mark both the humanistic and scientific poles of the discourse, *Sexuality in the Field of Vision* by Jacqueline Rose and *The Body in the Mind* by Mark Johnson. Johnson's title usefully names the phenomenon studied by those in one way or another influenced by Wilder Penfield's 1950 mapping of the "sensory homunculus"—"a greatly distorted representation of the body on the surface of the [cerebral cortex.]" Work that draws on Penfield's study poses such questions as, How and at what point(s) do mental representations of the body come into being? How are they altered as body configurations change (as with age, disease, loss of limb)? How do technological extensions of the body such as the camera, the typewriter, the computer, change the inner representation of the body? How do technologies of circulation and transportation (e.g., railway travel) bear on the psychic structuring of time and space? How do affective changes in the individual (such as an idiopathic depression) and in group experience (viz., Holocaust survivors and survivors' children) shape our most basic cognitive modes of self-other, mind-body experience? What evolutionary interests are served (or obstructed) by particular mind-body linkages? How might we describe the connections between long-term evolutionary interests and immediate social interests having to do with race, class, and gender?

I am also drawn to studies in both speculative and developmental biology that are developing fresh accounts of biological entities, environments, persistence, and causality. Thus far, most of our materialist readings of culture and literature have patterned their vision on Marx's picture of the laboring body; Freud's picture of the sexual, desiring/repressing body; and Darwin's picture of the historically evolving body. Each of these pictures has been to various degrees critiqued by the conditions of the present: in the case of Marx, a postindustrial world; a far less Oedipally and gender-determined world than Freud's; and, vis-à-vis Darwin, a world that includes genetic engineering and Daniel Dennett. Foucault's picture of the discursive body, which models the human as an endless practice of self-other definition, has offered a good alternative to the (so-called) essentialism of the Darwin/Marx/Freud paradigms. However, critics who work on the aesthetic per se, and who want to push their analysis to a place beyond or before verbal representation—that is, who want to study precisely those qualities in the text or practice that cannot be explained by its cultural conditions of being—are looking to cognitive research for fresh angles on the inherited dualisms of observer and observed, entity and environment, consciousness and behavior. It is my feeling that the "new formalism" in literary studies, which seems to conceive of itself as an institutionally conservative method, might well express a progressive interest of the kind I just sketched. To realize that interest, however, a new formalism would set aside Aristotle's normative picture of the human with its peculiar completeness, unity, and purposiveness (and Kant's extrapolation from the visually discrete natural body to the textually or graphically discrete aesthetic body) so as to acquaint itself with various mind-matter, part-whole, formal/material/final cause paradigms emerging from the cognitive sciences. A formalism conducted along these lines would be a re-invention not a retreat.

Short bibliography in the discourse of picture-theory:

Martin Jay, *Downcast Eyes: The Denigration of Vision in 20th-Century French Thought*, (U. Cal., 1993); David Michael Levin, ed., *Modernity and the Hegemony of Vision* (U. Cal., 1993); Leo Charney and Vanessa Schwartz, eds., *Cinema and the Invention of Modern Life* (U. Cal., 1995); Hal Foster, *The Return of the Real: The Avant-Garde at the End of the Century* (MIT, 1996); Rosalind Krauss, *The Optical Unconscious* (MIT, 1993); Griselda Pollock, *Vision and Difference: Femininity, Feminism and the Histories of Art* (Routledge, 1988); Johanna Drucker, *Theorizing Modernism: Visual Art and the Critical Tradition* (Columbia, 1994); Louis Marin, *To Destroy Painting* (trans. Mette Hjort; Chicago, 1995); James Elkins, *The Object Stares Back: On the Nature of Seeing* (Harcourt Brace, 1996); Elkins, *The Poetics of Perspective* (Cornell, 1994); Jonathan Crary, *Techniques of the Observer: On Vision and Modernity in the 19th Century* (MIT, 1990); Jacqueline Rose, *Sexuality in the Field of Vision* (Verso, 1986); Susan Bordo, *The*

Flight to Objectivity: Essays on Cartesianism and Culture (SUNY, 1987); Bordo, *Unbearable Weight: Feminism, Western Culture, and the Body* (U. Cal., 1993); Wolfgang Schivelbusch, *Railway Journey: The Industrialization of Time and Space in the 19th Century* (U. Cal, 1977; trans. 1986).

Short bibliography of representation-study in the cognitive and neuro-sciences:

W. Penfield and T. Rasmussen, *The Cerebral Cortex of Man: A Clinical Study of Localization of Function*; V. S. Ramachandran and Sandra Blakeslee, *Phantoms in the Brain: Probing the Mysteries of the Human Mind* (William Morrow, 1998); Daniel Dennett, *Consciousness Explained* (Little, Brown, 1991); Dennett, *Darwin's Dangerous Idea: Evolution and the Meanings of Life* (Simon and Schuster, 1995); Stephen Pinker, *The Language Instinct: How the Mind Creates Language* (Harper, 1994); Pinker, *How the Mind Works*; Paul M. Churchland, *The Engine of Reason, the Seat of the Soul: A Philosophical Journey into the Brain* (MIT, 1995); Gerald Edelman, *Bright Air, Brilliant Fire*; Terrence Deacon, *The Symbolic Species: The Co-evolution of Language and the Brain*; Edward Wilson, *Consilience*; Barkow, Tooby, and Cosmides, *The Adapted Mind: Evolutionary Psychology and the Generation of Culture*; Antonio Damasio, *Descartes' Error: Emotion, Reason, and the Human Brain*; Michael Ghiselin, *Metaphysics and the Origin of Species*.

Of related interest:

Francisco Varela and Umberto Maturana, *Autopoeisis and Cognition: The Realization of the Living* (D. Reidel, 1980); Varela, Evan Thompson, Eleanor Rosch, *The Embodied Mind: Cognitive Science and Human Experience* (MIT, 1991); Marvin Minsky, *The Society of Mind* (Simon and Schuster, 1986); Richard Dawkins, *The Selfish Gene* (OUP, 1976); Dawkins, *The Extended Phenotype* (OUP, 1982); Rupert Sheldrake, *The Presence of the Past: Morphic Resonance and the Habits of Nature* (Random House, 1988). From another angle, Robert Corrington, *An Introduction to C. S. Peirce: Philosopher, Semiotician, and Ecstatic Naturalist*; Eugene Gendlin, *Experiencing and the Creation of Meaning: A Philosophical and Psychological Approach to the Subjective* (NY: Free Press of Glencoe, 1962); Gendlin, *Language Beyond Postmodernism: Saying and Thinking in Gendlin's Philosophy* (Northwestern, 1997).

4. "Posthumous Critique," in *In Near Ruins: Cultural Theory at the End of the Century*, ed. Nicholas Dirks (U. Minnesota, 1998). The "theory-question," so-called, has never made much sense to me when it is posed by a community of critical readers. How could reading ever be anything *but* theory, a way of seeing and at the same time an effort to define and account for that way of seeing as best one can and acknowledging the error and partiality of the account? David Bohm frames the place of theory in science as follows: ". . . in scientific research, a great deal of thinking is done in terms of *theories*. The word 'theory' derives from the Greek 'theoria,' which has the same root as 'theatre,' in a word meaning 'to view' or 'to make a spectacle.' Thus, it might be said that a theory is primarily a form of *insight*, i.e., a way of looking at the world, and not a form of *knowledge* of how the world is." Bohm, *Wholeness and the Implicate Order* (Routledge, 1980; 1981), p. 3.

5. "Back to the Future," chap. 1, *Rethinking Historicism: Critical Readings in Romantic History* (Blackwell, 1990).

6. Where Romanticism defined the poet as a "prophet looking backwards" (Friedrich Schlegel), the Frankfurt School establishes the critic as a historian of the future.

7. Paul Mann, *Theory-Death of the Avant-Garde* (Indiana, 1991); Mann, *Masocriticism*, (SUNY, 1998).

8. I have only recently begun reading in this vein: Caroline Bynum, *Fragmentation and Redemption: Essays on Gender and the Human Body in Medieval Religion* (Zone, 1992); Bynum, *The Resurrection of the Body* (Columbia, 1995); Daniel Boyarin, *A Radical Jew: Paul and the Politics of Identity* (U. Cal. 1994); *Unheroic Conduct: The Rise of Heterosexuality and the Invention of the Jewish Man* (U. Cal., 1997); Sander Gilman, *The Jew's Body* (Routledge, 1991); Gilman, *Freud, Race, and Gender* (Princeton, 1993); Howard Eilberg-Schwartz, ed., *God's Phallus and Other Problems for Men and Monotheism* (Beacon, 1994); Eilbert-Schwartz, *People of the Body: Jews and Judaism from an Embodied Perspective* (SUNY, 1992).

9. I frame my description as an alternative to the work of "intervening" based on the Sartrean "project." For approaches to a notion of practice and value beyond work, see: André Gorz, *Farewell to the Working Class: An Essay on Post-Industrial Socialism*, trans. Mike Sonenscher (South End, 1982); Gorz, *Critique of Economic Reason*, trans. Gillian Handyside and Chris Turner (Verso, 1989); Kristin Ross, *The Emergence of Social Space: Rimbaud and the Paris Commune* (Minnesota, 1988); Paul Lafargue (La Droit à la Paresse, 1878); Jeremy Rifkin, *The End of Work: The Decline of the Global Labor Force and the Dawn of the Post-Market Era* (Putnam, 1995). My original aim was to develop a reading of Romanticism that began elsewhere than with Hegel and that was richer, more rigorous and independent, and conceptually more consequential, than the various swerves from orthodoxy one sees in Romantic period studies: e.g., rehabilitations of the gothic, of the literatures of sentiment and sensibility, and of performativity as defining modes of Romanticism.

10. Mark Johnson, *The Body in the Mind; The Bodily Basis of Meaning, Imagination, and Reason* (Chicago, 1987); Varela and Maturana, *Autopoeisis and Cognition*.

11. Gyanendra Pandey, "The Culture of History," in *In Near Ruins*; E. Valentine Daniels, "The Limits of Culture," in *In Near Ruins*; Ashis Nandy, *The Intimate Enemy: Loss and Recovery of Self Under Colonialism* (OUP, 1983); Partha Chatterjee, *The Nation and Its Fragments: Colonial and Postcolonial Histories* (Princeton, 1993).

12. See, for example, Varela and Maturana; Dawkins; and Sheldrake.

13. David Bohm and B. J. Hiley, *The Undivided Universe: An Ontological Interpretation of Quantum Theory* (Routledge, 1993); Bohm, *Causality and Chance in Modern Physics* (Routledge, 1957); Bohm, *Wholeness and the Implicate Order* (Routledge, 1980); Arkady Plotnitsky, *Configurations: Critical Theory and General Economy* (U. Florida, 1993).

14. Levinson, "State of the Art," *MLQ* (1993).

15. I find R. S. Crane's *neo*-Aristotelian (i.e., constructivist) shading more suggestive now than I did in the seventies: "what a poet does distinctively as a poet is to build materials of language and experience into wholes of various kinds, to which as we experience them, we tend to attribute final rather than merely instrumental value." *Critics and Criticism* (Chicago, 1952), p. 13.

16. Levinson, *The Romantic Fragment Poem: A Critique of a Form* (North Carolina, 1986); Levinson, *Wordsworth's Great Period Poems* (Cambridge, 1986); Levinson, *Keats's Life of Allegory: The Origins of a Style* (Blackwell, 1989). My essay, "Object-Loss and Object-Bondage: Economies of Representation in Hardy's Poetry," finds in the instance of Hardy's poetry a writing that neither mobilizes loss into value nor offers itself as a field of full presence. When modernity is defined not as nostalgia (as in Peter Laslett's *The World We Have Lost*) but as eternal return (the loss of loss itself), the experiment of a truly modern writing is to disable the breeding machinery of language and desire.

17. Thomas Travisano, "The Elizabeth Bishop Phenomenon," in *Gendered Modernisms: American Women Poets and Their Readers*, ed. Travisano and Margaret Dickey, 1966; Langdon Hammer, "The New Elizabeth Bishop," *Yale Review* 82 (1993).

18. Peter Bollas, *The Shadow of the Object: Psychoanalysis of the Unthought Known* (Columbia, 1987).

19. Naomi Schor, *Reading in Detail: Aesthetics and the Feminine* (Routledge, 1987).

20. Letter to Lowell, August 30, 1967, quoted in Brett Millier, *Elizabeth Bishop: Life and the Memory of It* (U. Cal., 1993), p. 394.

21. Mira Schor, *Wet: On Painting, Feminism, and Art Culture* (Duke, 1997), p. 35.

22. J. Laplanche and J. B. Pontalis, *The Language of Psycho-Analysis*, trans. Donald Nicholson-Smith (Norton, 1973), pp. 410–11.

23. Lee Edelman, "The Geography of Gender: Elizabeth Bishop's 'In the Waiting Room,'" in *Elizabeth Bishop: The Geography of Gender*, ed. Marilyn May Lombardi (U. Virginia, 1993), pp. 91–110 (rpt. from *Contemporary Literature* [summer 1985]).

24. Michel Foucault, *The Order of Things: An Archaeology of the Human Sciences* (Random House, 1970; rpt. 1994), chapters 2 and 3.

25. H. L. Mencken, *In Defense of Women* (1922).

26. T. J. Clark, quoted from manuscript version of "Freud's Cézanne," in *Representations* 52, (fall 1995), pp. 94–122.

27. Noreen O'Connor and Joanna Ryan, *Wild Desires and Mistaken Identities: Lesbianism and Psychoanalysis* (Virago, 1993), p. 79 (quoted from Melanie Klein, *The Psycho-Analysis of Children* [Virago, 1989], p. 196).

28. Susan McCabe (*Elizabeth Bishop: Her Poetics of Loss* [Penn State, 1994], pp. 214–15) assembles excerpts from Bishop's poetry that trope dangling, trailing, peninsular things and relations.

Textual note: in Bishop's posthumously published short story "The Country Mouse," probably written in 1961, the Aunt Consuelo figure is named Aunt Jenny, family pseudonym for Bishop's father's sister, Florence. In the story, Jenny keeps canaries, a trait in fact belonging to Bishop's mother's sister, Maud. The incident described in both poem and story—the visit to the dentist—occurred at the time of Bishop's move from the home of her paternal grandparents and aunt to that of her maternal aunt. In noting the derivation of "Consuelo" from "consolar," or "to console," Edelman brings out the maternal resonance of the name Bishop chooses for the poem. I detail these facts so as to bring out the way that a confusion or continuum of genders operates through these texts, not a progression or a layering.

8

JEFF NUNOKAWA

THE PROTESTANT ETHIC AND THE SPIRIT OF ANOREXIA: THE CASE OF OSCAR WILDE

I

FOR ALL HIS LAWLESSNESS, there is one venue where the subject of desire featured in *The Picture of Dorian Gray* has proven himself the most exemplary of citizens. At least by the lights of a contemporary sensibility concerned to expose what passes for natural proclivities as cultural constructions invented and imposed by the discourses which claim only to reveal them, the reprobate hero of Wilde's novel could hardly be more cooperative. As if pressed into the service of this sensibility *avant le lettre*, the story the novel tells of Dorian Gray's developing desire describes a trajectory of de-essentialism, in which his erotic passions appear less and less an expression of inherent attribute, and more and more a function of external influence, less and less like a natural hunger that arises from within the subject, and more and more like an infection or an affectation, picked up by the subject who is constituted in the very act of absorbing what is alien to him, a trajectory of de-essentialism celebrated by Lord Henry, its principal progragandist in the novel, as the conversion of "appetite into art."[1]

As the history of his sexuality begins, Dorian Gray's desires appear as the dormant urges of his nature, awakened by a famous speech that will sound, even to those who haven't read it already, like a line that they have heard before:

> There is no such thing as a good influence ... to influence a person is to give him one's own soul. He does not think his natural thoughts, or burn with his natural passions. ... To realize one's nature perfectly—that is what each of us is here for. People ... have forgotten the highest of all duties, the duty that one owes to one's own self. They feed the hungry and clothe the beggar, but their own souls starve.... Every impulse that we strive to strangle broods in the mind, and poisons us.... The only way to get rid of a temptation is to yield to it. Resist it, and your soul grows sick with longing. (61–62)

And those who have read Wilde's novel, as well as those who have not, will know full well the drama of revelation that comes next:

> "Stop!" faltered Dorian Gray, "stop! you bewilder me. I don't know what to say.... Let me think. Or rather let me try not to think."
> He was dimly conscious that entirely fresh influences were at work within him. Yet they seemed to have come really from himself. The ... words ... had touched some secret chord that had never been touched before, but that he felt was now vibrating and throbbing to curious pulses. (62)

Almost as soon as the speech praising them is done, though, the "natural passions" of Dorian Gray's "own soul" that Lord Henry's eloquence apparently brings out in this passage give way to the desires of another, and this displacement of "natural passions" by alien ones only grows more blatant as the chronicle of his erotic development continues. "[T]he ideology of ... essence implicit in Lord Henry's speech ... produces the very 'nature' or self that it seems only to reveal,"[2] Lee Edelman remarks, and whatever quibbles might attach themselves to his concise deconstruction of the repression hypothesis Lord Henry rehearses in the novel's primal scene are quite overwhelmed by the general direction of Dorian Gray's erotic development. If the scene of sexual instruction in *Dorian Gray* is somewhat more ambiguous than Edelman's brisk poststructuralist reading of it admits, he is surely faithful to the movement of the story as a whole. Any passion or proclivity that might have dwelt within Dorian Gray before Lord Henry gets to him, any desire

that might have been exposed and activated rather than wholly produced by his manipulations, has almost entirely disappeared by the
time they are recollected the morning after:

> [H]ow charming he had been . . . the night before. . . . Talking to
> him was like playing upon an exquisite violin. He answered to
> every touch and thrill of the bow. . . . There was something terri-
> bly enthralling in the exercise of influence. No other activity was
> like it. To project one's soul into some gracious form . . . to con-
> vey one's own temperament into another as though it were a
> subtle fluid or a strange perfume: there was real joy in that.
> (74–75)

And that's just the beginning. From this moment on, the prospect of
an essential self and a strain of desire which is the currency of that self
recedes further and further from view, displaced by an apparently inex-
haustible catalogue of alien ones that Dorian Gray absorbs instead, a
catalogue whose first entry is a "poisonous book," "a psychological
study of a certain young Parisian, who spent his life trying to realize in
the nineteenth century all the passions . . . that belonged to every century except his own" (141).

This rejection of essentialism is almost as famous an aspect of Wilde
as the one which has arrested the attention of his friends and enemies
since his command performance at the Old Bailey. No less well known
by now is the alliance between these things proposed or assumed by a
range of recent criticism, the alliance located in and then beyond Oscar
Wilde between perversity and postmodernism, between sexual dissidence and the denial of depth, an alliance whose most fundamental
link is the by now common sense that the concept of essence is the
prop of a heterosexual normativity whose propagations rely on the
claim that nature is on its side.[3]

The school of queer theory which congratulates for its political
subversiveness the habit of displacing the essential or natural by the
interpolated or performed subject of desire, a school of theory which
has found an inaugural genius in Wilde's life and work,[4] has been
much criticized lately, not least of all by the theorist whose own work
has been enlisted as the core curriculum of that school.[5] It is not my

intention to enter directly into this controversy. I will be concerned here not to assess the liberatory efficacy of the impulse to de-essentialize, but rather to consider the social character of this impulse along lines removed from the binary topography of subversion and containment altogether. I will read Wilde to trace a genealogy of this impulse, a genealogy which suggests that whatever its contemporary social effects, the theory and practice of de-essentialism is itself sometimes the effect of a social force situated far from the field of sexual politics where its dimensions have typically been taken in recent years, a social force quite foreign to the intimate affects which charge that field, but whose invisible hand, like the distant financial cataclysm whose reverberations shake the domestic economy, helps to define their terms.

A social force which takes form in the specter which briefly arises in *The Picture of Dorian Gray* to describe the fate of those who, evading what the libertine calls "the highest of duties," fail to appease their natural desires: "their souls starve." I will argue here that the swerve from essentialism in Wilde is as much a defense against this specter, as it is resistance to the ideological conditions of heterosexual hegemony; I will argue that this specter arises in the first place to punish a proclivity associated not with the party of sexual perversity, but rather with the leisure class; a taste not for unorthodox erotic passions and practices, but rather for the abstention from labor which constitutes the canon of that class; a tendency at odds not with any protocol of sexual propriety, but rather with the compulsion to work best known as the Protestant Ethic.

II

The resistance to work that usually goes without saying, a proclivity as generally understated as it is generally understood, is more blatantly exhibited in Wilde's colorful excursion into the regions of the dismal science. As removed, at least at first glance, from the charged terrain of sexual dissidence as "a more than usually lengthy lecture by the University Extension Scheme on the Influence of a Permanent Income on Thought" that nobody dreams of attending in *The Importance of Being*

Earnest, the spirit of nonconformity that animates the expanded version of that lecture Wilde called "The Soul of Man Under Socialism" (1891) is no less audacious than the one that landed him in Reading Gaol:

> Every man must be quite free to choose his own work. No form of compulsion must be exercised over him. If there is, his work will not be good for him, not good in itself, and will not be good for others. And by work I simply mean activity of any kind.... It is mentally and morally injurious to man to do anything in which he does not find pleasure, and many forms of labour are quite pleasureless activities and should be regarded as such.[6]

Like any utopian drive, Wilde's aspiration to end work as we know it, an aspiration sufficiently ambitious to oppose a rule of civilization hard to tell from a principle of reality, begins with conditions close to home. As things stand now, a happy few already have the high life where work is play, a site of liberty and a source of joy, a happy few dwell already in the House Beautiful where work takes its form from the disinterested delight of art, a happy few already inhabit the holiday pastoral where labor, changed utterly, cleansed of the element of compulsion to which it is typically yoked, has blossomed into pleasure; a happy few "who have private means of their own," and are thus "under no necessity to work for their living," the happy few "able to choose the sphere of activity that is really congenial to them and gives them pleasure" (1019).

But "*every* man must be quite free to choose his own work," and as things stand now

> there are a great many people who, having no private property of their own, and being always on the brink of sheer starvation, are compelled to do the work of beasts of burden, to do work that is quite uncongenial to them, and to which they are forced by the peremptory, unreasonable, degrading Tyranny of want. (1019)

By "converting private property into public wealth" and thus "ensur[ing] the material well-being of each member of the community," "Socialism, Communism, or whatever one chooses to call it" (1019) will dismantle the Tyranny of Want, and thus allow everyone, and not just the subsidized elite to do as they please. By "ensur[ing] the material well-being of each member of the community," "Socialism, Communism, or whatever one chooses to call it" will abolish the slavery of forced labor that Marx, in a waggish inversion that Wilde himself might well have savored, called "free." "Socialism, Communism, or whatever one chooses to call it," will liberate the working class from the obligation to toil for the food it needs to live and allow them to take their rightful place in the kingdom of leisure. And so, with a stroke of a pen like a wave of a wand, Wilde envisions total victory for a principle as dear to his heart as anything: "pleasure! What else should bring one anywhere?"[7] "What else is there to live for?"[8]

But if Wilde's socialist inclinations are in their own way as bold as a love that declines to heed a battery of discouragements as variously broad and deep as the culture that it occupies, they are even less frequently expressed. Aside from sporadic sightings here and there, Wilde's card-carrying involvement with the tradition of utopian prophecy is as brief as the length of a single essay. It may be that the yearning for a society where the tyranny of want and thus the obligation to work has been abolished seldom expresses itself in Wilde's book not, as with another yearning rarely disposed to speak its name, from a lack of nerve, but rather a lack of need; not because it is scandalous but rather because it appears superfluous.

For in the Society that Wilde was pleased to know, the tyranny of want is as good as gone. The compulsion to labor could hardly be further removed from the Society of conspicuous leisure which is the only one to show up on Wilde's map; the brilliant Society which usually eclipses any broader one, and not only in Oscar Wilde's eyes. How could the requirement to work for a living have a hold over anyone who's anyone on the stage where his spotlight is trained—the lounging exquisite, the sardonic dowager, the well-heeled misanthrope, the headstrong heiress—who saunter through the luxurious premises charted by a collection of writings which might just as well be called a more than usually lengthy lecture on the Influence of a Permanent Income on Thought?

What could the working stiff have to do with the society swell whose only occupation is a way of life defined by the "conspicuous abstention from labor,"[9] that its preeminent taxonomer identified as the signature style of what he called the leisure class? Perhaps a little more than either might have imagined: For as the dandy's defender knows, the labor of ostentatiously abstaining from it is no life for the slacker:

> idle ... How can you say such a thing? Why, he rides in the Row at ten o'clock in the morning, goes to the Opera three times a week, changes his clothes at least five times a day, and dines out every night of the season. You don't call that leading an idle life, do you? (*An Ideal Husband*, 393)

Nice work if you can get it, but High Society is no utopia, even in miniature: as routinized as the work week from which they distinguish themselves, its rituals of leisure hardly satisfy the condition of absolute freedom that is Wilde's standard for the good life; they hardly count as "the activity" detached from "compulsion of any kind," "the activity," "congenial," "pleasurable," and "quite freely chosen"—which is the only sort that Wilde's brand of socialism allows. Released from the requirement to work, the leisure-class subject is assigned instead the task of refraining from it, and if the task proves to be one, if not chosen, at least not minded by the subject to whom it is allotted, this is no more than the lucky coincidence of temperament and necessity that occurs to anyone not wholly done in by the job he has to do in any case: "It is awfully hard work doing nothing. However, I don't mind hard work where there is no definite object of any kind" (*Earnest*, 498).

No slouch himself, Wilde, when he wasn't spending it with reckless abandon, was busy throughout most his life working for his living: It may be, to take a page from the fairy tales, that his dedication to the protocol of the leisure class resembles the self-abnegating devotion of a misshapen troll for a haughty queen.[10] But whatever the sources of his fervor, the "conspicuous abstention from labor" is never more so than in Wilde's social register, even considering the wealth of gilded-age displays that surround it. If the pattern dandy in *An Ideal Husband* is "the idlest man in London," it must have been a hard contest to call, since the boulevards, houses, and clubs are crowded with others whose unemployment is no less assiduously underscored in Wilde's writings.

The concentrated pageantry of the dandy's daily rounds is sublimated and disseminated in the care with which Wilde generally asserts the indolence of the characters he features. Like the social arbiter whose eagerness he derides—"she treats her guests exactly as an auctioneer treats his goods"—Wilde wastes no time indicating their abstention from labor, announcing it either in so many words, or by habits and dispositions that may as well be: "He had set himself to the serious study of the great aristocratic art of doing nothing" (*Dorian Gray*, 71); He was "a delightful, ineffectual young man with a perfect profile and no profession";[11] "pleasure, pleasure! What else should bring one anywhere?"; "'Well, Harry . . . what brings you out so early? I thought you dandies never got up till twelve, and were not visible till five'" (*Dorian Gray*, 72).

However well documented Wilde's carelessness about other, more pressing prohibitions, no one is more respectful of the "tabu" as cardinal for high society as the one against incest for society in general, the tabu which by Veblen's account, "comes to be . . . not only an honorific or meritorious act, but a . . . requisite of decency." As much as he allows intimations of other transgressions to gather around his reprobate hero, Wilde is careful to certify his conformity to this rule of decency; as much as we are encouraged to suspect him of other vices, we are compelled to recognize his rectitude when it comes at least to this "index of reputability." Indeed, our suspicion of the first is the implicit certification of the second, since the late-night intrigues that absorb him could only involve one who, like his counterpart or alias in the pornographic adventure, never has to worry about getting to work in the morning; since leisure is the implicit condition for the trivial and even less reputable pursuits announced and insinuated in *The Picture of Dorian Gray*, amateur interests and serious addictions that can only be a way of life for someone who never has to worry about getting to work at all.

Less acute than the tyranny that compels labor, the pressure to abstain from it, a pressure as elusive, typically, as an ambiguous admonition—"In my day, one never met anyone in society who worked for their living. It was not considered the thing"[12]—all the force of gravity in the social world that Wilde charts; intangible, but by no means immaterial, the pang that enforces the rule of leisure is as effective in its own way as the one that enforces its counterpart. Apparently lighter than the tyranny that compels labor, the pressure to abstain from it is never too light to pass unfelt by the subject of Wilde's preferred Society, no matter how immune to social pressure he is generally. The "rough-mannered old bachelor . . . whom the outside world called self-ish because it derived no particular benefit from him, but who was considered generous by Society," is as indifferent to the judgment of the first as he is sensitive to that of the second. Deaf to the disapproval of the outside world, the misanthrope who "set[s] himself to the serious study of the great aristocratic art of doing nothing" could hardly be more alert to the appearance of what High Society counts as the essence of impropriety:

> [He] . . . paid some attention to the management of his collieries in the Midland counties, excusing himself for this taint of industry on the ground that the one advantage of having coal was that it enabled a gentleman to afford the decency of burning a wood on his own hearth. (*Dorian Gray*, 71)

A joke, of course—but like fire in a theater, or firearms at the airport, the "taint of industry" is a grave-enough charge in Wilde's leisure-class canon that even its most facetious assertion calls for immediate investigation. If the aristocrat in question can't be serious, or only half so about a taint of industry attached to his slight attention to the management of his coal mines, a taint of industry itself tainted by the coal miners to which it is slightly connected, he still takes the trouble to mention and dispel it. If no one else apart from the defendant himself hears the accusation of this taint, that is because it is delivered by what Simmel calls the "voice of conscience": "The voice of conscience we hear only in ourselves, although in comparison with all subjective egoism, we hear it with a force and decisiveness which apparently can stem only from a tribunal outside the individual."[13] Mildly mocking the overwrought supervision that he nonetheless effectively embraces, the aristocrat in question, like an ironic but ultimately friendly witness before the committee on subversion, seeks to clear his name of the suspicions attached to it by the remotest of associations. His fleeting identification with the working class is terminated when, at the conclusion of his testimony, the aristocrat recalls his affiliation with the class that doesn't, when he "excus[es] himself for this taint of industry on the ground that the one advantage of having coal was that it enabled a *gentleman* to afford the decency of burning a wood on his own hearth."

But more is at stake in avoiding work than the profits of invidious comparison that Veblen's contemporary counterpart calls symbolic capital.[14] If the urge to abstain from labor is an elementary form of the drive for distinction that Veblen and his heirs locate at the center of Society,[15] it is also the means of evading the corrosive grip of Work as we know it, a regime of Industry that touches all parts of the everyday hell that Wilde, in "The Critic as Artist," calls Action:

> There is no mode of action . . . that we do not share with the lower animals. . . . Action, indeed, is always easy, and when presented to us in its most aggravated, because most continuous form, which I take to be that of real industry, becomes simply the refuge of people who have nothing whatsoever to do. . . . It is to do nothing that the elect exist. Action is limited and relative. Unlimited and absolute is the vision of him who sits at ease and watches. . . . Thought is degraded by its constant association with practice. . . . Each of the professions means a prejudice. The necessity for a career forces every one to take sides. We live in the age of the overworked, and the undereducated; the age in which people are so industrious that they become absolutely stupid. (256, 275, 278)[16]

A specter haunts this vision of action: that specter is labor. More than mere instances of the "being we share with the lower animals," its aspects constitute the essence of this abject sphere. Action in its "most aggravated" "form" is "real industry"; if thought is corrupted in general by "its constant association with practice," it is compromised in particular by overwork ("We live in the age of the overworked, and the undereducated"), and negated utterly by industriousness ("people are so industrious that they become absolutely stupid").[17]

As familiar as the pangs of hunger, the hardness of labor with which action in general is identified here has the feel of an inflexible sentence, like the speed of light or the Fall of Man. But no less than the pleasures of sexuality, the pains of labor can be read as social symptoms; no less than the pulsations of the erotic, the dull or acute strains of working for a living may be read as political promulgations masked as mere facts of life. No less than sexuality, what Marcuse calls "the fundamental fact" of "more or less painful arrangements and undertakings for the procurement of the means for satisfying needs" is shaped by social contingencies that make a permanent fixture of the human condition as much the artifact of the epoch it inhabits.[18]

The tradition of critical thought most notably concerned with the social specificity of work has concerned itself in particular to take the dimensions of a historical regime of labor close to home, a historical regime that defines work as we know it, a regime we can glimpse in the figure of "real industry" that Wilde denigrates and more extensively in another phase of his quarrel with Action in "The Critic as Artist":

> don't talk about action. It is a blind thing dependent on external influences, and moved by an impulse of whose nature it is unconscious. It is a thing incomplete in its essence, because limited by accident, and ignorant of its direction, being always at variance with its aim ... the man of action ... knows neither the origin of his deeds nor their results. From the field in which he thought that he had sown thorns, we have gathered our vintage, and the fig-tree that he planted for our pleasure is as barren as the thistle, and more bitter.... Each little thing that we do passes into the great machine of life which may grind our virtues to powder and make them worthless, or transform our sins into elements of a new civilization. (256, 257)

Like the abstract art which sublimates a concrete passion, or the diffuse despair that camouflage a local pain, this panoramic picture of the *vita activa* bears signs of a more particular historical circumstance, a circumstance located in the specific figure that Wilde employs here to comprehend human action, the figure of the factory where individual acts melt into the impersonal process of labor: "Each little thing that we do passes into the great machine of life which may grind our virtues to powder and make them worthless, or transform them into elements of a new civilization." The amputation of agency that is the casualty of action generally in Wilde's account describes in particular the condition of capitalism that Marx called alienated labor:

> the worker is related to the *product of his labour* as to an *alien* object. . . . What is embodied in the product of his labour is no longer his own. The greater this product is, therefore, the more he is diminished. The *alienation* of the worker in his product means not only that his labour becomes an object, assumes an *external* existence, but that it exists independently, outside himself, and alien to him, and that it stands opposed to him as an autonomous power. . . .
>
> [A]lienation appears not merely in the result but also in the process of production, within productive activity itself . . . work is external to the worker . . . he does not fulfill himself in his work but denies himself.[19]

"If we follow the path taken by labour in its development from the handicraft via co operation and manufacture to machine industry," Lukács remarks in his decisive report on the condition of alienated labor,

> we can see a continuous trend towards greater rationalization, the progressive elimination of the qualitative, human and individual attributes of the worker . . . the process of labour is progressively broken down into abstract, rational, specialized operations so that the worker loses contact with the finished product and his work is reduced to the mechanical repetition of a specialized set of actions. . . . The . . . stance adopted towards a process mechanically conforming to fixed laws and enacted independently of man's consciousness and impervious to human intervention, i.e. a perfectly closed system, must likewise transform the basic categories of man's immediate attitude to the world. . . . Here, too, the personality can do no more than look on helplessly while its own existence is reduced to an isolated particle and fed into an alien system.[20]

Circulated by the broad ideological apparatus Lukács calls reification, the condition of the working class covers the entire sphere of human action in "The Critic as Artist." Here, "the stance adopted towards a process mechanically conforming to fixed laws and enacted independently of man's consciousness and impervious to human intervention" is the depressed condition of anyone who does anything; here the machine to which Wilde in "The Soul of Man Under Socialism" remarks "man has been . . . the slave" (1028), the machine of "real industry" where the alienation of labor is concentrated has expanded to become "the great machine of life which may grind our virtues to powder and make them worthless, or transform our sins into elements of a new civilization," but which defeats in any case even our most artful intentions.

To escape the shadow of the machine broad enough to cover all forms of human effort, Wilde invokes a vision of absolute idleness quite distinct from the conspicuous abstention from labor that characterizes the condition of the leisure class, an absolute idleness which echoes what Hannah Arendt calls the "error" of an ancient idealism that condemns all action as the annulment of the actor's agency and autonomy, and which, in her words, locates their "salvation" "in non-acting, in abstention from the whole realm of human affairs as the only means to safeguard one's sovereignty and integrity as a person":[21]

> Let me say to you now that to do nothing at all is the most difficult thing in the world, the most difficult and the most intellectual. To Plato, with his passion for wisdom, this was the noblest form of energy. To Aristotle, with his passion for knowledge, this was the noblest form of energy also. It was this that the passion for holiness led the saint and the mystic of medieval days. . . . It is to do nothing that the elect exist. Action is limited and relative. Unlimited and absolute is the vision of him who sits at ease and watches. . . . The gods live thus. . . . We, too, might live like them, and set ourselves to witness with appropriate emotions the varied scenes that man and nature afford. We might make ourselves spiritual by detaching ourselves from action, and become perfect by the rejection of energy. (275, 277–78)

Behind its classical sound, the cold pastoral retreat that Wilde proposes bears the traces of a distinctly modern pattern of flight. To evade the specter of labor that haunts all human activity in a world where the machine of "real industry" has become "the great machine of life," Wilde points to a region of unbroken ease, a recess illuminated now less by the wisdom of the ages than the light of the television screen; a sphere of leisure less like the condition of classical contemplation than a day spent in bed. "[W]ith its fragmentation of labour, modern industrial civilization creates . . . a need for leisure," Henri Lefebvre observes, whose "most striking imperative"

> is that it must produce a *break*. . . . Thus there is an increasing emphasis on leisure characterized as distraction: rather than bringing any new worries, obligations, or necessities, leisure should offer liberation from worry and necessity. Liberation and pleasure—such are the essential characteristics of leisure, according to the parties concerned. . . . So those involved tend to reject ambiguous forms of leisure which might resemble work or entail some kind of obligation. . . . They mistrust anything which might appear to be educational and are more concerned with those aspects of leisure which might offer *distraction, entertainment* and *repose,* and which might compensate for the difficulties of everyday life.[22]

What Lefebvre diagnoses here as an aversion to labor sensitive even to the slightest insinuation of its hold—the tendency "to reject ambiguous forms of leisure which might resemble work or entail some kind of obligation"—determines the idleness that Wilde exults in "The Critic as Artist," an idleness as hollow as the holiday dedicated to "do[ing] nothing at all." For it is only when the sphere of leisure has been drawn to the point of pure passivity that it is sufficiently removed from the regime of labor whose grasp comprehends the whole category of action.

And as if this resort to the rigorous purity of utter inanition were not enough to insure it, Wilde strives further to defend the separation of leisure and labor by propping the difference between them on to the more dramatic distance charted by an ancient opposition. Like the nineteenth-century campaign on behalf of a sexual minority which sought substantiation in classical antecedents, the Platonic scheme on which it rests in "The Critic as Artist" magnifies the modern divide between work and rest, a divide which, for all its decisiveness, is often no grander than the quotidian separation of a day at work from a day off. Dressed as the difference between the Ideal and the Real, a distinction elsewhere as easy to overlook as a lost weekend or a dull rerun is radiant now in the timeless style of the Western thinker's master dichotomy. The vacuity ("do[ing] nothing at all") at the heart of the vacation rises to a height as far from the workplace as the serenity of philosopher and saint from the push and shove of everyday life.

The aura of ease that describes Wilde's vision of idleness here is as different, at least at first glance, as freedom and necessity from the thin atmosphere of High Society where leisure is a duty which, while preferable to its counterpart, remains, nonetheless, another job to do. While the conspicuous abstention from labor which is the lifestyle of High Society is marked by a panopticon pressure to conform to its canon, the leisure enjoyed by the charmed circle of the elect is marked by the ease of just looking: "Unlimited and absolute is the vision of him who sits at ease and watches." Compared to the exhibitory exertions of High Society ("you don't call that idle, do you?"), this higher mode of leisure seems like a night at the movies after a day in the spotlight. "'Ah! I have talked quite enough for today,' said Lord Henry. . . . 'All I want now is to look at life'" (80).

A night at the movies, but, of course, by Wilde's lights, more like the antecedent forms of just looking whose collective name is the key term of his glossary. To "make ourselves spiritual by detaching ourselves from action," to aspire successfully to the condition of the elect "who sit at ease and watch," is to possess "the aesthetic temperament"; to enter the company of the gods who "watch[] with the calm eyes of the spectator the tragi-comedy of the world" is to join the society of the spectacle that Wilde calls the work of art, or, more precisely, the society of the spectacle that Wilde calls the detached ease of aesthetic appreciation:

> [T]he contemplative life, the life that has for its aim not doing but being . . . that is what the critical spirit can give us. The gods live thus: either brooding over their own perfection, as Aristotle tells

us, or as Epicurus fancied, watching with the calm eyes of the
spectator the tragi-comedy of the world that they have made. We,
too, might live like them, and set ourselves to witness with appropriate emotions the varied scenes that man and nature afford. We
might make ourselves spiritual by detaching ourselves from action
and become perfect by the rejection of energy.... Calm, and self-
centred, and complete, the aesthetic critic contemplates life, and
no arrow drawn at a venture can pierce between the joints of his
harness. (278)

Like the contemporary advertising which promises access to the
glamor of old romance by the purchase of the new commodity, Wilde
promotes the aesthetic sphere as a modern facsimile of a classical ideal.
Contemplating life as art, the aesthetic critic "calm, and self-centred,
and complete," occupies the easy chair of a modern pantheon where
"we might make ourselves spiritual by detaching ourselves from action
and become perfect by the rejection of energy." "[W]atching with the
calm eyes of the spectator" "the world" as "tragi-comedy," the aesthete
manages to miss the bullet which never fails to reach the man of action,
the arrow whose unerring aim shatters the agency of any actor, no matter how regally armored.[23]

But if the fine art of leisure appears far closer to the Utopia arranged
for "The Soul of Man Under Socialism" than to the arduous regions of
High Society, it is no less haunted, as we might surmise even from
Wilde's busy efforts to defend against it, by the form of labor whose
transcendence is Utopia's prehistory. For just as the rule of leisure that
defines High Society is enforced by a pressure softer than the threat
that enforces the imperative to work, but coercive still, the ease of this
higher idleness only extends by other means the passivity that prompts
the flight from work in the first place. Like the committed liar who dis-
covers much to his chagrin "that all his life he has been speaking nothing but the truth" (*Earnest*, 538), he who rejects the Protestant Ethic
in order to follow "the great creed of Inaction" (222), embraces the dis-
sipation of agency he meant to escape; like the epigram whose insur-
rection against the tyranny of common sense is confined to the
acrobatics of inverting it, the passive pleasure of just looking that is the

main feature in Wilde's house of art is less an escape from the regime of alienated labor than a repetition of its primary aspect.

In a variation on "the irony" attached to the modern ruse of power that Foucault calls the deployment of sexuality—"The irony of this deployment is in having us believe that our 'liberation' is in the balance"—Wilde celebrates as the "fastidious rejection" of that regime what is, after all, only its sublimated afterlife:[24] An extension of labor's passivity which, like a mode of subjection embraced as the means of freedom, functions to deepen its hold. Rewriting that passivity as a refined and passionate repose, the high art that Wilde celebrates renders the condition of our imprisonment an experience to be enjoyed rather than merely endured. To praise as the highest glory "the mere joy of beholding," a joy like the serenity of the gods who "watching with calm eyes" passively regard "the world that they have made" return in a spectacle of alienated majesty, is to support the "self-alienation" that for Walter Benjamin is the standard of modernity, a "self alienation [that] has reached such a degree that . . . mankind . . . can experience its own destruction as an aesthetic pleasure of the first order."[25]

III

But no depth of collaboration between the idle and the rule of labor they resist can suspend the sentence imposed by that regime, with the regularity of a natural law, on those who do not work. As uncompromising as the most severe sexual censorship, the regime of labor is rigorous enough to mobilize itself against any exception to its rule, even those as inscribed as the weekend in the schedule of compulsory labor they appear to abjure. Even here, as we will see in a moment, the compulsion to work knows no bounds.

Were it not for the fact that no further confirmation of its wide-spanning potence could possibly surprise us, we might be more amazed that the conviction that Weber located at the heart of the Protestant Ethic, the conviction that no one is ever exempted "from the unconditional command to labour,"[26] is a law whose arm is long enough to reach the heart of its most dedicated discontents. "Work is the mission of man in this Earth," Carlyle declares,[27] but such *ex cathedra* pronouncements have nothing over the authoritative *éclat* with which Wilde expounds the opposing theory of the leisure class: "There is something tragic about the enormous number of young men there are in England at the present moment who start life with perfect profiles, and end by adopting some useful profession";[28] "The condition for perfection is idleness" ("Phrases and Philosophies," 573); "It is to do nothing that the elect exist."[29] If Wilde's book renders the injunction against labor as compelling for the "elect," for those who aspire to the condition of "perfection," or who by virtue of their good looks manifest their arrival there, as the commandment to perform it is for the working class, this is partly because his sense of this injunction is borrowed from the prescriptive character it opposes. Resisting authority by mirroring it, mimicking the judicial confidence attached to the law whose spirit it inverts, the trademark *attitude* that Wilde displays when he peremptorily reverses conventional verdicts would seem, by virtue of its reflective relation to them, immune to the ideological forces it mocks. As self-assured as the stern law-giver whose authority he mimics, it's hard to see how, short of military intervention, Wilde's disdain for his rules could ever be undone, since the power that drafts them appears to be by definition no greater than Wilde's own.

Yet in the very essay where his endorsement of idleness, usually no more expository if no less effective than an enigmatic epigram, expands to become a full-blown defense of leisure, even in "The Critic as Artist," where the taboo on labor takes on the force and compass of a cosmology as articulate as the one it opposes, Wilde submits to the categorical imperative to work. In the very essay which, gathering to itself the authority that underwrites the doctrine it reverses, inverting the hierarchal order of the Protestant Ethic, hails idleness as the sign and instrument of election, and condemns work as an everyday hell, in the essay where the abstention from labor spells not merely social distinction, but existential salvation, Wilde, as if from a sudden failure of nerve, briefly concedes everything to the enemy.

Even with the backing of an alternate cosmology, Wilde's defense proves insufficient to stand against a rule of labor which makes no exceptions, a rule of labor whose agency of enforcement we will have occasion to examine again in a moment. For it is here, in the middle of his most systematic defense of indolence that Wilde, like a deathbed convert, as if momentarily overwhelmed by a suddenly irresistible power, accepts briefly, but completely, the doctrine that he spent a good portion of his genius refuting:

> Society . . . demands, and *no doubt rightly* demands, of *each* of its citizens that he should contribute some form of productive labour to the common weal, and toil and travail that the day's work may be done. (274, emphasis added)

No doubt *rightly*? Since when? Like the split personality in the comedy who half the time disavows the pleasure-driven character he embraces when he is Ernest, the arch-antinomian who presides over "The Critic as Artist," as if snatched by the spirit of the law that Carlyle worded, suddenly turns himself into the channel of the universal work ethic that he elsewhere disdains. As if reeducated by a regime quite opposed to the one he propagates in "The Soul of Man Under Socialism," Wilde renounces absolutely the aspiration he charted there, endorsing now the ubiquity rather than the annulment of the compulsion to labor.

As the passage continues, the dandy recovers his voice, but only by means of a crucial compromise with an enemy now powerful enough to exact it:

> Society often forgives the criminal; it never forgives the dreamer. . . so completely are people dominated by the tyranny of this dreadful social ideal that they are always coming shamelessly up to one at Private Views and other places that are open to the general public, and saying in a loud stentorian voice, "What are you doing?" whereas "What are you thinking?" is the only question that any single civilized being should ever be allowed to whisper to another. They mean well, no doubt, these honest beaming folk. Perhaps that is the reason they are so excessively tedious. But some one should teach them that while, in the opinion of society, Contemplation is the gravest sin of which any citizen can be found guilty in the opinion of the highest culture it is the proper occupation of man. (274–75)

Ditching the good citizen act, the dandy becomes again the patrician *refusenik* we readily recognize, rediscovering the self-assurance that seems briefly to have abandoned him, a self-assurance sufficiently haughty to treat Society, not the high one now, but rather those "honest beaming folk," with utmost condescension—"they mean well no doubt." The steadfast elitism forgotten long enough not merely to accept but to endorse the idea of a law that applies to everyone returns now to dismiss such "dreadful" dogma with the confidence of a snob consummate enough to crown himself Philosopher King, and restore the *ancien régime* which excuses the aristocrat of high culture from the rules that apply to little people.

But this is a potentate who has given Caesar his due. For now his dissent from the Protestant Ethic, elsewhere as *outré* as Cardinal Newman's costumes, is as obscure as the sublimated essence of homosexuality which everyone suspects but no one can locate specifically in the vague ether of Hellenism that Wilde and his Oxford cronies breathed. The dandy's derogation of the general category of "action" in general has discreetly dropped any reference to work, in particular, just as his correlative defense of the "social sin" of contemplation tactfully avoids any allusion to the indolence with which it is elsewhere, as we have already noticed, identified. Quietly changing the subject so as to avoid directly flouting the work ethic, the dandy takes back his bad attitude, but at the cost of giving up a good part of its edge, like the offensive entertainer who, under network pressure, tones down her show to a dimness that reveals no more than the now phantom form of opposition.

I want to suggest that the agency that so magnetizes the universal commandment to labor that its enemy now bends before it is what Wilde in the essay on Socialism calls the "Tyranny of Want," which compels "a great many people who, having no property of their own, and being always on the brink of sheer starvation . . . to do the work of beasts of burden, to do work that is quite uncongenial to them." For a tradition of thought at least as old as the Puritan foundations of the Protestant Ethic, it isn't enough that the working class on the actual brink of it should be harrowed by the prospect of starvation. According to the most emphatic Victorian prophet of the Protestant Ethic, even those who by means of a permanent income are sure of a dinner whether they work for it or not must be made to feel the threat of going without it if they don't. As happy to condemn the idle rich to starvation as he was the idle poor, Carlyle's vicious authoritarianism, quite unlike that of its contemporary counterpart, has at least the virtue of consistency:

> He that will not work according to his faculty, let him perish according to his necessity: there is no law juster than that. Would to Heaven one could preach it abroad into the hearts of all sons and daughters of Adam, for it is a law applicable to all; and bring it to bear, with practical obligation strict as the Poor-Law Bastille, on all! ...That this law of "No work no recompense" should first of all be enforced on the *manual* worker, and brought stringently home to him and his numerous class, while so many other classes and persons still go loose from it, was natural to the case. Let it be enforced there, and rigidly made good. It behooves to be enforced everywhere, and rigidly made good;—alas, not by such simple methods as "refusal of out-door relief," but by far other and costlier. (*Chartism,* 132)

It is the broadcast effect of what Carlyle calls the most just of laws that overwhelms Wilde's *summa theologica* for indolence, a law which makes a slight but decisive appearance when "The Critic as Artist" describes the fate of the modern subject who aspires to the heights of classical thought, a sphere of pure thought which is at the same time the height of pure idleness:

> It is to do nothing that the elect exist. Action is limited and relative. Unlimited and absolute is the vision of him who sits at ease and watches, who walks in loneliness and dreams. But we who are born at the close of this wonderful age, are at once too cultured and too critical, too intellectually subtle and too curious of exquisite pleasures, to accept any speculations about life in exchange for life itself. To us the *citta divina* is colorless, and the *fruitio Dei* without meaning. Metaphysics do not satisfy our temperaments, and religious ecstasy is out of date. The world through which the Academic philosopher becomes "the spectator of all

> time and of all existence" is not really an ideal world, but simply a world of abstract ideas. When we enter it, we starve amidst the chill mathematics of thought. (275)

In the midst of an essay where the fear of going without dinner seems as inappropriate as the bill collector who briefly darkens the premises of *The Importance of Being Earnest*, the specter of starvation appears, cast to figure the fate of the modern sensibility when it enters the sphere of pure indolence: "When we enter it, we starve amidst the chill mathematics of thought." Starting with its most immediate context— why would we *starve*, rather than freeze amidst a *chill*?—the figure Wilde introduces here clashes with its surroundings; like the voice or suit rather too loud for Society, it is slightly but distinctly out of place. It is surely a little excessive to describe even the acute alienation, not to mention the duller *ennui* suffered by "temperaments" "too intellectually subtle and too curious of exquisite pleasures" to be "satisfied" by the religious ecstasies and the philosophical abstractions which provided sufficient fare for our more ascetic ancestors.

Like the raised voice, really meant to reach someone out of earshot, but more like the anxiety which has floated free from its source, the lurid threat that Wilde mentions here, hard to explain by its most proximate circumstance, is better illuminated when we consider a circumstance somewhat remoter from view, namely the idleness which defines the condition of those who are subject to it. By a drift of metaphor as slight as a slip of the tongue, Wilde is made to reproduce the law whose annulment he regards as humanity's only hope, the law which orders people to work or starve. And like a reaction to the raised voice, or to military maneuvers designed to intimidate those who witness them, Wilde's otherwise inexplicable submission to the doctrine of compulsory labor is best read as a response to an object lesson on the consequences of defiance, consequences which take shape here in the shadow of starvation that falls upon the palace of the indolent.

Finally, like the conclusion drawn from a sudden awareness that the range of a bullet has no limit, Wilde's concession that the demand for labor should apply to everyone, no less odd coming from him than his concession that the demand should apply to anyone at all, may best be read as a submission to the sense that no one is excused from the continuous exertions required to avoid a universal threat. For the shadow of starvation on Wilde's social map extends beyond those who live on the actual edge of it, those "who have no property of their own, and being on the brink of sheer starvation, are compelled" to work in order to get food, and are compelled to go without it when they can't; it falls as well upon those who aspire to join the elect "who exist to do nothing."

As removed from the brink of starvation as the unconscious fear of catastrophe is from the fact of it, the modern subject who aspires to the condition of classic idleness is susceptible nonetheless to a spectral emanation of the threat that Wilde, elsewhere in "The Critic as Artist," calls "the strongest, because most sordid, incentive to industry." Thus, like the police whose disciplinary operations enjoy novel extensions in a domestic literature that is formally opposed to them, the rule of labor is magnified by the offices of an essay dedicated to belittling it. For the sanction which enforces this rule is not merely reproduced in the essay; rather, by means of its sublimation there, its jurisdiction is expanded to cover even the charmed circle of those who would otherwise be immune to its powers. "[E]ven the wealthy shall not eat without working," Weber remarks, giving voice to the Puritan frame of mind that Wilde, despite his best efforts, could not keep from haunting his own.[30]

IV

But as soon as the specter of starvation falls upon the region of idleness, Wilde proposes a regimen for its subjects that would render this specter irrelevant to them again, not by inducing them to abandon their affiliation with the elect by conforming to the rule of labor, but rather by transforming their appetites and thus diminishing to the vanishing point their vulnerability to the "tyranny of want" which enforces this rule. In the lines that follow the revelation of its presence in the precincts of sublime idleness, Wilde introduces a program to dismantle this tyranny by means of a personal reformation that renders want tolerable rather than a social reform that would abolish it once and for all.

Like a holistic diet program that concerns itself less with a low-calorie appeasement than a radical reform of appetite, Wilde answers the challenge of satisfying the modern hunger for sensuous particularities that goes unsated in the old dispensation of idleness, the hunger whose more advanced stage we have just heard called starvation, not with a different bill of fare, but rather a different brand of desire:

Gilbert. Who as Mr. Pater suggests somewhere, would exchange the curve of a single rose leaf for that formless intangible Being which Plato rates so high? . . . Like Aristotle, like Goethe after he had read Kant, we desire the concrete, and nothing but the concrete can satisfy us.

Ernest. What do you propose?

Gilbert. It seems to me that with the development of the critical spirit we shall be able to realize not merely our own lives, but the collective life of the race. . . . Is this impossible? I think not. By revealing to us the absolute mechanism of all action . . . the Scientific principle of Heredity has become, as it were, the warrant for the contemplative life. It has shown us that we are never less free than when we try to act. It has hemmed us round with the nets of the hunter, and written upon the wall the prophecy of our doom. . . . And yet . . . it comes to us, this terrible shadow, with many gifts in its hands, gifts of strange temperaments and subtle susceptibilities, gifts of wild ardours and chill moods of indifference. . . . And so, it is not our own life that we live, but the lives of the dead, and the soul that dwells within us is no single spiritual entity, making us personal and individual, created for our service, and entering into us for our joy. It is something that has dwelt in fearful places, and in ancient sepulcres has made its abode. It is sick with many maladies, and has memories of curious sins. It is wiser than we are, and its wisdom is bitter. It fills us with impossible desires, and makes us follow what we know we cannot gain. (275–76)

What is to be done to sate our hunger for the concrete, the student asks, and Wilde's dandy, never closer to the condition of stoicism with which Baudelaire associated him, answers not directly, but rather by robbing the question of its urgency, proposing not to satisfy our longing but rather to lighten it. In place of the want whose satisfaction appears indispensable for survival, the want that is mantled in the naturalized urgency that Baudrillard calls "the grace of need," the "terrible shadow" that Wilde here designates the "Scientific principle of Heredity" and "the soul that dwells within us," and whose other names we will expose in a moment, offers "impossible desires" and the inclination to "follow what we know we cannot gain," offers a species of yearning insatiable but also entirely bearable, interminable, but never terminal.

The state of enduring but endurable desire may recall the incurable nostalgia of the recovering smoker, but a more felicitous representation is Wilde's famous advertisement for the positive pleasure of the cigarette itself: "You must have a cigarette. A cigarette is the perfect type of the perfect pleasure. It is exquisite, and it leaves one unsatisfied. What more can one want?" (*Dorian Gray*, 107). For what this passage hails as "impossible desires" and the inclination to "follow what we know we cannot gain," are more than merely endurable; they are, rather, forms of pleasure lustrous enough to eclipse the satisfaction that would terminate them. Ranged amongst the glamorous psychological dimensionalities which Wilde designates as our inheritance, such endless desires, like the "wild ardours" and the "subtle susceptibilities" to which they are closely related, constitute the currency of our affective affluence, rather than a form of poverty that leads finally to the specter of starvation. What more can one want, at least in a Society everywhere haunted by this specter? What more can the subject of this society wish for than that the lack which defines want take form as pleasure rather than lethal need?

But if such desires are sometimes as light as the "broken heart that runs to many editions" (*Dorian Gray*, 56), the reformation that delivers them to us is as harrowing as an alien abduction. While the terrible shadow that Wilde calls heredity in "The Critic as Artist" appears to "mirror" our "soul," appears as the agent that delivers and defines our own essential genetic character, it nevertheless fills us with affects that are not our own. If the desires that this "terrible shadow" offers are "impossible" because they cannot be fulfilled, they are impossible as well because, being the desires of an other, they never cease to be implausible as *our* desires.

As common, for all their strangeness as "the tears we shed at a play," these alien desires, as light as the natural need they displace is heavy, desires whose endless deferral is as easy to bear as that of the other would be impossible to live with, are calculated by Wilde, with all the rhetorical resources at his disposal, as a central benefit of art. The synthetic fervors he pictures our systems absorbing belong to a genus of inorganic affects, what Wilde praises as "the exquisite sterile emotions that it is the function of Art to awaken"; exquisite sterile emotions which offer a safe substitute for the potent ones they replace:

> Art does not hurt us. The tears that we shed at a play are a type of the exquisite sterile emotions that it is the function of Art to awaken. We weep but we are not wounded. We grieve, but our grief is not bitter. It is through Art, and through Art only ... that we can shield ourselves from the sordid perils of actual existence. (273–74)

Frankly proposing art's "exquisite sterile emotions" as a form of prophylaxis, Wilde both enlists and revises the traditional doctrine of aesthetic disinterestedness. To admit to the region of aesthetic experience along with the tears of the unwounded and the grief that brings no bitterness "wild ardours" and "impossible desires" is to bend the rule of admission that Kant codified in *The Critique of Judgement*. Bend without breaking: for while Wilde populates this region with a species of affect ruled out of court by Kant, he nevertheless upholds the conception of the aesthetic as the zone where the force of that affect is transcended. For Wilde, the aesthetic experience consists in part of the category of longing excluded by the Kantian scheme (the "interest" from which "the delight which determines the judgement of all taste" is "independent" according to Kant's famous account, "always involves a reference to the faculty of desire"), but it is a longing divested of its dangerous dimension, the element of need. There is an infinite amount of desire in Wilde's more promiscuous vision of the aesthetic experience, but it is a desire whose subject is as immune from its vicissitudes as the disinterested one who inhabits the more canonical grounds of the aesthetic, the disinterested subject who has succeeded in abandoning desire altogether.[31]

Despite his most emphatic protestations, the aesthetic sphere in

Wilde's book proves no more immune to the hegemonic rule of reification than it does to the judgments of popular morality and the law. But if the idleness that high art offers according to Wilde's measure, like the dispensation furnished by mass culture according to a familiar critique,[32] does no more than extend our engrossment in the atmosphere of alienated labor, it offers relief at least from its most dire dimension. If the aesthetic subject in Wilde's book, held captive as mere spectator to a picture of the world, is no freer than her laboring counterpart from the rigors of alienation, she is spared at least the terror by which that régime is enforced.

But as glamorous as he makes it, the spectrum of affective color that Wilde allows the aesthetic subject doesn't exactly sell itself. His enthusiasm for the alchemy which "converts an appetite into an art," the process of introjection and displacement by which organic needs give way to impossible desires suggests the apostolic determination to convert the unbelieving. The determined profession of the aesthetic, the tireless promotion of "the exquisite sterile emotions that it is the function of Art to awaken" as the material that shields us from "the sordid perils of actual existence" may put us in mind of the contemporary campaign to convince a skeptical audience that safe sex can conduct all the electric charge of risk:

> *Gilbert.* Yes, we can put the earth back six hundred courses and make ourselves one with the great Florentine, kneel at the same altar with him, and share his rapture and his scorn. . . . Pass on to the poem on the man who tortures himself, let its subtle music steal into your brain and colour your thoughts, and you will become for a moment what he was who wrote it. . . . We sicken with the same maladies as the poets, and the singer lends us his pain. . . . Life! Life! Don't let us go to life for our fulfillment or our experience. It is a thing narrowed by circumstances, incoherent in its utterance, and without that fine correspondence of form and spirit which is the only thing that can satisfy the artistic and critical temperament.
>
> *Ernest.* Must we go, then, to Art for everything?
>
> *Gilbert.* For everything. Because Art does not hurt us. The tears that we shed at a play are a type of the exquisite sterile emotions that it is the

function of Art to awaken. We weep but we are not wounded. . . . It is through Art, and through Art only . . . that we can shield ourselves from the sordid perils of actual existence. (273–74)

Judging by the force of Wilde's advertisement on their behalf, art's "exquisite sterile emotions," for all of their potence, do not invade us without support. Like the vampire, whose Paterian shadow we have already seen arise amongst them, these alien raptures must be invited to enter us. We must be persuaded to want them in.

The triumph of yearning's benign strain in Wilde's book, what may appear as inevitable as the exposure of the star-crossed passion as the teenage crush in the sober light of maturity, requires a specific act of conversion—an act of conversion which is central to Wilde's life and work, the act of conversion called seduction. This figure of seduction is easier to make out elsewhere in Wilde's book, but even in the passage from "The Critic as Artist" that we have already considered, it almost emerges from the shadow where it dwells there; even here we can glimpse the agent of insinuation who annuls the boundaries of our individuality by inculcating strange desires in the place of our own. Its identity is intimated by the aura of seduction that surrounds "this terrible shadow, with many gifts in its hands," an aura of seduction all the brighter for the light that it borrows from the picture that Pater called *La Gioconda*, the picture of "what in the ways of a thousand years men had come to desire."[33] Even in "The Critic as Artist," the agent who instills desire in another is difficult to distinguish from the figure desired by the other; hard not to read the desires this figure incites as desires for this figure himself.

Elsewhere in Wilde's book, this figure of seduction is unclosted altogether, entirely visible in all the old familiar places where the desire of the other is hard to tell from a desire for the other. We have, of course, already encountered this figure fully fledged; we have encountered it as "the tall, graceful young man" that Dorian Gray "could not help liking," "the tall, graceful young man" whose "low, languid voice was absolutely fascinating." The shadow that constitutes the essential character that it appears only to reveal, the shadow that incites the passions that it seems merely to discover, is made flesh in the figure of

Lord Henry with whom we began, Lord Henry whose insinuations conduct the exodus of Dorian Gray from the life-threatening tyranny of want to the softer genre of endurable desire, Lord Henry who in the early turn in the text we have already surveyed, plots the displacement of "passions" that lead to "starvation" if left unsatisfied by a species of desire that does not.

Thus the perverse implanations which form the currency of seduction in *The Picture of Dorian Gray*, the insinuations of alien desire that work to impeach the very idea of inherent ones is a propagation of de-essentialism which, if not certifiably strategic, is certainly convenient in more ways than one. If the novel's unsettling of natural desire abets a campaign to liberate perversity from the ideological shackles of a conventional heterosexism that anchors itself in an alibi of nature, it offers as well a route of escape from the harshest of penalties reserved for those indisposed to follow to the letter a sentence of hard labor whose end no one can predict.

NOTES

1. *The Picture of Dorian Gray*, in The Oxford Authors Edition of *Oscar Wilde*, ed. Isobel Murray (Oxford: Oxford University Press, 1989), p. 194. All subsequent citations of *Dorian Gray* refer to this edition.

2. Lee Edelman, *Homographesis* (New York: Routledge, 1994), p. 17.

3. See of course, Judith Butler, *Gender Trouble: Feminism and the Subversion of Identity* (New York: Routledge, 1990) for an inaugural situation of de-essentializing apprehension as an instrument of resistance to heterosexual hegemony, an account which inaugurates, amongst other things, a central strain of queer theory.

4. For elaborations of Wilde's status as avatar of a queer theory which identifies the announcement and apprehension of de-essentialism as an instrument of resistance to heterosexual hegemony, see Christopher Craft, "Alias Bunbury: Desire and Termination in *The Importance of Being Earnest*," in *Representations* 31 (Summer 1990); and Jonathan Dollimore, *Sexual Dissidence: Augustine to Wilde, Freud to Foucault* (Oxford: Oxford University Press, 1991). For a skeptical account of this affiliation see Eve Kosofsky Sedgwick, "Tales of the Avunculate: Queer Tutelage in *The Importance of Being Earnest*," in *Tendencies* (Durham: Duke University Press, 1993), pp. 52–72. "Each of these readings traces and affirms the gay possibility in Wilde's writing by identifying it—feature by feature, as if from a Most Wanted poster—with the perfect fulfillment of a modernist or post-modern project of meaning-destabilization and identity-destabilization" (p. 55).

5. Judith Butler, *Bodies That Matter: On the Discursive Limits of "Sex"* (New York: Routledge, 1993). See especially chapter 8.

6. Oscar Wilde, "The Soul of Man Under Socialism," in *The Works of Oscar Wilde* (London: Blitz Editions, 1990), p. 1021. All subsequent citations of the essay refer to this edition.

7. *The Importance of Being Earnest,* in The Oxford Authors Edition of *Oscar Wilde,* p. 481. Subsequent citations of this play refer to this edition

8. *An Ideal Husband,* in The Oxford Authors Edition of *Oscar Wilde,* p. 401. Subsequent citations of the play refer to this edition.

9. Thorstein Veblen, *The Theory of the Leisure Class,* Introduction by C. Wright Mills (New York: New American Library, 1899; 1912; 1953), p. 43. Citations of *The Theory of the Leisure Class* refer to this edition.

10. "The Birthday of the Infanta," in *Oscar Wilde: Complete Shorter Fiction,* ed. with an Introduction by Isobel Murray (New York: Oxford University Press, 1980), pp. 185–202.

11. "The Model Millionaire," in *Complete Shorter Fiction,* p. 88.

12. *A Woman of No Importance, The Collected Plays* (London: Methuen, 1988), p. 304.

13. Georg Simmel, "Superordination and Subordination," in *The Sociology of Georg Simmel,* trans. and ed. Kurt H. Wolff (New York: The Free Press, 1950), p. 254.

14. Pierre Bourdieu, *Outline of a Theory of Practice,* trans. Richard Nice (Cambridge: Cambridge University Press, 1977); *Language and Symbolic Power,* trans. Gino Raymond and Matthew Adamson, ed. with an Introduction by John B. Thompson (Cambridge, MA: Harvard University Press, 1991).

15. See Pierre Bourdieu, *Distinction: A Social Critique of the Judgement of Taste,* trans. Richard Nice (Cambridge, MA: Harvard University Press, 1984).

16. My reading of "The Critic as Artist" emphasizes one element of its historical situation. For an account of other elements of this situation, one that takes up some of the sexual and professional pressures that form a crucial part of the essay's social context, see Lawrence Danson's *Wilde's Intentions: The Artist in His Criticism,* chapter 6 (Oxford: Clarendon Press, 1997).

17. In *The Human Condition* (Chicago: University of Chicago Press, 1958), Hannah Arendt situates at the center of a degraded modernity this reduction of action in general to labor in particular:

> [W]e live in a society of laborers . . . we have almost succeeded in leveling all human activities to the common denominator of securing the necessities of life and providing for their abundance. Whatever we do, we are supposed to do for the sake of "making a living"; such is the verdict of society, and the number of people, especially in the professions who might challenge it, has decreased rapidly. . . . The same trend to level down all serious activities to the status of making a living is manifest in present-day labor theories. . . . (pp. 126–27)

For Arendt, this leveling down is a dark chapter in the history of ideas, which by her concentrated lights, is another name for History itself.

18. Herbert Marcuse, *Eros and Civilization: A Philosophical Inquiry into Freud* (Boston: Beacon Press, 1955; 1966), p. 35. Readers of Marcuse may recognize the debt this essay owes to his work. I am indebted especially to Marcuse for a habit of connecting the social forms of sexuality with those of labor, and thus for a way of connecting the intimacies of the erotic with the macropolitics of the economic. My differences from Marcuse will also be evident: while Marcuse relies on an essentialist model of sexuality consistent with the repression hypothesis, I am concerned with a version of the erotic in Wilde consistent with the de-essentialist, constructivist perspective of Foucault in particular and postmodernism in general. Most importantly, while Marcuse casts sexuality as the target of the capitalist regime of labor, the target of a surplus repression which extends and deepens that regime, my reading of Wilde seeks to notice how the sexuality featured in his book furnishes its subject some relief from that regime. For a canny recent revival of the alliance politics proposed by Marcuse, one that reads one form of transgressive sexuality as a characteristically indirect expression of a utopian impulse to resist a work ethic that extends itself into the realm of "responsible relationships," see Laura Kipnis, "Adultery," in *Critical Inquiry*, vol. 24, no. 2 (Winter 1998), special issue on Intimacy, ed. Lauren Berlant (Chicago: University of Chicago Press, 1998), pp. 289–327. Not the least persuasive, not to say eloquent, aspect of Kipnis's article is its insistent recognition that the utopian intensities of the transgression she treats can hardly escape an idiom as banal as the familial ideologies it seeks to evade.

19. Karl Marx, "Alienated Labour," in "Economic and Philosophical Manuscripts," from *Early Writings*, trans. and ed. by T. B. Bottomore (New York: McGraw Hill, 1963), pp. 122–27.

20. Georg Lukács, "Reification and the Consciousness of the Proletariat," in *History and Class Consciousness: Studies in Marxist Dialectics*, trans. Rodney Livingstone (Cambridge, MA: MIT Press, 1971), pp. 88–90.

21. Arendt, *The Human Condition*, p. 234.

22. Henri Lefebvre, *Critique of Everyday Life: Volume One*, trans. John Moore (New York: Verso, 1991), p. 33.

23. Wilde alludes in this passage to 1 Kings 22:34, in which Ahab is killed in battle: "And a certain man drew a bow at a venture, and smote the king of Israel between the joints of the harness."

24. Michel Foucault, *The History of Sexuality—Volume I: An Introduction*, trans. Robert Hurley (New York: Vintage Books, 1978), p. 159.

25. Walter Benjamin, "The Work of Art in the Age of Mechanical Reproduction," *Illuminations*, ed. with an Introduction by Hannah Arendt, trans. Harry Zohn (New York: Schocken Books, 1969), p. 242.

26. Max Weber, *The Protestant Ethic and the Spirit of Capitalism*, trans. Talcott Parsons (Los Angeles: Roxbury Publishing Company, 1995), p. 159. Subsequent citations of this work refer to this edition.

27. Thomas Carlyle, *Chartism,* in *Critical and Miscellaneous Essays* (London: Chapman and Hall, 1896–1899), p. 133. All citations of Carlyle refer to this edition.

28. "Phrases and Philosophies for the Use of the Young," in The Oxford Authors Edition of *Oscar Wilde,* p. 573. All citations of this text refer to the Oxford edition.

29. "The Critic as Artist," in The Oxford Authors Edition of *Oscar Wilde,* p. 275. All citations of this text refer to the Oxford edition.

30. Weber, *The Protestant Ethic,* p. 159. The specter that haunts all leisure in Wilde's essay suggests a failure of the treaty between "an aristocratic morality of 'otium' and a puritan work ethic" that Jean Baudrillard detects in his study of conflicts correlative to the collision between the imperatives of labor and leisure that I have sought to trace. Thus, he heralds a compromise between the valorization of useless objects, and "a social morality that no more wants the object to be unemployed than the individual":

> the functional object pretends to be decorative, it disguises itself with non-utility . . . the futile and indolent object is charged with a practical reason . . . objects are caught in the fundamental compromise of having to signify, that is, of having to confer social meaning and prestige in the mode of otium . . . and of having incidently to submit to the powerful consensus of the democratic morality of effort, of doing. (p. 71)

>> From "The Genesis of Need," in *For a Critique of the Political Economy of the Sign,* trans. Charles Levin (St. Louis: Telos Press, 1981).

Similarly, he discerns a continuity between the demands of production and consumption, demands respectively associated with labor and leisure, reading them as twin aspects of a single social imperative:

> [T]he ethos of "conspicuous" consumption is an uninterrupted performance, a stress for achievement, aiming always at providing the continual and tangible proof of social value . . . which under inverse influences, is the heir of the principles that were the foundation of the Protestant ethic and which, according to Weber, motivated the capitalist spirit of production. The morality of consumption relays that of production, or is entangled with it in the same social logic of salvation. (p. 33)

But if the hostilities between the compulsion to work and the compulsion to abstain from it are suspended in a confusion of instrument and ornament, or dissolved in the long-term alliance between production and consumption, they remain, as Baudrillard notes, "fundamentally incompatible." The cooperation and convergences that take place between these forces can do nothing to quell the figure which rises on behalf of the work ethic to punish those who fail to follow its law to the letter, even if, as Baudrillard suggests, they manage, by the labor of their protestations, to sustain its spirit.

31. Immanuel Kant, "Analytic of the Beautiful. First Moment," *The Critique of Judgement,* trans. with Analytical Indexes by James Creed Meredith (Oxford: Oxford

University Press, 1952), p. 42. The immunity that Wilde awards to aesthetic experience differs from disinterestedness in another way as well. Where Kant identifies disinterestedness as the character that defines the relation between the subject and object of the aesthetic, the soft desire in Wilde's account, as good as disinterestedness, is an affect passed from the aesthetic object to the subject.

32. See for example, Theodor Adorno, "On the Fetish Character in Music and the Regression of Listening," in *The Essential Frankfurt School Reader*, ed. with Introductions by Andrew Arato and Eike Gebhardt (New York: Urizen Books, 1978), pp. 270–299.

33. Walter Pater, *The Renaissance*, ed. Adam Phillips (Oxford: Oxford University Press, 1990), pp. 79–80.

JONATHAN CULLER 9

THE

LITERARY

IN

THEORY

THE TITLE "What's Left of Theory?" asks what place the discourse called "theory" occupies today: how does it relate both to its past and to other discourses that claim a place on a political spectrum? As the opening speaker at this year's English Institute Conference, my job is to serve as an instantiation of what's left of theory—a living remnant—a remainder of theory, whose example would allow other speakers to situate themselves without great contortions to the left of theory. No doubt the way to do this is to tackle the question of theory's relation to its past: what's left of theory?

When in the 1960s I first became involved with what our title calls simply "theory," this term—so very odd, theory of what—made a good deal more sense than it does today. In the structuralist moment there was a growing body of theory—essentially the generalization of the model of structural linguistics—which, it was claimed, would apply everywhere, to all domains of culture. *Theory* meant a particular body of structuralist theory that would elucidate diverse sorts of material and be the key to understanding language, social behavior, literature, popular culture, societies with and without writing, and the structures of the human psyche. Theory meant the specific interdisciplinary body of theory that animated structuralist linguistics, anthropology, Marxism, semiotics, psychoanalysis, and literary criticism.

But despite the broad interdisciplinary ambitions of theory, in those heady days, the question of literature lay at the heart of the theoretical project: for Russian formalism, for Prague structuralism, and for French structuralism—especially for Roman Jakobson, who introduced Claude Lévi-Strauss to the phonological model that was decisive for the development of structuralism—the question of the literariness of literature was the animating question. Theory sought to treat the objects and events of culture as elements of so many "languages," so it was concerned above all with the nature of language; and literature was what language was when it was most deliberately and most ludically, most freely and most self-reflectively, being language. Literature was the place where the structures and the functioning of language were most explicitly and revealingly foregrounded. To investigate the crucial aspects of language, you had to think about literature. Thus, amid the array of functions of language defined by Roman Jakobson—the referential, the emotive, the phatic, the conative, the metalingual, and the poetic, which involve, respectively, the foregrounding of or stress on the context, the speaker, the contact, the addressee, the code, and the message itself—it is the poetic function of language, that, in Jakobson's famous phrase, brings "the focus on the message for its own sake" (where "message" means the utterance itself).[1] And, in a formulae that all of us relics of theory knew by heart, Jakobson declared that "The poetic function of language projects the principle of equivalence from the axis of selection into the axis of combination."[2] The poetic function of language involves the superimposition of the two fundamental axes of language.

Now even at that time, when the nature of the literariness of literature was a question that every good theorist had to address, it was clear that in some sense theory was displacing the literary—clear, at least to all those who attacked theory, accusing us of foreswearing literary values and undermining the prestige or the special character of literature. Narratologists studied the narrative structures of Balzac and Ian Fleming with equal assiduousness. Roman Jakobson, notoriously, took as his key example of the poetic function of language not Baudelaire's "Les Chats" but the political slogan "I like Ike," where the object liked (Ike) and the liking subject (I) are embraced in and contained by the act, *like*, so that the necessity of my liking Ike seems inscribed in the very structure of the language.[3] The special status of literature as privileged object of study was in an important sense undermined, but the effect of this sort of study (and this is important) was to locate a "literariness" in cultural objects of all sorts and thus to retain a certain centrality of the literary.

The attempt to theorize the distinctiveness of literary language or the distinctiveness of literature was central to theory in those early years, but it hasn't been the focus of theoretical activity for some time. This is not, I should add, because we answered the question of the nature of literature. Neither of the principal lines of thought led to an answer that resolved the question. The first approach was to treat literature as a special kind of language; but each definition of literariness led not to a satisfactory account of literature but to an often extremely productive identification of literariness in other cultural phenomena—from historical narratives and Freudian case histories to advertising slogans. The alternative approach was to posit that literature was not a special kind of language but language treated in special ways; but despite valiant efforts by Stanley Fish, who sought to show, for instance, that a list of names of linguists written on the blackboard could be read as a religious lyric, this never proved very satisfactory either.[4]

There are two morals here, I think. First, just as meaning is both a textual fact and an intentional act and cannot be adequately theorized from either one of these points of view alone or through a synthesis of the two,[5] so in the case of literature, we must shift back and forth between the two perspectives, neither of which successfully incorporates the other to become the comprehensive framework: we can think of literary works as language with particular properties or features and we can think of them as language framed in particular ways, but any account of particular properties or of perceptual framing leads us to shift back ultimately into the other mode. The qualities of literature, it seems, can't be reduced either to objective properties or to consequences of ways of framing language.

The second moral, I think, is that questions about the nature of literariness or of literature were not, in fact, attempts to discover criteria by which we could distinguish literary from non-literary works and sort them into the right categories. On the contrary, attempts to answer these questions always functioned primarily to direct attention to certain aspects of literature. By saying what literature is, theorists promote the critical methods deemed most pertinent and dismiss those that neglect what are claimed to be the most basic and distinctive aspects of literature—whether literature is conceived as the foregrounding of language, or as the integration of linguistic levels, or as intertextual construction. To ask "what is literature?" is in effect a way of arguing about how literature should be studied. If literature is highly patterned language, for instance, then to study it is to look at the patterns, not to focus on the authorial psyche it might express or the social formation it might reflect. Investigations of the nature of literature seem to have functioned above all as moves in arguments about critical method.

Recently, as I say, the nature of literature or of the literary has not been the focus of theory, and what we call "theory" for short is manifestly not theory of literature. I wrote the article on "Literary Theory" for the second edition of the MLA's *Introduction to Scholarship in Modern Languages and Literatures* in 1992, and I realized afterwards I had left out the theory of literature.[6] Busy talking about race and gender, identity and agency, distracted by the skirmish of Steve Knapp and Walter Benn Michaels's anti-theory theory, I forgot the theory of literature. I think it's important not to forget it: narrative theory, for example, is crucial for the analysis of texts of all sorts. These days, beginning graduate students often have little acquaintance with basic narratology (they've read Foucault but not Barthes or Genette, much less Wayne Booth). They may not know about identifying narrative point of view or the analysis of implied readers or narratees, despite the centrality of such matters to questions that *do* urgently concern them, such as the analysis of what is taken for granted by a text.

Trying to make good my omission of the theory of literature from my MLA account of literary theory, I have written a little book called *Literary Theory: A Very Short Introduction*, which leaves out Knapp and Michaels and puts in not just "what is literature?" (in a chapter entitled "What is Literature and Does it Matter?"), but also discussion of narrative and of poetry and poetics, as well as of identity, identification, and performative language. I am thus engaged in keeping the literary in theory, and I hope that it will stay there.

But what of "literature after post-theory"—to take up the title John Guillory offers us? I take "post-theory" to be theory after the supposed death of "grand theory," as the phrase has it. If one wants a concrete reference, one might go back to an article of 1982, "Against Theory" by Steve Knapp and Walter Benn Michaels.[7] Now largely forgotten, that article claimed that theoretical arguments have no consequences; thus, theory had no useful work to do and theory should simply stop. Since, as many commentators remarked, this argument against theory was manifestly an instance of theory, and provoked many and divergent responses that were themselves instances of theory, this case may define "post-theory" for us: the theoretical discussions animated by the questions of the death of theory.

If this is our point of reference, then it is particularly striking—and, I confess, for me a source of a certain perverse pleasure—that in recent years, the purest example of that traditional theoretical project, the theoretical investigation of the nature of literature, is a book by one of the proponents of the death of theory, Steve Knapp. His book *Literary Interest: The Limits of Anti-Formalism* takes up the traditional questions of literary theory: "Is there such a thing as a specifically *literary* discourse, distinguishable from other modes of thought and writing? Is there any way to defend the intuition that a work of literature says something that can't be said in any other way?"[8] Knapp's book surprises by giving positive answers to these questions. Philosophically more rigorous than most such investigations, and, I should say, more doggedly determined not to end up with the patently unsatisfying answers that so often end such enquiries—such as that literature is whatever a given society means by literature—Knapp's enquiry concludes that, Yes, there *is* a distinctiveness to literature. Yes, literature does do something special.

Knapp's approach takes up and refines traditional kinds of answers but under a different rubric. Having committed himself in the anti-theory article to the position that the meaning of a literary work is simply, by definition, what the author meant by it (and that any other notion is incoherent), he approaches the distinctiveness of literature not through the special kinds of meaning that a literary work might have—there are none—but through what he calls "literary interest." Since he admits that our interest in literary language exceeds our interest in figuring out what its author might have intended by it, that surplus is available to be called something else, and is baptized "literary interest."

The distinctiveness of the literary lies not in the specificity of literary language: "I came to see," Knapp writes, "that what could not be defended as an account of literary language could be defended instead as an account of a certain kind of representation that provoked a certain kind of interest" (2). Literature is a "linguistically embodied representation that tends to attract a certain kind of interest to itself; that does so by particularizing the emotive and other values of its referents; and that does *that* by inserting its referents into new 'scenarios' inseparable from the particular linguistic and narrative structures of the representation itself" (3). And crucial to the particular structures of the representation itself are what in other theoretical schemes are called the homologies between levels of structure and the self-referential aspects of literary discourse, but which Knapp presents as relations between analogical structures involving different levels of agency: is what the author is doing in writing a poem analogous to what happens in the poem? "This sort of recursion," Knapp writes, "—where a problem of agency located as it were outside the work also shows up inside it—is the kind of effect that turns an interpretive problem into a source of literary interest" (3). We are dealing with literary interest when interpretive problem becomes not just a source of interest, but the source of an interest in the analogical structures whose particularity and complexity give the work its peculiarly literary status.

An example—this is my example, not Knapp's, but it has the virtue of great economy—might be Robert Frost's two-line poem "The Secret Sits."

> *The Secret Sits*
> We dance round in a ring and suppose,
> But the Secret sits in the middle and knows.[9]

The interpretive problem, "what is the poet saying or doing here?," becomes a source of distinctively literary interest, one might say, when it is transformed into a question about the relation between what the speaker or the poem is doing and what the agents within the poem, "we" and "the Secret," are doing. The poem contrasts our dancing and supposing with the Secret's sitting and knowing. We can ask what attitude the poem takes to the contrasted actions or modes of being. Is the poem a sardonic comment on the futility of human activity, or can we contrast the dancing of communal supposing to the dour and immobile knowing? But to address the question of the poem's take on these oppositions, one needs to ask whether the poem itself is engaged in dancing and supposing or in sitting and knowing. Is the poem itself in the mode of supposing or knowing?

The answer is somewhat complicated. The poem certainly sounds knowing, but as a verbal construction, can it be other than an act of human supposing? And if we ask about the status of knowing in the poem, what we can discover is that the subject supposed to know, the Secret, is produced by a rhetorical operation or supposition that moves it from the place of the object of "know" to the place of the subject. A secret is something one knows or does not know. Here the poem capitalizes and personifies the Secret and, by metonymy, shifts it from the place of what is known to the place of the knower. The knower is thus represented as produced by a rhetorical supposing or positing that makes the object of knowledge (a secret) into its subject (the Secret). The poem says that the secret knows but shows that this is the performative product of a rhetorical supposition.

Since Knapp wants to locate literary interest in analogies of *agency*, what would he say here? His claim would be that literary interest inheres in the relation between the act that Frost is performing in this poem and the acts represented. Is Frost knowing or supposing, dancing round or sitting in the middle, and what difference does it make? Are the difficulties of deciding what act Frost is performing illuminated by the difficulties of sorting out the relation between the acts of the poem's "we" and the acts of the Secret? This poem would, I think, be a good example for Knapp's approach, though in insisting that we focus on analogies of *authorial* agency, he has us ask what Frost is doing rather than what the poem is doing. I am not convinced that this is helpful, much less necessary. It may be more pertinent and productive to ask what the speaker or the poem is doing and how that relates to what is done in the poem than to focus on what Frost is doing and its relation to actions in the poem. But this may well be a separate issue. I do think that the problem of literariness is sharpened and illuminated by Knapp's suggestion that a text has literary interest insofar as our interest in it exceeds our interest in figuring out what the author intends.

Knapp seeks to reinterpret in terms of agency the kind of complexity of structure that has generally been taken to characterize literariness. He then proceeds to argue that, while literature does indeed have the distinctiveness that it has recently been denied, often on general political grounds (as an unwarranted, elitist privileging of certain modes of discourse), still, literature does not have the moral and political benefits that those defending literature are wont to claim for it. He thus hopes, as in the anti-theory articles he wrote with Walter Benn Michaels, to succeed in irritating everyone, on both sides of the question.

But there are probably few of us left in theory who will be surprised or annoyed by the conclusion that literature does not necessarily have moral and political benefits: arguments for the disruptive and emancipatory value of the avant-garde can always be countered—we know this all too well—by claims about the normalizing and policing functions of literary scenarios. Knapp's example certainly illustrates, however, albeit in an unusual traditional mode, what has been the tendency in recent thinking about the theory of literature: to relate the defense of the literary and the specificity thereof not to questions of the distinctiveness of literary language or to the radical potential of disruptions of meanings, but to the staging of agency on the one hand and to engagements with otherness on the other.[10]

Knapp's argument is that literary representations, which foreground analogically complex representations of agency, do not tell us how to act but help us to discover what our evaluative dispositions are and enhance our awareness of the complex relations—perhaps relations of contradiction—among our evaluative dispositions. An example he offers is Chinua Achebe's *Things Fall Apart*, where the colonial intervention into traditional Ibo culture is presented simultaneously as a cruel act of aggression and as an answer to the often extreme injustices of Ibo custom (the subordination of women, the exposure of twins, the murder, if an oracle so commands, of an adopted child). For readers, the novel may set up a clash between sets of values readers hold. Reading the novel, Knapp writes, "a feminist anti-colonialist might discover that her negative response to patriarchal customs far outweighed her commitment to preserving indigenous cultures (or the reverse)" (100–101). If literature helps to make us self-conscious agents, it does so by promoting thick description over simplifying principle, so that potential conflicts of value and principle may emerge. Knapp cites Locke's account of freedom of the liberal subject as the possibility of suspending decisions to examine carefully the alternatives and their values, and he concludes that literary interest provides a model for the exercise of liberal agency. "It isn't," he warns, "that literary interest makes someone a better agent." (He is not convinced that self-conscious agency is better agency.) But it "does give an unusually pure experience of what agency, for better or worse, is like" (103).

Agency involves a structure akin to that of what literary theory has called "the concrete universal," that special combination of particularity and generality that enables Hamlet, for instance, to be more than a merely actual person: Hamlet is embodied in particular details yet nevertheless open and general in ways that actual persons are not. To understand myself as agent is to see myself both in a concrete situation determined by my particular past and yet able to consider alternative courses of action by debating what it is appropriate for *someone* in my situation to do and thus to consider choices open to a certain type of agent—a type of which I am only one possible example. Since the ideal of full agency is that of the fusion of particularity and generality—that the determined particular which I am would be able effectively to choose any of the courses open to an agent—it is no surprise that, as Knapp puts it, encountering literary interest "should feel like glimpsing the ideal condition of practical agency itself" (140).

Such arguments go some way toward explaining the common intuition that the experience of literature has a bearing on the act of making judgments. Literature offers, as others have often said, a kind of mental calisthenics, a practice that instructs in exercise of agency.[11] Knapp explicitly denies that literary interest makes someone a better agent, but his work marks a general tendency in recent theory: to locate the distinctive features of literature not in particular qualities of language or framings of language, but in the staging of agency and in the relation to otherness into which readers of literature are brought. The effects of literature here depend, I think, on the special structure of exemplarity in literature.

A literary work is more than an anecdote, a singular example that is offered as an instance of something (though a detailed and well-told anecdote can accede to the condition of literariness). The literary representation has greater autonomy, so that the question of what it exemplifies can be left in abeyance at the same time that that question subtends the significance of the representation. This is why through the years people have often been led to speak of the "universality" of literature. The structure of literary works is such that it is easier to take them as telling us about the human condition in general than to specify some narrower category they describe or illuminate. Is *Hamlet* just about princes, or men of the Renaissance, or introspective young men, or people whose fathers have died in obscure circumstances? Since all such answers seem unsatisfactory, it is easier for readers not to answer, thus implicitly accepting a possibility of universality. Novels, poems, and plays, in their singularity, decline to explore what they are exemplary *of* at the same time that they invite their readers to become involved in the predicaments and the consciousness of narrators and characters who are in some sense posited as exemplary.

This structure of exemplarity has been important to the relationship of literature to the problem of identity, which as been so central to recent theory. Is the self something given or something made and should it be conceived in individual or in social terms? Literature has always been concerned with such questions and literary works offer a range of implicit models of how identity is formed. There are narratives where identity is essentially determined by birth: the son of a king raised by shepherds is still fundamentally a king and rightfully becomes king when his identity is discovered. In other narratives characters change according to the changes in their fortunes: they acquire identity through identifications, which may go awry but have powerful effects; or else identity is based on personal qualities that are revealed during the tribulations of a life.

The explosion of recent theorizing about race, gender, and sexuality in the field of literary studies may owe a good deal to the fact that literature provides rich materials for complicating political and sociological accounts of the role of such factors in the construction of identity. (I think, for instance, of Eve Sedgwick's and Judith Butler's discussions of cross-gendered identifications in Willa Cather's novels—accounts undreamt of by sociologists.)[12]

Consider the underlying question of whether the identity of the subject is something given or something constructed. Not only are both options amply represented in literature, but the complications or entanglements are frequently laid out for us, as in the common plot where characters, as we say, "discover" who they are, not by learning something about their past but by acting in such a way that they *become* what then turns out, in some sense, to have been their "nature."

This structure, where you have to *become* what you supposedly already were, has emerged as a paradox or aporia for recent theory, but it has been at work all along in narratives. Western novels reinforce the notion of an essential self by suggesting that the self which emerges from trying encounters with the world was in some sense there all along, as the basis for the actions which, from the perspective of readers, bring this self into being. The fundamental identity of character emerges as the result of actions, of struggles with the world, but then this identity is posited as the basis, even the cause of those actions. Isn't that what we're struggling with in theory's debates about essentialism?[13]

A good deal of recent theory can be seen as an attempt to sort out the paradoxes that often inform the treatment of identity in literature. Literary works characteristically represent individuals, so struggles about identity are struggles within the individual and between individual and group: characters struggle against or comply with social norms and expectations. In theoretical writings, arguments about social identity tend to focus, though, on group identities: what is it to be a woman? to be Black? to be Gay, to be a man? Thus there are tensions between literary explorations and critical or theoretical claims. The power of literary representations depends on their special combination of singularity and exemplarity: readers encounter concrete portrayals of Prince Hamlet or Jane Eyre or Huckleberry Finn, and with them the presumption that these characters' problems are exemplary. But exemplary of what? The novels don't tell. It's the critics or theorists who have to take up the question of exemplarity and tell us what group or class of people the character instantiates: is Hamlet's condition "universal"? Is Jane Eyre's the predicament of women in general?

Theoretical treatments of identity can therefore seem reductive in comparison with the subtle explorations in novels, which are able to finesse the problem of general claims by presenting singular cases while relying on a generalizing force that is left implicit—perhaps we are all Oedipus, or Hamlet, or Emma Bovary, or Janie Starks. And it is for this reason that theoretical reflection on the structures of exemplarity of literature are crucial to both the kinds of uses theory is making of literature these days, in its reflections on identity and agency, and to any attempt, as in Nussbaum and Knapp, to link the distinctiveness of literature to its bearing on questions of agency.

But if the literary can function as exemplary representation of agency for theory it can also be a source *of* agency in theory, as literary works provide leverage for theoretical argument. One impressive case where the role of literature is complex and overdetermined (and hence hard to define) is Judith Butler's *Antigone's Claim*.[14] Antigone, notoriously, makes a claim in Sophocles' play (precisely what sort of claim is the major issue in the history of the play's reception) and thus functions as a potentially exemplary literary representation of agency. Luce Irigaray has suggested, for instance, that Antigone can offer an identification for many girls and women living today. But the terseness of Butler's title suggests that Antigone—representation or text—has a claim on us. If Butler can use the words and deeds of Antigone and the text of Sophocles' play *Antigone* in a sustained argument about the relations between psychoanalysis and politics, focused on the problem of ways of theorizing kinship relations and family structures, it is not just because Antigone the agent is in some ways exemplary, but rather because the figure of Antigone has given rise to a powerful tradition of interpretation—from Hegel to Lacan and Irigaray—which has had effects on our conceptions of kinship and of the possible relations between the family and the state.

We can ask what would have happened if psychoanalysis had taken

Antigone rather than Oedipus as its point of departure, foregrounding the question of exemplarity. Butler writes,

> it is interesting to note that Antigone, who concludes the Oedipal drama, fails to produce heterosexual closure for the Oedipal drama, and that this may intimate the direction for a psychoanalytic theory that takes Antigone as its point of departure. . . . She does seem to deinstitute heterosexuality by refusing to do what is necessary to stay alive for Haimon, by refusing to become a mother and wife, by scandalizing the public with her wavering gender, and by embracing death as her bridal chamber. (Lecture 3)

Her case offers alternatives to the conceptual routes that Western culture has taken. But, more important, the interpretation of Antigone has undergirded a discourse about kinship and its relation to political structures that continue to exercise its effects today. As Butler puts it, "In her act she transgresses both gender and kinship norms, and though the Hegelian tradition reads her fate as a sure sign that this transgression is necessarily failed and fatal, another reading is possible in which she exposes the culturally-contingent character of kinship, only to become the repeated occasion for a rewriting of that contingency as immutable necessity" (Lecture 1). Butler's intervention does not simply cite the figure of Antigone as an agent exercising certain choices or making claims. It undertakes detailed readings of Sophocles' text, *Antigone*, to expose the reductive simplifications in the readings by theorists, have set kinship (as a configuration of "natural relations") against the state and have produced an idealization of kinship as a structural field of intelligibility, and have thus established certain forms of kinship as intelligible and legitimate. This idealization, which legitimates a certain form of family structure as supposedly prior to and outside of politics, has drawn on the story of Antigone, but, in so doing, has denied the challenge that Sophocles' text offers to its peremptory inscription of intelligibility. If Hegel attends to Antigone's acts but not her speech, regarding that language today reveals the instability of the conceptual apparatus erected on her example. And it is in the appeal to the complexities and indeterminacies of this literary work that Butler intervenes, in the name of those who today are attempting to work out alternative family structures—where two men or two women may parent, for instance—and whose practice encounters the stigmatizing idealization in psychoanalytic, cultural, and political theory of the supposedly primordial, symbolic positions of Father and Mother.

Claude Lévi-Strauss in his structuralist studies of myth and totemism maintained that myths are central to culture because they are "good to think with." Butler's use of *Antigone* in an argument about the legitimacy of models of kinship and politics, shows that literature is better to think with, in that its language provides powerful resources for a critique of constructions that it has been used to sustain and thus of the institutional arrangements it has helped to subtend.

So far I have approached the literary in theory by discussing some forms the theorization of the literary has taken in recent theory. But one could also argue that what has happened to the literary in theory is that it has migrated from being the object of theory to being the quality of theory itself: what we in America call "theory"—after all, an American invention—is elsewhere the broad movement of modern thought which takes as its "other" instrumental reason and empirical science (some other names for this other are: the restricted economy of utility, the logic of enframing, the logic of reification and reifying rationality, the totalizing logic of technological efficiency, the binary logic of the metaphysics of presence, and so on).[15] What if theory is the exfoliation, in the sphere of thought in general, of the literary? Freud, notoriously, said that the poets had been there before him; he tried to found a science on literary insights, and his critics have in our day tried with some success to beat him back into the position of failed scientist and successful storyteller. More generally, one could say that insofar as thought seeks to find passages beyond the familiar, the known, the countable, it is cognate with the literature, or at least the literary efforts of Romanticism and Modernism.

One striking signal of this is that philosophical texts have become literary in the classic sense that, like poems, they are not supposed to be paraphrased: to paraphrase is to miss what is essential. People often say this of Derrida, of course, but here is Adorno, a philosopher not usually identified with the literary: in *Negative Dialectics* Adorno writes,

> Instead of reducing philosophy to categories, one would in a sense have to compose it first. Its course must be a ceaseless self-renewal, by its own strength as well as in friction with whatever standard it may have. The crux is what happened in it, not a thesis or a position, the texture, not the deductive or inductive course of one-track minds. Essentially, therefore, philosophy is not expoundable. If it were, it would be superfluous; the fact that most of it can be expounded speaks against it.[16]

This is a literary way of conceiving philosophy—philosophy as writing that achieves literary effects. This is not to imply that exposition of such texts is not necessary or desirable—only that such texts also require the kind of rhetorical readings and the contextual analysis as acts, as performances, that we take for granted when engaging literary works and, thus, that the literary has migrated into theory.

Insofar as theory is the discourse that seeks the opening of the subject to the nonidentical, to alterity, the other, the indeterminate, or some other site or event beyond instrumental reason, it inscribes itself in the literary lineage of post-Enlightenment poetry. Adorno has a striking passage in *Minima Moralia: Reflections from Damaged Life* on the task of thought, which brings together the goals of literature and of theory.

> Perspectives must be fashioned that displace and estrange the world, reveal it to be, with its rifts and crevices, as indigent and distorted as it will appear one day in the messianic light. To gain such perspectives without velleity or violence, entirely from felt contact with its objects—this alone is the task of thought. It is the simplest of all things, because the situation calls imperatively for such knowledge, indeed because consummate negativity, once squarely faced, delineates the mirror-image of its opposite. But it is also the utterly impossible thing, because it presupposes a standpoint removed, even though by a hair's breadth, from the scope of existence, whereas we well know that any possible knowledge must not only be first wrested from what is, if it shall hold good, but is also marked, for this very reason, by the same distortion and indigence which it seeks to escape. The more passionately thought denies its conditionality for the sake of the

> unconditional, the more unconsciously, and so calamitously, it is delivered up to the world. Even its own impossibility it must at last comprehend for the sake of the possible. But beside the demand thus placed on thought, the question of the reality or unreality of redemption itself hardly matters.[17]

The literary nature of this project emerges in that difficult concluding sentence: beside the demand thus placed on thought, the question of the reality or unreality of redemption itself hardly matters. As in literature, it is the demand of otherness placed on thought that counts. But rather than venture further down this road, where the specter of redemption lurks, let me address in a different mode the pervasiveness of the literary.

In the course of his discussion of literary interest, Steve Knapp remarks that the New Historicism involves the transfer of literary interest from the literary work itself to the literary work grasped in a historical context: as a result, the new construct that is the object of literary interest is, in fact, the complex interrelations between text and context (context, which is, of course, more text). Literary interest comes no longer from the complex relations between form and meaning or between what the work says and what it does, but, for instance, from the dialectic of subversion and containment which it provokes and in which it participates. The explanatory vagueness of much New Historicism comes from the fact that the goal is not to decide whether, say, "the theater in a particular era is an effect or a cause of a certain monarchical ideology," but to illuminate a complex interdependent structure, like that of a literary work. "The point," Knapp writes, "is to see how the theater, as it exists in its hard-to-define relation to the state becomes (to someone who notices the right affinities) the theater as suggesting, and suggested by, the state" (104). The object of literary interest—approached as a complex literary structure—is the work in a posited context. The historical investigations of the New Historicism take as their object not historical explanation but elucidation of an historical object that displays the structures of literary interest.

A similar point is taken further in a recent book by David Simpson, *The Academic Postmodern and the Rule of Literature*, which argues—in a mode of critique and complaint, I should make clear—that literature, far from being ignored or relegated to the margins in the university, as conservative critics claim, has conquered: in the academy, literature rules, even though that rule is disguised as something else. Simpson seeks to show that a range of scholars and disciplines have been willing to accept, for the description of the world, terms that come from the realm of literary studies. He surveys various dimensions of this phenomenon: the return of storytelling to centrality in history (Simpson speaks of the "epidemic of story-telling"), which had thought itself rid of that sort of humanistic, literary issue; the general recourse to anecdote or autobiography, the celebration of "thick description" and "local knowledge," and the use of the figure of "conversation," in the fields of history, philosophy, feminism, anthropology. Such is the transformation of the humanities that knowledge now takes literary forms. The calls for concreteness, and historical specificity are, as Simpson explains, not part of a renewed empiricism but versions of an appeal to the values of literary singularity, to that presence of the general in the particular that distinguishes literary discourse. Clifford Geertz's *local knowledge*, for instance, brings not empirical mastery but the incompleteness and instability of all knowledge claims and the appeal, instead, to vividness of realization as the substitute for claims to mastery. The literary reigns.

But "how," Simpson asks, "can I make this claim at a time when some of our most astute commentators on the contemporary condition"—he cites Fredric Jameson and John Guillory—"are describing a move *away* from the literary as most urgently definitive of the postmodern condition."[18] (Jameson says that the replacement of literature by video is the signature of the postmodern condition, and John Guillory describes the flight of cultural capital from literature as the most characteristic element in the evolving state of the humanities.) Since these folks are Simpson's friends and co-religionists, he answers, politely, that "culture is not a monolith" (they are looking at different phenomena in the panoply of culture) but fundamentally he thinks that he is right and they are wrong. Literature may have lost its centrality as a specific object of study but its modes have conquered: in the humanities and the humanistic social sciences everything is literary.

Indeed, if literature is, as we used to say, that mode of discourse which knows its own fictionality, then, insofar as the effect of theory has been to inform disciplines of both the fictionality and the performative efficacy of their constructions, there seems a good deal to be said in favor of Simpson's account of the situation of disciplines. Insofar as disciplinary discourses have come to engage with the problem of their positionality, their situatedness, and the constructedness of their schemes, they participate in the literary.

If the literary has triumphed, as Simpson claims (and for him the postmodern is the name of the triumph of the literary), then perhaps it is time to reground the literary in literature, to go back to actual literary works to see whether the postmodern condition is indeed what should be inferred from the operations of literature. It seems to me quite possible that a return to ground the literary in literature might have a critical edge, since one of the things we know about literary works is that they have the ability to resist or to outplay what they are supposed to be saying. David Simpson's book claims quite explicitly that what's left of theory is the literary. If so, all the more reason to return to literary works for the critique of the literary that has historically been one of the tasks of literature.

NOTES

1. Roman Jakobson, "Closing Statement: Linguistics and Poetics," in *Style in Language*, ed. Thomas Sebeok (Cambridge, MA: MIT Press, 1960), p. 35. For a discussion of theory in this structuralist moment, see Jonathan Culler, *Structuralist Poetics: Structuralism, Linguistics, and the Study of Literature* (Ithaca: Cornell University Press, 1974).

2. Jakobson, *op. cit.*, p. 358.

3. *Ibid.*, p. 357.

4. Stanley Fish, "How to Recognize a Poem When You See One", in *Is There a Text in This Class?* (Cambridge, MA: Harvard University Press, 1980), pp. 322–37. For general discussions of the problem of literariness, see Terry Eagleton, *Literary Theory: An Introduction* (Minneapolis: University of Minnesota Press, 1983), pp. 1–12; Jonathan Culler, "La littérarité," in *Théorie littéraire*, ed. Marc Angenot et al. (Paris: Presses universitaires de France, 1989), pp. 31–43; and Culler, *Literary Theory: A Very Short Introduction* (Oxford: Oxford University Press, 1997), pp. 18–42.

5. See William Ray, *Literary Meaning: From Phenomenology to Deconstruction* (Oxford: Blackwell, 1984).

6. Jonathan Culler, "Literary Theory," in *Introduction to Scholarship in Modern Languages and Literatures*, 2nd ed., ed. Joseph Gibaldi (New York: Modern Language Association, 1992), pp. 201–35.

7. Steven Knapp and Walter Benn Michaels, "Against Theory," *Critical Inquiry* 8 (1982), pp. 723–42.

8. Steven Knapp, *Literary Interest: The Limits of Anti-Formalism* (Cambridge, MA: Harvard University Press, 1993), flyleaf copy. Further references to this book are given in the text.

9. Robert Frost, *The Complete Poems* (New York: Holt, Rinehart, 1958), p. 495.

10. Literature's relation to otherness is a large topic which I cannot broach here. For an incisive and suggestive approach to the question, see Derek Attridge, "Innovation, Literature, Ethics: Relating to the Other," *PMLA*, 114.1 (January 1999), pp. 20–31. The writing on this topic is considerable; some aspects of it are surveyed by Lawrence Buell in "In Pursuit of Ethics," *PMLA* 114.1 (January 1999), pp. 7–19. See, in particular, Jacques Derrida, "Psyche: Inventions of the Other," trans. Catherine Porter, in *Reading de Man Reading*, ed. Lindsay Waters and Wlad Godzich (Minneapolis: University of Minnesota Press, 1989); and Derek Attridge, "Literary Form and the Demands of Politics: Otherness in J. M. Coetzee's *Age of Iron*," in *Aesthetics and Ideology*, ed. George Levine (New Brunswick: Rutgers University Press, 1994), pp. 243–63.

11. A recent articulation of the traditional view is Martha Nussbaum's *Poetic Justice: The Literary Imagination and Public Life* (Boston: Beacon Press, 1995), which claims that literature is distinctive for its success in enabling us to appreciate the situation of the other. She stresses the potential role of literary representations in bringing us to exercise agency in the interests of justice, because the literary imagination, or more specifically, literary representation and the dealings with the kind of representations that characterize the literary imagination, lead the reader to enter vicariously into the circumstances of other lives and to ground judgment on a rich and comprehensive understanding of the situation and experiences of other people.

    But Nussbaum's case illustrates the difficulty of sustaining an argument that literary representations make us better agents, since her vicious attacks on other feminist theorists who dare to promote something other than the reformist feminism she espouses display a manifest inability to assume a rich and comprehensive understanding of the position of others.

12. See Eve Kosovsky Sedgwick, "Across Gender, Across Sexuality: Willa Cather and Others," *South Atlantic Quarterly* 88:1 (Winter 1989), pp. 53–72; and Judith Butler, "Dangerous Crossing: Willa Cather's Masculine Names," in *Bodies That Matter: On the Discursive Limits of "Sex"* (New York: Routledge, 1993), pp. 143–66.

13. See, for example, Diana Fuss, *Essentially Speaking* (New York: Routledge, 1989). The most powerful and influential exploration of this aporia, through the theorization of a performative notion of identity, comes in Judith Butler, *Gender Trouble: Feminism and the Subversion of Identity* (New York: Routledge, 1990), and *Bodies That Matter: On the Discursive Limits of "Sex"* (New York: Routledge, 1993).

14. *Antigone's Claim* (New York: Columbia University Press, 2000). Versions of these three lectures were delivered as the Christian Gauss lectures at Princeton University, the Messenger Lectures at Cornell University, and the Wellek Library Lectures at University of California, Irvine, in 1998.

15. I am indebted for some of these formulations, as for the quotations from Adorno below, to a remarkable doctoral dissertation by Robert Baker, now of the University of Montana: *Poetic Form, Poetic Fiction, and the Way of Extravagance: Twentieth-Century Inventions* (Cornell University, 1997).

16. Theodor Adorno, *Negative Dialectics*, trans. E. B. Ashton (New York: Continuum Books, 1973), p. 33.

17. Adorno, *Minima Moralia: Reflections from Damaged Life*, trans. E. F. N. Jephcott (London: Verso, 1974), p. 247.

18. David Simpson, *The Academic Postmodern and the Rule of Literature: A Report on Half-Knowledge* (Chicago: University of Chicago Press, 1995), p. 38.